Parts of this book have been previously published in the following: "Prologue" and "Uncle Wiggly in Darfur" appeared in "Back From the Brink: War, Suicide, and PTSD" in *Health Affairs*, July 2010, Volume 29, Number 7; "Yellow" in the journal *JMWW* in a special non-fiction issue, Fall 2011; "The French Lieutenant's iPod" in the Press 53 Open Awards 2011; "The Whole Mehgilla," originally titled "Writing My Way Home" in *The Delmarva Review*, Volume 6; "Writing My Way Home" appeared on TIME Magazine's Battleland Blog, 2011; and in *Healing War Trauma: A Handbook of Creative Approaches* (Routledge, 2009), edited by Ray Scurfield and Kathy Platoni.

For other permissions and copyright information, see Publisher's Note at back of the book.

For permission to reprint, contact:
Permissions Dept., Schaffner Press, Inc.
POB 41567, Tucson, AZ 85717

First Hardcover Edition: May, 2014

ISBN: 978-1936182-58-9 (hardcover ed); 978-1936182-59-6 (adobe); 978-1936182-60-2 (epub); 978-1936182-61-9 (kindle)

For Cataloging-in-Publication Information, see back of the book

For B.C.

AUTHOR'S NOTE

The opinions and characterizations in this book are those of the author, and do not necessarily represent official positions of the United States Government.

Table of Contents

SERIOUSLY NOT ALL RIGHT

Five Wars in Ten Years

PROLOGUE

WHEN THE PHONE RANG I jumped—startled—and nearly shot myself. This would have been somewhat ironic, because I was sitting in a truck, about to kill myself and was already holding the pistol in my hand. But I would have pulled the trigger while the pistol was pointed at my foot rather than my head. After all the crying and shaking, the moralizing and justifying, the calming of hands and nerves, the intense focusing on the immediate act of charging the weapon to put a bullet into the firing chamber, and then taking off the safety and preparing to put the barrel in my mouth, the sudden ringing broke the spell, and pulled me back from the brink.

I looked down at the phone lying on the seat of the pickup. It was my wife, Maureen, calling from Washington, D.C. I then looked up just as a boy with a camel in tow walked past my truck. The boy's face was dirty—he'd probably been walking in the desert all day—and he was wearing a stained, full-length *thawb* (the classic garment worn by many Arab men) and dusty sandals. He looked at me, our eyes locked for a second. Then he turned away and pulled the camel's rope bridle a little harder. I picked up the phone.

"Hello?"

The static on the phone cleared up.

"Hey," Maureen said. "What's up?"

I paused. I certainly couldn't answer with the truth.

"Not much," I said. "What's up with you?"

I swallowed hard to clear my throat and fought to get control of my breathing. The pistol felt good in my hand. I felt surprisingly deft with it. The selector switch had two painted dots, one red and one white. White is safe; red is not. With my thumb, I put the pistol back on *safe* and laid it on the seat. While I talked to my wife for a few minutes, I stared out through the windshield and watched the sun setting over the rocky brown desert of Darfur.

"I'll be careful, don't worry. I'll be home in a few weeks."

I started the truck's engine and drove back to the United Nations guesthouse where I was staying. On the way, I returned the pistol to the peacekeeper sergeant I'd borrowed it from. We had served together for five months. He had loaned me the pistol, no questions asked, because he knew me and because I was a senior officer with more than twenty years of field experience whom he believed to be competent and trustworthy. I'd given him no reason to think otherwise.

This book tells the story of how I got to that point in my life when I was sitting alone in a pickup truck in the middle of the African continent ready to end it all, and how I came back from there. It is the story of five wars in ten years.

But, it is only in the vaguest sense a war story, in that it takes place in the midst of wars. During the story people will die and people will be horribly wounded, lives will be destroyed along with villages and towns. During part of the story I am a soldier in a war, but I don't kill anyone. There is no moment where I level a weapon towards an enemy and recognize in that brief instant before I kill him that we are both human beings sent by our masters to kill and die for vague concepts like honor and patriotism.

There are no massed movements of forces on an epic scale, nor small unit combat pitting handfuls of warriors against each other. There are no moments of stark courage in the face of sustained enemy rifle and machine gun fire, nor the ungodly fear of an artillery bombardment. No, it's not that kind of war story.

This is instead the story of one person going in and out of wars, sometimes as a soldier, sometimes as a Foreign Service political officer for the State Department—a bystander for the most part to hideous violence, an observer among hundreds of thousands of dead on three continents.

I joined the Army in 1983. I had been in and out of different colleges for seven years, first studying music and then working off and on towards an English degree. I wasn't making much progress at school until I decided I wanted to join the military. I guess I didn't have a real reason to want to graduate, so it wasn't a priority. But I realized that playing my guitar and singing in bars around Virginia Beach and the Outer Banks of North Carolina wasn't going to hold my interest for too much longer, so I decided I would try to get in to flight school. I was too old for an ROTC scholarship, so when I enrolled in ROTC I simultaneously enlisted in the National Guard to make a little extra money. When I graduated from school a couple of years later, I was commissioned as a second lieutenant in armor branch—not aviation, so no flight school—and went on active duty in the regular Army.

After training at Fort Knox, Kentucky, I was assigned to the 11th Armored Cavalry Regiment on the East-West German border. The Cold War was in its death throes and the Army had just passed the height of the build-up begun under President Reagan. Everything we did in my unit had to be bigger and shinier and faster than any other unit in the Army. For three years I cruised around Germany on M1 Tanks and Bradley Fighting Vehicles, patrolled the East German border, and shot up boatloads of ammunition on the ranges at Grafenwoer.

At the end of that tour, I was transferred to Military Intelligence branch and assigned to Korea for a year. My first assignment was in Seoul as a liaison officer to the Korean Defense Intelligence Agency. I wore a suit and shiny shoes to work. I was told to get a membership—using government funds—at the local golf course and to plan to play a lot of golf with senior Korean officers. The joke was that this was the only job in the Army where your golf handicap was a part of your evaluation. It wasn't far off, and it wasn't what I had in mind when I joined the intelligence corps; I thought I would be the staff intel officer in a combat arms unit rather than doing strategic collection among allies. I volunteered to move north to the De-Militarized Zone and spent the second half of my year in Korea in the Second Infantry Division.

At the same time, the U.S. was preparing to go to war with Iraq in Operation Desert Shield. Because of the war, the regular assignment process was disrupted and officers who had been assigned to schools were deployed, leaving seats to highly competitive schools open. So while I was in the 2nd Infantry Division, two guys walked into my office to ask if I would be interested in attending some specialized training as a case officer. The training would take me out of the big Army—the regular Army—and into the small world of clandestine intelligence operations. I said yes.

For the next four years I worked in units based in the Washington, DC and Fort Meade, MD area as a case officer, a team chief, and a company commander. It was challenging. But, although I worked with, and eventually led, a team of talented and creative people, I wasn't happy. I still wanted something else. I had served for seven years in the regular Army, but hadn't yet found a real niche. I was constantly looking around the corner for the next cool thing to do.

I went to graduate school at Johns Hopkins University. I applied for another special program in the Army—this one to become a Foreign Area Officer, a regional specialist who would more than likely be working as a military attaché out of an embassy. One evening in 1992, I was sitting in a lawn chair out in my yard, drinking wine with my wife and a friend, and listening to John Miller call a Baltimore Orioles game on the radio. I remember complaining about being sort of brain dead because I had taken the Graduate Record Exam that day as preparation to enter the Foreign Area Officer program. As our conversation went on, the talk turned to other hard, standardized tests. My friend asked if I had ever taken the Foreign Service Exam. I hadn't even heard of it.

He explained that the Foreign Service Exam was considered the *ne plus ultra* of standardized tests—for liberal arts majors, anyway. He said only a tiny percentage passed the test, and then applicants had to take and pass an in-person oral exam that lasted a full day before they could actually join the Foreign Service. We were drinking. We decided to give it a shot.

On test day in the fall of 1992, three of us—we had recruited a third friend to join us—showed up to take the exam. My friend was right. It was a butt-kicker of a test. But a few weeks later we learned that we had all passed. Neither of my friends was interested in taking the oral boards, but I signed up. I went to the Foreign Service Institute in Arlington one morning the next spring for the day-long series of interviews, writing exercises and tests that comprised "the orals." At the end of the day, I was told I had passed. I was given a packet of materials to complete that would get my medical exams and security clearance background checks started.

I had then to decide whether to stay in the military or move to the State Department. I was in company command, in theory at least the best job an officer can ever have in the Army, and I wasn't having fun. I talked it over with my wife and we decided to jump, but only partway. A year later, I left the regular Army and joined the State Department as a Foreign Service officer. But I stayed in the Army Reserve.

After a year of training in Virginia, I was assigned to the American Embassy in Yaoundé, Cameroon. At about the same time, I was assigned as an Army reservist to Special Operations Command-Europe, the headquarters and staff of U.S. military special operations forces for Europe and Africa.

About halfway through my tour in Cameroon, in May of 1996, I started an odyssey of assignments alternating between the Department of State as a political officer, and mobilized from the Army Reserve onto active duty as a Military Intelligence officer or military attaché.

From 1996 to 1998 I served in Cameroon and the Central African Republic as an FSO, and in Uganda and Zaire as a soldier. From 1998 to 2000, as an FSO, I was an international diplomatic observer in

Kosovo. Then I returned to Central Africa—to Rwanda—until 2002 as an FSO, assigned as chief of the political section of the American Embassy in Kigali. Nearly every day of those six years I was in the midst of murder, rape, mutiny, the burning of villages, crimes against humanity, war crimes, ethnic cleansing, or genocide. I was left with deathly images of the hacked and burnt bodies of men, women and children stuck in my head. Images that would and will never leave me.

After the attacks on the United States on September 11th, 2001, and until 2007, I served in Afghanistan as a soldier, Iraq as an FSO, Darfur and Chad as a soldier, and back to Darfur as an FSO.

Against the tableau of the two larger wars and the genocide in the desert of over 300,000 people, I lost my sanity, took a pistol in hand ready to end my life, and saw a successful career disintegrate along with my twenty-year marriage.

In five wars—Central Africa, Kosovo, Afghanistan, Iraq, and Darfur—I was a party to, witness to, and a survivor of unthinkable violence. It changed me as I assume it would change anyone. My mind, once my most potent weapon, grew treasonous. The government that sent me to war, that encouraged me to return again and again, dropped me as soon as I stumbled.

During these wars one of my jobs was to talk to people and report their stories and what I thought about them back to my readership—U.S. government policy makers. Early on in my work I began keeping personal notes about what happened because I wanted to remember details. We were instructed to write crisp, dry reports about messy, horrible acts of cruelty. I knew those reports were not sufficient to tell the tale. I needed to tell the deeper story of what was happening in these "small wars." So I wrote in order to remember.

Over time, I didn't want to remember any longer. But that's not how these things work. Once an image is in your head, it's there forever. And a traumatic memory causes the body to react in the same way it did during the original event, and operate in fight-or-flight mode. This is a part of Post-Traumatic Stress Disorder.

Writing helps me control the memories through repeated, controlled exposure to them. Writing is a learned skill, so it brings higher brain functions back into service rather than allowing the brain and body to remain in fight-or-flight mode. Just as a glove protects a hand around hot iron, writing allows me to hold onto the memory long enough to shape it. It allows me to distance myself from it. In a very real way, I wrote my way into it, and this book is my attempt to write my way out of it, to write my way home.

Throughout the book I have relied on my memory of events to reconstruct dialogue and scenes. My memory, once exceptional, is alas imperfect. I used field notes and journals whenever possible, but there may be small errors in time and place. There are as well a few points where I have had to excise names or blur details of events for reasons of security.

This is a small story, one person's story. Mine. There are lots of other people in it or it wouldn't make sense. No one goes to war alone.

Kosovo

2000-2002

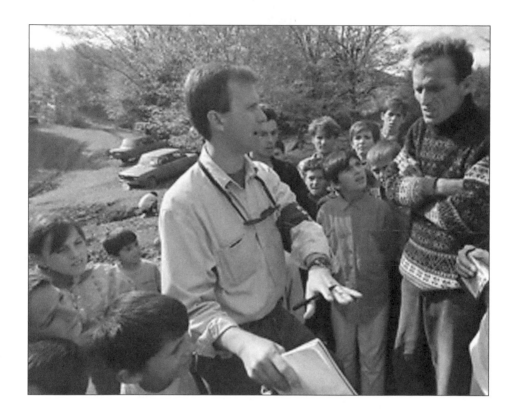

You can only love one war; afterwards,
I suppose, you do your duty.

MARTHA GELLHORN
(Attributed)

My New Favorite Person

THE MAN AT THE VISA window stood still, his head wobbling only slightly from side to side as he fought millennia of cultural programming to present himself to the American consul precisely as his documentation showed him to be: a young, well-educated, affluent, New York financial analyst.

"How long have you been with Merrill?" I asked. I looked up briefly then back to the documents the corporation's immigration lawyers had assembled, which showed he was employed by Merrill, Lynch, Pierce, Fenner & Smith.

"Not quite three years," he responded.

"And how long do you anticipate staying on?" This was probably the only question he could get wrong. One line, deep in the Immigration and Naturalization Act of 1980, Section 214(b), stipulated that "every alien shall be presumed to be an immigrant until he establishes to the satisfaction of the consular officer... that he is entitled to a nonimmigrant status..." The chance he would screw up and say something to convince me he really intended to stay illegally in the U.S. was about nil, but I was supposed to ask nonetheless.

"Another three years, probably," he responded perfectly. Good, I thought, this one is quick and easy. I had about thirty more interviews

I

ahead of me that morning, many of which would surely be neither quick nor easy.

Just then, my boss slipped halfway into my booth and dropped an inch-high stack of papers butterfly-clipped together into my in-box. It was the daily read-file, the collected message traffic from Washington each officer was supposed to read.

"You should look at the top one," he said and tapped his finger on the stack. I glanced at the title, VOLUNTEER CABLE: KOSOVO DIPLOMATIC OBSERVER MISSION. "As if you'd let me go," I said.

He shrugged. "We'd think about it."

A volunteer cable is a notification sent out from the Department of State to embassies and consulates worldwide announcing that a position needs to be filled badly enough that the human resources bureau is looking for volunteers. It also means that if you want to go, your boss isn't supposed to say no. At that point, the applicant could have said almost anything and still gotten his visa. It was June, the height of the visa season in Canada, and I was bored out of my skull conducting interviews. A chance to go on mission to some place called Kosovo sounded like just the ticket.

"Thanks," I said, returning to the applicant at the window. "You can come back this afternoon at three o'clock to pick up your visa."

"Thank you very much," he said, smiling broadly.

I picked up the telephone at my elbow and dialed the number listed to volunteer to go to Kosovo, wherever that was. The officer on the other end of the line had been tasked with building a team of diplomatic observers to go into a hot war during the peak season for job changes, international moves, and getting kids into schools. Apparently, the recruitment process wasn't going particularly well. When I called to volunteer, he said, "You're my new favorite person." A couple of weeks later, I was on my way to Kosovo.

The Air France gate agent took pity on me. She called me up to the counter a few minutes before boarding began and handed me an upgrade to Business Class.

"You look like you could use a comfortable seat," she said.

I didn't argue. It was a relatively short flight to Belgrade from Paris, but having some additional legroom and a couple of free drinks sounded nice. So I took the new boarding pass and proffered a sincere *merci bien* in return.

The JAT Airlines 737 had about a dozen seats in the front set aside for Business Class. I got a window seat. Just after takeoff, as Paris disappeared beneath the cloud layer, I pulled out what had been my near constant companion in the weeks since I had bid Montreal adieu: Noel Malcolm's *Kosovo: A Short History*. It was the newest book available on Kosovo's political, economic and cultural history.

Quite honestly, I had never heard of Kosovo when I volunteered to go there. I wasn't a Europeanist. I wasn't really a typical Foreign Service officer. I had come to the Foreign Service after nine years in the Army rather than directly from one of the several international relations graduate programs that serve as feeder schools for our diplomatic corps. So Malcolm's book, alongside *Yugoslavia: Death of a Nation* by Laura Silber and Allan Little, became my crash graduate course on where I was headed and why.

On the opening page of their book, Silber and Little wrote:

> "The war in Yugoslavia was not the international community's fault. The war was planned and waged by Yugoslavs. It was not historically inevitable. To attribute the calamity that engulfed the peoples of Yugoslavia to unstoppable forces is to avoid addressing oneself to the central dynamic of the war. It also lets the guilty off the hook…Yugoslavia did not die a natural death. Rather it was deliberately and systematically killed off by men who had nothing to gain and everything to lose from a peaceful transition from state socialism and one-party rule to free-market economy."

They continue for about four hundred pages to explain how Slobodan Milosevic and his regime had destroyed so many lives in the course of dismantling their country.

Yugoslavia was in some ways a fiction. The word Yugoslavia means, roughly, "land of the southern Slavs." Three nations have carried the name. All three sprang from the ashes of war: in 1918 and 1946 and, finally, in 1992.

Marshal Josip Broz Tito ruled Yugoslavia from 1945 until he died in 1980. Tito understood that in order for there to be a strong and successful Yugoslavia there needed to be a weakened and compromised Serbia. I imagined Tito standing astride Yugoslavia for forty years like the Colossus of Rhodes, with a foot in Macedonia, a foot in Slovenia, and his hand firmly upon the head of Serbia, holding down the Serbs in order that all the other ethnic groups—the Croats, the Slovenes, the Bosnians and Montenegrins, the Kosovar Albanians, and the Macedonians—could stand freely. I'm sure this is how some Serbians viewed their position in Yugoslavia.

Yugoslavia was also horrifyingly real. Scarcely ten years after Tito's death, the nation was well on its way to a bloody, murderous, and all too public dissolution in the Balkan Wars of the 1990s. We need only say the word to recall the horror of Srebrenica, or the terror of the siege on Sarajevo.

Noel Malcolm's book opens with this line: "The Yugoslav crisis began in Kosovo and it will end in Kosovo." He is quoting an often-heard bromide rather than his personal, well-informed opinion. But the final dissolution of Yugoslavia came about because of the war in Kosovo.

About halfway through the flight to Belgrade, I put down Malcolm's book and stared out the window. I remember wondering what I was in for. I had previously worked, both as a soldier and a diplomat, on the edges of wars in Central Africa—in Uganda, Rwanda, Zaire, and the Central African Republic. But the violence there was distant. I reported on the aftermath of fighting, often simply by interviewing victims of violence days afterwards and after they had traveled hundreds of miles. I guessed this would be different, that I would be much closer.

My job was usually described as a reporting officer: I would go and observe, then report what I saw. I've joked over the years that at its core, my job was to talk to people and write down what they said. It sounds simple, and it is to a point. But it becomes exponentially more interesting and difficult if there is shooting and burning and killing and dying going on around you.

Restless, I dug through the seat pocket in front of me. In it, I found the JAT in-flight magazine. As I absent-mindedly flipped through the pages, I found a map of Serbia at the back. I tore the map out and stuck it in my notebook; it was, for a time, the best map I had of the country. As we began our descent, I put away my books and finished off my drink.

The Ministry of the Interior officer at the immigration booth examined my diplomatic passport and visa, carefully going through each page of the passport, pausing to read other visas. Then she passed it to her colleague, who left the booth with it. The woman looked at me and smiled. We stayed that way, looking at each other for a moment until her colleague returned with my passport, nice and warm from the photocopier. She returned it to me and nodded in the direction of the luggage carousels.

Outside, an embassy driver picked me up and delivered me to the Belgrade Hilton. He told me that someone would pick me up in the morning to take me to the embassy. Once checked in, I went upstairs to my room and dropped my bags on the floor. I sat on the edge of the bed and told myself I had to stay awake until at least 10 p.m. I woke up about four hours later. I've always sucked at jet lag.

At the embassy the next morning, I met the team I would work with. I knew none of the Foreign Service officers, but one of the military planners and I had worked together in Uganda and Zaire a couple of years before on a humanitarian mission. He warned me about the politics between the members of our team and the embassy's permanent staff. Nothing unusual, he said, but there was a clear sense that the embassy staff felt the need to protect their interests against some perceived incursion by outsiders. It was true to some degree, I would learn, but it was primarily an uneasiness of the Foreign Service staff with the military. As an FSO who had spent nine years on active duty in the Army, this wasn't news to me.

It took about three days for the Serbian government to prepare my *Licna Karte*, the diplomatic pass that would allow me to work in Serbia. While I waited, I had a chance to catch up on sleep and see some of Belgrade. One evening, a colleague and I walked northwards from the embassy towards Kalemegdan, the historic center of the city and its old citadel. The evening was warm and people were spilling out of cafes at sidewalk tables, drinking coffees and beers, and smoking—everyone smoking. Storefronts were lighted and filled with European fashions. Couples strolled arm in arm; people rushed home from work with groceries. It was lovely. There was a park near the fortress, and as we walked through, an old woman sitting on a stool at the edge of the lawn offered to sell us 100,000 Dinar notes of the former currency. I bought a stack of twenty for about five Deutschmarks that I would use later as bookmarks and party invitations.

From the edge of the fortress, looking over the confluence of the Danube and Sava Rivers, my colleague told me that, at one time, the lands to the west were part of the Austro-Hungarian empire, its people Catholic; the lands to the north and east were Slavic, the people Orthodox; and the lands to the south were Ottoman, and the people Muslim. I'm not sure he was precisely accurate, but it was a good illustration of the complexities we faced just ahead.

The next afternoon I received my *Licna Karte*. The Deputy Chief of Mission (DCM) told me that I was going south to Kosovo, and to focus on working with the non-governmental relief agencies there to learn as much as I could about what they were doing and why.

In the morning, an embassy driver loaded my bags into the back of the Suburban and we headed south out of Belgrade. The highway was clear once we'd left the city limits, and we made good time, arriving in the province around mid-day. Just outside the line dividing Kosovo from Serbia was a small restaurant. I thought it was probably a place like so many on county lines in the U.S., called the State Line Bar or Last Chance for Cheap Gas. In reality it was where the Serbian Army (called the VJ) and the Ministry of the Interior Police (called the MUP) would hang out between missions.

We passed through a number of military and police checkpoints as we entered Kosovo. At each stop I was asked for my *Licna Karte*— the Serbs are sticklers for protocol, and any chance to stick it to an American seemed a welcome diversion for the officials at that point. The road was poorly maintained, the houses shabbier than those in Serbia proper. But other than a few military vehicles on the road, I initially saw nothing to suggest that I was entering a war zone.

The team I was joining remained only partially formed. Its basic structure was simple: twelve officials, half from the military and half from the Foreign Service. This structure had been designed by a Special Forces colonel on detail to the Department of State. Special Forces teams had twelve men, so he probably figured that would be a good system for the Kosovo Diplomatic Observer Mission. The operational model was that teams would consist of one military officer and one FSO, plus a translator. We were to travel in Chevy Suburbans that had been specially modified to withstand small arms fire, and were equipped with satellite phones and radios, plus some specialized tracking gear.

While most of the team remained in Belgrade, writing standard operating procedures and security/evacuation plans, a couple of military officers had taken up residence in the Pristina U.S. Information Service building and had begun to conduct missions. So that's where we started.

When the military gets an assignment like this, one of the services, let's say the Army, finds a unit nearby and sends it off to carry out the mission. The unit will have been together for years in some cases. All of the soldiers will have undergone basic and advanced training in their specialties, plus additional training on working together as a team to complete their mission. When the State Department gets a mission like this it's a little different. The Department isn't organized into platoons and companies and battalions. Individual officers have their specialties, but there are no formed units. When something like this comes up, the Department sends out a volunteer cable and hopes for the best.

In effect, you get whoever is available. In Kosovo, we initially had a team of seeming misfits: an intern from Ambassador Bob Gelbard's office who had to go back to graduate school at Harvard in September; our communications technician; the desk officer for Kuwait, who was to start Arabic language training in three weeks; and me. On the military side we had a couple of attachés from western European posts, an F-111 pilot nicknamed Moon from London, a Special Forces officer from Fort Bragg, and some staff officers from the planning cell at U.S. European Command in Stuttgart.

None of us spoke any of the relevant languages, so we hired translators. Most of the translators were young Albanian women who spoke English, Albanian, and Serbian. We probably would have hired Serbians to translate for us, but we couldn't find any Serbs who were willing and who spoke Albanian.

We stayed for a few days in the USIS office, sleeping on cots and doing business over macchiatos in the coffee shop around the corner. Within the week we moved a few kilometers to the south to a hotel the Embassy staff had rented for us in the Serbian enclave of Kosovo Polje—the Hotel Herzegovina.

I shared a room on the third floor in a back corner of the hotel with Moon, the Air Force pilot and attaché. It was divided into what could only in the loosest terms be called a suite, with a front room where a couch might plausibly be placed but now featured a bed, and a back room, barely big enough for a single bed and a side table, my space. There was one window, about a foot and one half square, and high up on the wall. In the July heat, it was our only source of air.

At night, any breeze was welcome, but in late summer the dominant weather pattern featured a wind from the west that carried with it the soot and smell of a lignite coal plant a few miles away. After a few nights of this we started sleeping with the window closed, but it had little effect. We woke each morning covered in soot, with our mouths and noses caked, coughing from the pollution.

My first few days on the team were spent getting to know the area. Pristina itself was a mostly charmless, Socialist-architectured burg. A few Mercedes—someone said they all were stolen from Western

Europe or the U.S. and brought to Serbia through Albania—wove between the Ladas and Yugos downtown. Coffee shops lined the streets and customers spilled out onto the sidewalks, smoking and sipping espressos from beautiful, Italian-made machines. Older women wore headscarves—this was the only real sign of the dominant Muslim culture—while younger women wore tight skirts. Our first trip outside Pristina was a tour d'horizon with the defense attachés from the American and British embassies, mostly just getting a feel for the roads and how to manage the innumerable checkpoints (government) and roadblocks (rebels). Kosovo is small enough that you can drive across it in a couple of hours, and we would be covering all the main roads and hitting all the major towns in a matter of days.

I went on my first real mission a couple of days later. We were out in the area west of Malisevo and came across a small cluster of houses where there had obviously been a firefight. The locals said the VJ had attacked the day before with tanks. Earlier in my career, when I was on active duty in the Army, I had been an armor officer, a tanker, and had learned over the years that civilians, and even some military, figure that anything bigger than an SUV is a tank. So I was a bit skeptical. Then we walked around to the back of the house.

Most of the back wall was missing, completely disintegrated. The owner of the house told us through our translator that the tanks had fired from the wood-line a couple hundred meters away. We walked over there and found two shells from a 100mm tank cannon lying on the ground. I threw them in the back of our Suburban, and we continued our chat with the owner. As we were talking to him, a Swedish film crew showed up and started filming. We continued our work. The owner showed us where pieces from one of the tank rounds had pushed all the way to the front wall of the house. He pointed to a small hole at the base of the house's foundation, and said the second round was embedded there.

I paused for a moment and thought about what that might mean. Tanks generally fire two types of rounds: high explosive or sabot. Sabot rounds are designed to destroy other tanks. They are usually made of some highly dense alloy of tungsten or of depleted uranium and designed to penetrate the heavy armor of the enemy tank. High Explosive (HE) rounds are designed to blow up other things, like trucks or houses. A tanker would have fired an HE round at the house, thus the huge hole where the back wall used to be. If this guy was right, there was a chance that an unexploded HE round was stuck in the ground under the house.

I looked into the hole. I didn't see anything. I gingerly got down on my hands and knees. The Swedish cameraman leaned over me and I joked with him, "Don't show this film to my mother." I dug around a bit in the hole but couldn't find anything. I tried to explain to the man what he might be living on top of, but he didn't seem particularly phased by the possibility that another of his house's walls might disappear given that the back half was already gone.

That evening I triumphantly carried the two tank shells into the team office. Our boss was less than pleased. I was the first to bring in what could even in the wildest sense be termed souvenirs of the fighting. I saw them as evidence that the Serbs were using heavy armor against unarmed civilians—a war crime. My boss told me I should have left them out there. We weren't supposed to be bringing in stuff from the battlefield, he said. I suspected at the time it was because the Serbs would think we were unduly targeting them.

Later that month, this new rule would come back to bite one of our military officers in the ass. My friend from Uganda and Zaire had brought something small back from the field. I don't even remember what it was. Regardless, he was gone the next morning. It seemed like this was part of the ongoing squabble between the Foreign Service and the military over control of the team.

Little things like the level of detail in our reports about personnel and equipment present at checkpoints highlighted fundamental differences in the way in which soldiers and diplomats went about their work. The military wanted as much detail as possible in every report: how many people, what were they wearing, how many and what kind of weapons, communications equipment, vehicles, etc. Each point of data helped to create for analysts and planners a coherent picture of the opposing forces.

The Foreign Service officers were more accustomed to what I referred to as the Impressionist School of reporting. Typical reports would include a high level of detail and precision over the words and actions encountered, but spare coverage of the equipment. Frankly, FSOs aren't generally trained to be able to tell the difference between a howitzer and a tank. This, one might think, would augur well for pairing up the two sides and combining their reports at the end of the day to create a coherent whole. But it never worked that way. Both sides simply became recalcitrant, and our lone reports officer—tasked to make sense of a half dozen field reports daily—struggled with the mix. Eventually, the State Department's methods prevailed. We were a diplomatic observer mission, after all.

My friend packed out and was gone the morning after he committed the minor infraction. The military officers felt that they had been put on notice, and that our boss, a Senior Foreign Service officer (the civilian equivalent of a General Officer in the military), had demonstrated his hegemony over the team.

On a mission in August, we were driving in the west of the province trying to get to a village west of Klina. We were stopped at a checkpoint by some MUP reservists who told us there were terrorists operating in the village just ahead, and that we couldn't proceed. In reality, what this meant was that the MUP were clearing out a village and likely burning a bunch of houses and they didn't want us in the way. We had been stopped at every road leading into the villages.

This was an everyday or almost everyday occurrence. Usually, we would come back the next day and find a bunch of burned houses and reports of missing people. Sometimes we could talk our way through these checkpoints by explaining that we were willing to take our risks—if this happened, we understood the MUP were simply screwing around with us—but other times we weren't going to get through. It usually took about half an hour to figure out which situation we were facing. On this day, after forty-five minutes, we were getting ready to take off when one of the MUP guys motioned for our translator, Sanije, to come speak with him. They walked a few feet away and talked quietly for a minute or two. He handed her something and she turned to join us in the car.

"What was that all about? I asked. "He's from Podujevo, my town, and he asked me to call his girlfriend to tell her he's OK."

"Are you going to do that?"

"Sure. I know who she is. I've seen her around."

With this simple interaction, the binary world of ethnic hatred I was constructing in my head dissolved. These weren't two peoples whose long-standing enmity had boiled over into civil war. These were neighbors, their lives intertwined in nearly every possible way. They shopped in the same markets. They watched the same football and basketball teams. They used the same public transportation. They shared a common history—although they chose to view this in a different light. They were killing each other every day, and I was supposed to stop it.

Klaxon

A S THE INSURGENCY SPREAD ACROSS Kosovo that summer, the lines between Serb and Albanian were clear. But even among themselves, ethnic Albanians were forced to take sides. On one side were Ibrahim Rugova and his Kosovo Democratic League (LDK) that had represented Kosovar Albanians for a decade as Milosevic had systematically destroyed Yugoslavia in the name of Serbian nationalism. Rugova was a Sorbonne-educated intellectual, a professor of literature, who had organized a shadow government that managed everything from holding university classes in people's homes, to delivering health care, to picking up the trash. Rugova was a pacifist.

The other choice that summer was the KLA, the group of mostly young dissidents who had gathered enough arms after the Albanian government collapsed in the wake of the pyramid scheme to set up a pretty efficient insurgency.

In February the Serbs had attacked the Jashari family compound in Gornje Prekaze, killing Adem Jashari along with fifty-three others, mostly members of his extended family, as retribution for attacks on police stations in the area that they thought Jashari had organized and led. Within weeks there was war.

In those early days there were several KLAs. There was one in

Southwest Kosovo, in Dukagjini; another in Drenica, the heartland; a third in the east, in Llap. Each group had its own organizational personality and each group was particularly good at certain complementary skills. The Drenica bunch were the organizers, the Llap group expert smugglers, and the Dukagjini group were arguably the toughest fighters. Slowly, the groups merged and strengthened. By June, the KLA had established "Free Kosova" with the headquarters in Malisevo.

There was a small well in the garden of a café near the center of Malisevo, known as the Well of Freedom. Kosovars would drive from all over the Province in those heady days to drink from it. But, on June 24 the MUP and the VJ moved against Malisevo. That morning, the VJ commander blocked three of the four roads leading into Malisevo and began to roll tanks towards the town. The KLA beat a strategic retreat and the entire civilian population—save one old woman—moved a few kilometers south into the Pagarusha valley.

At one point in early August I asked my Kosovar Albanian translator if a person we had just interviewed was KLA or not. She smiled and said, "Don't you understand? We're all KLA." While Rugova's picture may still have hung in thousands of homes across Kosovo, the KLA was fighting back and gaining supporters and strength.

Malisevo became a center of gravity to my work. Its axial position in the province meant that I drove through the town almost daily going to one place or another. We really thought the town was empty until one afternoon on the way through we saw that old woman sweeping her stoop. We stopped to talk with her.

Her house was on the main road that ran out from the town center to the southeast. It must have been one of the oldest homes in the town. She wasn't fully in control of her faculties, but she wasn't totally around the bend either. We asked her if she lived alone. She told us her husband—we later learned he had died years before—was out and expected back. She didn't seem concerned that she was the only person remaining in the town. We talked to her for a few minutes and then left her to continue sweeping the stoop. Every once in a while afterwards, we would check in on her to see how she was getting along.

Driving around the province day after day in our Suburbans, we spent time talking and listening to music on cassettes. My regular partner was Rob, a retired Marine master sergeant, who had joined the Foreign Service as a communications technician. We were paired up, I suppose, because there were actually more Foreign Service personnel on the team than military, and since both of us had military experience it seemed to balance out the lack of a career military officer.

We were also about the same age—Rob a few years older —and had roughly the same musical taste. Rob had made a bunch of tapes before leaving Frankfurt, and he always had one in his bag for the mission. My favorite was one with lots of Creedence Clearwater Revival, Steve Miller, and The Who. He hadn't labeled them but somehow seemed to know which was which. Our translators were all considerably younger and had different musical tastes, I'm sure. One of them had got her hands on this specific cassette at some point and scrawled "Geezer Rock" on the label. Fair enough.

Back in Pristina my work with the NGOs was being supplanted a bit: USAID had brought in someone who actually knew what he was doing, so I was off the hook. I still made the rounds sometimes, particularly to groups that served as information clearing houses like the UN High Commission for Refugees (UNHCR) and International Red Cross (ICRC). Both groups kept maps of where mines had been reported or had actually gone off. With our teams running around the province, we stopped in regularly to see not only what others had reported, but also to update the maps with what we had learned.

At one point in late August we were driving on a road that was mined, or at least so the locals thought. We had no idea. It was a small road just south of Lladrovac and the hills where the KLA had their headquarters. We were driving along slowly, looking for a way into a small town the Serbs were said to have attacked the night before, when a couple of guys with Kalashnikovs stood up next to the road and flagged us down. They told us the road had been mined a few hundred meters ahead and that we should turn around. We decided this was probably good advice and followed it.

Not far back down the road we met a man leading a donkey cart. We stopped to speak to him. His eyes were red-rimmed, and tears, now dried, had carved little trails down through the dirt on his cheeks. I asked him where his family was, fully expecting him to point up into the hills near Sedlare where a large number of IDPs had settled. He looked down for a moment and then stepped over to the trailer. He looked directly into my eyes.

He said, "I'd like to introduce you to my family," and flipped back the tarp covering the trailer.

In the trailer were the mutilated bodies of his wife and children. He named them all and then waited for us to react.

I was too stunned to speak. The man stood staring at me through those red-rimmed eyes, daring me or maybe imploring me to say something, anything. I was mute. My translator, Mimoza, was silent as well. There was nothing to translate.

After a moment, Mimi said something to the man in Albanian. He nodded. I asked, "What will you do now?" But stopped her with a hand on her forearm before she could translate. "Where are you taking them?" I asked instead.

"I have to bury them," was all he managed to say.

Again, there was nothing to say.

"I'm glad I found them," the man said. "I'm lucky I found them."

At least we knew the rumors of an attack were true. We warned him of the mines along the road. He said he knew about them, but thanked us. He thwacked the donkey on its haunch with the branch in his hand and they moved off down the road.

When we got back to town, I went over to the UNHCR and ICRC to mark that the road was mined on their maps. Our relationship with the UN agencies, like the High Commission for Refugees and the World Food Program (WFP) was guided—some might say clouded—by the fact that the U.S. is one of, if not the biggest, donor to their operations. In fact, when congressional staffers came to Kosovo to look in on what was happening, they always asked to meet with the

UN leadership.

In one case, after a dinner we had put together for a senior congressional staffer, she questioned the UNHCR and WFP leaders so intently, others in the room quietly left until just four of us remained. After our talk the staffer looked like she needed a cigarette. The UN staff mockingly complained later of being interrogated and tortured.

Our team was growing. We gained an Air Force lieutenant named Eric as our intelligence officer. He would work through the night to pull together a morning briefing for us that was supposed to give us what the military refers to as situational awareness. The problem was that we were the only reporting element for the U.S. Government in the area so there wasn't any additional reporting except that received from the Top Secret signals intelligence or imagery satellites. And we couldn't get access to that information because we didn't have a Secure Compartmentalized Information Facility (SCIF), a place where we could keep a computer that could link into those systems and store the information we'd downloaded. Still, every morning, Eric would dutifully put together as best he could a morning report to brief us on.

After a couple of weeks, he was joined by an Army intel officer. I knew this guy from my time in Germany in the cavalry; he had joined my squadron just before I left at the end of my three-year tour. Doug took over the night shift from Eric, but was no more effective at putting substance into the briefing—there simply wasn't substantive intelligence to be had. And the night shift was grueling. Doug would start at around two a.m., and work through until our morning brief at about eight a.m. He would try to catch up on sleep during the day while we were out. It apparently didn't work well.

He wanted to find a place that would be quieter than his room in the middle of the hotel. He nosed around, found my little space in the back, and decided he wanted it. I wasn't keen to swap, but told him that if all he needed was a quiet space to sleep, he could crash on my rack when I was out. For whatever reason, this wasn't enough. He complained to our boss that I wasn't a team player because I wanted to keep my space. My boss pulled me aside and asked that I give up my space for Doug so he could sleep. I explained that I had offered him the space during the day and he had refused it. We were stubbornly at a bit of a deadlock over what seemed at the time to be a very minor issue.

But one afternoon when we came back from a mission, I learned that Doug had collapsed. He had gone for a few days with almost no sleep. His boss, an ambitious Army lieutenant colonel, had been constantly on his back over the character of the morning briefings. While we had been out, Doug had gone into a rage, throwing things around the office and breaking up some furniture in his room. His roommate, a very sturdy Marine Corps major, had finally been forced to restrain him, holding him in a bear hug until he relented and calmed down. That evening the Deputy Chief of Mission from Belgrade came down, and the next morning the two left Kosovo together. The DCM said that, on the way back, as soon as they had left Kosovo and crossed into Serbia proper, Doug seemed to come to—like a flower opening, he said.

Doug's collapse should have been a klaxon, warning us of what was to come. But, if it was, we failed to heed it. Either we didn't understand what we needed to learn from it, or we refused to accept that it could happen to any of us. We would endure other, less spectacular crashes on our team. Some came during our tours, and a few hit long afterwards. Some of us would learn the hard way that working around ethnic cleansing and war crimes leaves an indelible mark on the psyche and, possibly, the soul.

Yellow

Y ELLOW. THEIR SKIN WAS YELLOW. They had dirt under their fingernails and their feet were dirty. There were six of them, all women, under the tarpaulin. Some of them had lived long enough to have their wounds bandaged before they died. Some of them were killed more or less instantly as shrapnel or 7.62mm rounds had entered their bodies. They had been dead for about 24 hours. We knew this because we had come to witness their funeral—to witness and to stand a type of guard. If we were present, the Serb snipers would not shoot at the family members as they buried their dead.

It was the first time I had ever seen war dead. I remember being surprised that their skin was yellow. My experiences with death before that day had been to a few funerals: a friend's older brother, my grandmother. None of them had been yellow. So I was surprised at the color. This was the first time I had ever seen what dead people looked like if no embalming was done. What they looked like without make-up and a nice suit of clothes. They were just dead.

Lying in a tangle of limbs under a blue UN tarp on a trailer that only a week before had carried peppers and corn to the market in Malisevo. Only parts of their bodies were visible. I couldn't see all of their faces. One had an arm resting across her forehead. One had a bandage covering most of her head.

One of the dead was missing, an eighteen- month-old child. We had seen some dogs on the way up the trail. Morgan Morris, the dauntless UN refugee agency field officer who had led us to the scene, said what all of us were thinking, "The dogs probably got the body." She was right, of course, but none of us wanted to be the one to say it. We had just seen the mother, resting in a house in the village a couple kilometers away. She had a bullet in her upper arm. The bullet had passed through her baby, then through her breast before lodging in her arm. The father said the baby was killed instantly. "The bullet tore the child in half," he said. He had dragged the mother away to safety. A doctor from the Red Cross was treating her wounds in a small house in the village. There were ten women and a seventy-two year-old man in one stifling, airless room of the house. All of them had been wounded in the attack. They sat silently on the floor, their backs against the walls of the room, lost in their pain and their thoughts, waiting.

Standing in that house on the day after the attack, with the smell of sweat and blood and wounds mingling with the smell of fear in the air, I was overwhelmed with the sense that I was in the middle of something I didn't, and maybe couldn't, understand, and that people's lives depended on my doing the right thing. The old man's eyes were filled with something between hate and incomprehension: hatred for the Serbs and incomprehension that an American and a Brit—representatives of the United States and the United Nations— were standing in his living room doing nothing about the Serbian infantry a couple of kilometers away who had just killed six women and an infant, and wounded all these others.

Senik was a village of roughly five hundred people, consisting of no more than a couple of dozen houses at a three-way intersection on a dirt road. Hardly enough to warrant a spot on the map; it was too small to have a school. There was an elementary school at the base of the hill a couple of kilometers away. Even in the winter the kids could walk that far. There was only one small store. Everyone went into Malisevo to do their shopping. The trouble with Senik, in the eyes of the Serbian military police who attacked it was that it was on the edge of Berisha Mountain and near Lladrovac, a Kosovo Liberation Army stronghold and headquarters. It was becoming Serbian policy to attack villages that supported the KLA. We never really knew if the villagers supported the KLA before this attack, but afterwards they certainly did—after they had buried six of their women and watched as doctors treated eleven more.

Morgan and I stood at the edge of a trail a couple of kilometers up the road from the house where the doctors were tending the wounded. Some men and women from the village walked slowly behind a tractor pulling the bodies on a trailer into the valley. She had told me the story the night before over a beer in my office in Kosovo Polje. She led us—me, another American and our translator, and several members of the European Union's mission—to the scene. She, and several men from the village, walked us around the area explaining what had happened the previous afternoon, and in the days leading up to what was to be the first event our team would document in which Serbian special police had attacked civilians. As we moved from yard to yard, they would point out a grenade or mortar fragment in a wall, some dried blood on the ground of a garden still full of tomatoes and peppers. They spoke calmly as if they were merchants showing us used furniture on sale in a warehouse.

The basics of the story went like this. Three days before, ethnic Albanians living in the village of Senik had seen a Serbian T-55 tank roll up the road towards their village from the direction of Malisevo. Many chose not to wait to see what the Serbs had in mind. They packed what they could onto tractors and headed for the higher ground to the northeast. But, the tank did not enter the village. It was simply a demonstration by the Army of what was to come.

The following morning, six mortar rounds hit in the village. We thought the rounds had come from the high ground to the northwest, beyond the draw of a small canyon where those who had departed were hiding. But that was probably too far.

The base of the canyon was surrounded by cliffs three or four hundred feet tall on three sides and led to a narrow gorge that continued to climb to the east. The villagers had spread out in the flat, rocky area at the bottom of the draw on both sides of an intermittent stream. They had parked their tractors and Zastavas helter-skelter around the canyon center. Some had erected small windscreens and shelters from plastic sheeting, and covered them with branches. Many had erected shelters on the trailers they pulled behind their tractors. These looked for all the world like the Conestoga wagons of the American West as they moved along Kosovo's roads that summer.

One woman had been injured in the first shelling, hit by some 60mm mortar fragments as she was tending to the tomatoes in her garden. We discovered some fragments in the wall of her house, and found her resting inside with the others, waiting for the Red Cross doctors to treat her wounds. The rest of the village, except for those too old to move, had left that afternoon.

The next day, mortar shells rained down on the families in the draw and the trees nearby. Minutes later a platoon of special police, who had been trained as infantry, moved through the canyon, firing automatic weapons. We found dozens of shell casings littering the ground. This was when the six women and the baby had been killed, and most of those in the house down below had been wounded. Unarmed women and children were shelled and shot, and seven civilians murdered by the police, the protectors of the State. I had to keep reminding myself that this was Europe at the end of the 20th century.

The villagers wanted to bury the dead in plain sight of the ridgeline where we could still see Serbian snipers. The land, they said, had been taken from them in the 1940s, and they had reclaimed it in the 1970s. It belonged to these people, and they were going to be sure that the Serbs understood that. The women they were burying were born in this valley and had spent their lives raising crops in its fields and giving birth to their children in the small houses that made up the hardscrabble town.

We had parked our vehicles in plain view as a deterrent to further shooting. Certainly, the Serbs wouldn't shoot at EU and U.S. observers or the white and blue UNHCR vehicle. Nonetheless, I admit I was shaky standing about at the base of the draw.

The ground was hard and it took some time to bury the dead. The men worked with shovels and picks for about an hour to dig graves for the women. Afterwards, we stopped on the way out of the draw and used our satellite telephone to call Washington and tell the State Department's Operations Center what we had seen. It seemed very far away from that hillside. The officer on the line was a colleague, a classmate and a friend. Had it been someone else, I might have been more animated in my description of the scene. But he understood what was happening without my resorting to histrionics.

"Eleven wounded: ten women and one seventy-two year-old man. Seven dead: six women and one child."

"Yes, I counted them myself."

"Yes, we're sure they were dead. I verified it personally." I left out the part about the dogs.

We made one more stop on the way off the hill. An old man flagged us down as we were leaving the draw for the village, and told our interpreter he wanted to show us something the Serbs had done. I glanced through the window of the house and saw a group of women sitting on the floor and rocking slowly, comforting each other. They surrounded the body of another woman. She was laid out on her back and wrapped in a blanket. Part of her face and head were missing, what remained was veiled in a colorful scarf. The man said a mortar round had exploded within a meter of her head. He held his hands out in front of his body to demonstrate the distance. The sitting women wailed in unison as he said this. He was the dead woman's father. Amid the crying and the smell and the flies, we listened to his story.

Having felt safe enough in her house to remain there with her husband and children rather than moving up with the others, she had decided to take some food up to her neighbors hiding in the small canyon. She was at the base of the draw when the attack started. The mortar shells probably came in groups of three. *Poonk, poonk, poonk* as they left the tubes, then the breathless, agonizing five or six second wait while they flew, and finally the brittle *kahrump, kahrump, kahrump,* barking and echoing off the walls of the canyon as they exploded. The gunners probably set the fuses to go off about one and one half or two meters above the ground—about head high.

It was an awful story. I couldn't wait to get out of there, away from the smell and the crying and the death. I felt outraged and horrified that soldiers would fire mortars at women and children. I had to look away. I concentrated on the colors in the woman's headscarf rather than her wounds. I watched the other women slowly rocking. I looked at the woman's father. My partner Rob photographed her body, and I took notes about what her father said. Then we left. Eight dead.

Down the hill, at the intersection marking Senik proper, a crowd of women and a few men had gathered. Some boys were sitting by the edge of the road with a wooden box filled with cigarettes, crackers and Chiclets—entrepreneurs. They sat expressionless as a small crowd swarmed our vehicle. I pushed open the door and stood pinned against the truck by the crowd as my translator echoed staccato pleas for help. One woman pushed through the crowd and held her baby at arms length in front of me. I was face to face with the child while the mother spoke deliberately but calmly.

"She wants you to take her son out of here so the Serbs won't kill him," Mimoza said.

I looked at the woman and said to Mimi, "Make sure she knows we can't do that. Say this, 'We are observers. We can't relocate you or your son. If we do, the Government in Belgrade will order all of us out of the country.'"

I felt feckless and impotent as the words spilled out. For the first time, I understood the folly of being in the war only to observe—a tourist among the victims. It was hot and, with the sun beating down on me, I felt cowardly, yellow, hiding behind my sunglasses. I waved my notebook at the Red Cross panel truck and said that was the vehicle that would take them to safety. I thought the Red Cross would probably refuse, but I was unable to muster the courage to tell the woman and the fifty other people crowded around me that there was little hope she would get out that day with an International. I found out later that I had been wrong. Several UNHCR officers arrived late in the day, and one of them took it upon herself to evacuate some of the children to a safer village.

Before we left, I went back into the house where the wounded were being treated. I had to tell the mother of the missing child that we didn't find her baby. It would have served no purpose to tell her what we thought had happened. I couldn't have found those words anyway.

That evening after we had returned to our office, after we washed our truck, I drafted my report. It was only about three pages long: no speculation, just the things we understood to have happened based on what we saw and what was reported to us. I said it appeared that a Serbian infantry unit had swept through the valley from north to south, preceded by a barrage of mortar fire. During the barrage and subsequent infantry sweep seven women and one infant had been killed, and eleven others wounded including a 72-year-old man. Vehicles and clothes, food and other supplies were burned in the sweep. I said we had seen no evidence of weapons or of any insurgent activity in the village or among the villagers.

I didn't mention the funeral or the dogs. I didn't mention the woman begging me to take some action to save her children. I didn't mention the look on the old man's face. I carefully caveated what was told to us versus what we saw ourselves with qualifiers like reportedly and allegedly. I carefully made the people and the events in the village the center of the report rather than my actions or my feelings—never star in your own report. I let my teammates read the report to ensure we all agreed with it, and then I turned it in to the reports officer, our editor. I had written a crisp, dry account of a messy, horrible act of cruelty. In doing so, I had documented a war crime.

Istinic

W E HEARD ABOUT A LARGE group of IDPs near the town of Istinic, in the far west of the province. I went to the town, but was intercepted along the way by Kurt Schork, who was covering the insurgency for Reuters. Clearly infuriated, he was leaning out of his armored vehicle and frantically waving to stop me. As I pulled alongside his land rover, he yelled, "Where's the international community now?!? There are twenty thousand people being herded like cattle down there and what are you doing about it? Where's the sense of outrage!?!"

Kurt was one of my closest contacts at that point. He was a mature, professional journalist who had covered Bosnia and Chechnya, and was now spending his time covering the most difficult and dangerous flashpoints in Kosovo. Our paths crossed regularly, and often when I arrived to cover an event, Kurt was there to fill me in on what had happened. He was usually unflappable, and the fact that he was yelling at me rather than talking to me was disturbing. I assumed the worst lay ahead, waved, and noted that I was on my way.

I worked my way to the town through a series of west Kosovo farm roads. Peja (the Serbians called it Pec), the largest town in western Kosovo sits at the base of the Prokletije Mountains and the Prester Plateau that separate Kosovo from Montenegro. The mountains rise unannounced and nearly vertically from the fields of vegetables and villages scattered across the lowlands at their feet. Although the Patriarchate of the Serbian Orthodox church had been re-established here in 1557—only a few kilometers away, in Glodjane, stood the largest Catholic cathedral in the province—by this time the majority of the population were Albanian Muslims.

I knew there were several roads leading to Istinic but, as we got close, we found that a Serbian police vehicle blocked each of them. We got to the last turn into the town and argued our way past the Serbian police manning the checkpoint. We crept along in our vehicle, passing police buses and dozens of trucks and armored vehicles parked helter-skelter along the roadside. At the town center hundreds of Albanians were sitting on curbs or standing around in knots. We parked and began our work. Within minutes we began to understand the scope of what we were seeing.

The town center was little more than a cobblestone square with a small fountain at its center, surrounded by a dozen small buildings. Beyond the square, there were only a handful of buildings. Probably no more than 150 or 200 people called Istinic home. Just beyond the edge of the square, pastures and orchards began. A couple hundred meters east of the square was an intersection of farm roads. We later estimated 30,000 Albanians were crowded into five pastures at that intersection.

A handful of police officers stood between the square and the pastures. They wanted little to do with us, but brusquely told me that the Albanians were being taken to their homes, or if they had no homes, they would be taken to collective centers in Djakovica (Gjakova to the Albanians) or Pec. When I asked if the Albanians were being moved against their will, the Major said that the people were being moved for their safety, and then he turned away to let me know he was through answering my questions.

Dozens of men and women stood in the square. Most looked terrified whenever we approached them. I decided to ask a few of them if they wanted to leave Istinic. Several quietly said, "Don't talk to me," but some were more forthcoming. One young man said that he was from Glodjane, the Catholic village. He said the police had come to Glodjane three days before and accused the villagers of supporting the KLA. A police officer had ordered his family out of their home and told them to move towards Istinic. They had been living in the pastures under plastic sheeting for three nights. He did not want to go to Peja or to Gjakova, he said, but would go home if the road was safe. The woman next to him said she didn't want to go anywhere if the Serbs could come after them again. After those two spoke out, others came and told their remarkably similar stories. Some families were from Lodi, some from Glodjane, some from areas that had only names like "the area by the hill." They were all displaced now.

We walked out of the village center towards the pastures. Most of the major humanitarian agencies were already on the scene. I saw a *Medecins Sans Frontieres* truck parked just outside a large house in a small pasture at the eastern edge of town. Dozens of women with babies in their arms crowded against the front door. One local Albanian MSF employee was holding back the deluge of need as two staffers conducted triage in the foyer of the house. We decided not to press our way in. Doctors rarely need to talk to diplomats when they've got sixty or so patients in the waiting room. As we were turning to leave, we heard someone inside yell down the stairs, "It's a girl!"

We got into our vehicle and made our way down the road towards the largest of the five pastures. At the edge of the field a UN press officer from Australia was sitting atop her land rover with a video camera filming the events. A handful of new officers had arrived to join our team and this was their first mission introduction to Kosovo: 20,000 civilians being herded like cattle. I asked the two new guys— Nick, a Marine artilleryman, and Len, an Army Special Forces officer, both majors—to stay with the truck while I waded into the crowd with a translator.

Inside the pasture hundreds of families had spread out their lives on blankets or carpets under plastic sheeting. The Serbs had ordered everyone out of the pasture, so most people had packed what they had onto trailers and were simply waiting for instructions to move, or for an unlikely intervention by the international community. As we walked through, simply taking account of what we were witnessing, people implored us to do whatever we could.

An enervating wailing seemed to grow from near the eastern edge of the pasture, drawing us to where just a few meters away we saw a group of women holding each other and sobbing hysterically while a handful of men were comforting one old man who was near collapse. Several women were on the back of a farm trailer under a makeshift shelter built of plastic sheeting and tree branches. The women in the trailer were covering a body, what we found out was the body of their grandmother, the matriarch of the family. She had died just moments before at about the same time the mother was giving birth to the baby girl in the makeshift clinic.

As I looked around the group of women, it was painfully evident to me that they were simple farm women dressed in typical Albanian farmer clothes: baggy pants and sweaters, with black plastic slip-on shoes, their heads covered with scarves. The older man, who I assumed to be the husband and patriarch, stood silently holding in his arms a younger man, who I took to be his son, who sobbed unashamed. A few other men stood uncomfortably about the group in their farm clothes, their hands hardened by their work and their eyes misty.

I felt my jaw tighten against the sadness as we walked close to the group. One of the men looked at me as if he wanted to grab me by the collar and shake me for not stopping this from happening. I must have looked hollow and grey because in a second his glance seemed to go right through me. We passed quietly.

Inside the largest of the pastures, I met some workers from Mercy Corps International. One was snapping photos and trying to document what was happening. He introduced me to Rruk Berisha, the LDK's representative in the area who lived in Glodjane. Berisha calmly detailed the story of how the IDPs had come to Istinic in fear of attacks on their home villages. The police were now driving them out of the area because, he said, they were becoming an embarrassment to the Serbian government. The crowd around us agreed.

I wandered around a bit more and found the World Food Program team leader, a mountain of a man, easily 6'5" and about 250 pounds. He was a former Royal Marine commando and as intimidating a physical presence as one could imagine. He was clearly outraged at what was happening, and was moved almost to tears of fury at the situation surrounding us.

As I walked through the pastures, I watched the police order the Albanian families onto the road and towards the collection point at the fountain. The police were using their rifles to prod the slow movers and just behind them two wheeled armored vehicles called BOV-Ms were moving slowly around the field with steel grates folded across their fronts, crushing the remaining small shelters, and herding the very last stragglers towards the gates. Atop each of the vehicles, a soldier sat poised behind a machine gun. There was nothing we could do, save document the forced eviction of thousands of people and send the reports back to Washington. Maybe, I thought, the NGOs and the UN might actually be helpful.

Podujevo

THE CALLS BEGAN LATE in the evening. We were sitting around the hotel restaurant that served as our dining room, done with writing our reports about that day's mission and more or less through planning the following day's mission, and probably drinking a beer. The first call came from Liz at Oxfam.

"Have you heard?" she asked. "A compound was burned with four people locked inside the houses." Within minutes other contacts had called with similar stories.

We drove out the next morning under a granite sky. We stopped in Podujevo and Mimoza, my translator and teammate, called a friend familiar with the area to act as a guide to the village a few kilometers away.

Zastavas and Toyotas lined the roadside for a few hundred meters before we got to the entrance to the compound. Inside, there were probably a hundred people standing around in groups of four and five. They stared and motioned towards us as we got out of our vehicle. A woman nearby said something in Albanian.

"It's going to be all right," Mimi answered her softly. A restless rain fell, and the ground was slippery as we came up to the crowded compound. I knew that, despite what Mimi said, it was not going to be all right.

There were three buildings on the compound, two houses and an outbuilding. All three had been burned. All three had sections of their roofs that had collapsed. Even in the light rain, smoke still floated up from blackened and broken rafters. A Volkswagen Golf smoldered in the muddy yard. One door hung open, there were bullet holes in the doors and front end, and several of the windows were shattered.

Mimi spoke for a moment with a young man standing at the edge of the drive, and he pointed us to the smaller of the two houses. The house was typical for this part of Kosovo: concrete block walls painted white with a red tile mansard roof, a door in the center and a couple of windows on the facade.

The roof was mostly burned away. Window glass lay shattered on the muddy ground outside; a curtain fluttered through a window frame on the front of the house. The door was burned through and a locked padlock hung from a hasp on the wooden doorframe. As I stepped inside, I instinctively but needlessly wiped my feet. The walls more or less had survived the fire; they were blackened and wet from the rain. I splashed a bit through small puddles as I moved about the room. The furniture was charred. I carefully noted the damage and tried to find the right words to describe what I saw while a small crowd gathered at the doors and windows, watching and whispering.

The room was strewn with ordinariness gone awry. Some shoes and a pair of children's rain boots left by the door had filled with rainwater, and a sack of flour cut open and spilled now made a pallid, muddy batter on the floor. There were dishes in the sink and a leaf floated in the ashen grey water. Some jelly jar glasses lay overturned on the edge of the counter. A man in a *plis*, the distinctive conical hat worn by older Albanian men, stared at me through the window over the sink. Silently, he watched me observe the scene.

There were two bodies lying on the floor of the kitchen. They were monstrously disfigured. Nothing remained of their faces; their hands and feet had been burned off. No clothing or jewelry or hair remained. Their skin was charred almost to cinders. They looked like they were made of some dusky obsidian crystal that would shatter or collapse if I touched them. Only their form gave them away as human. I couldn't tell their gender.

The first corpse I guessed was a woman, but it was no more than a guess. She lay on her back with her legs bent upwards at the hips and then folded at the knees. What remained of her arms pointed upwards from her elbows. She looked as if she had been sitting and had fallen off the chair onto her back or as if she had been crawling and simply turned over but remained in the same position.

A few feet away, nearer to the sink, lay another corpse. I guessed this one was a man. He lay on his right side, frozen into the same position with his legs bent and arms extended. I wondered why they were in the exact same configuration. Dead people on television always lay in tortured, random positions with an arm underneath the torso and legs akimbo.

I took notes and nodded to Mimi when I was ready to move on. Someone asked if we wanted to see the bedroom. I felt we had already intruded enough on the dead, helping their murderers rob them of any final dignity. Looking into the bedroom seemed coarse and invasive, like rifling uninvited through their most personal belongings. But still we went to look at the other room of the house.

The fire hadn't spread too far into the bedroom. The paint on the door had bubbled off, but it remained in one piece. The windows were still in place. Part of the roof had burned away because of the fire in the main room I thought, and a breeze loosed cinders hanging on the wall amid wan grey streaks from the smoke. A few cinders floated on the air. I watched one ride a draft upwards and out through the hole where the roof had been. One landed on the leg of my jeans and hung there just for a moment like a butterfly.

A poster of pacifist political leader Ibrahim Rugova that must have hung on the wall lay ripped in half on the floor surrounded by the detritus of lives: shoes, clothes, and books littered the wet floor like jetsam on the shore of some ruined lake.

We stepped outside through a side door and circled around to the front of the house. A low wall surrounded the main house. Just inside the wall stood what was left of a small outbuilding. We pushed past the door hanging on one hinge to get inside. The family had stored grain and tools here. Shards of broken red tiles from the collapsed roof covered the dirt floor of the shack. Along the back wall, under a window, was another body.

This one was smaller than the others and so fully burned as to be unrecognizable. I wondered if it was a child or a big dog. Had the family hidden their child in this shed or did the killers lock the dog in there to keep it out of the way? I stood for a moment looking at the window and wondered if, whatever this creature was, it had fought to get out of the building while the roof burned and crackled and collapsed. As the room filled with smoke, did this child or dog try to claw its way up to the window to escape until it was overcome with the smoke? I imagined how terrified it must have been to be locked in a burning shed. I could picture the smoke and heat and flame. I imagined voices outside, screaming and crying, and gunfire. I imagined that whatever creature this was, it had curled into a ball where, as it lay in the space between the wall and floor, death came to it.

I needed to focus on something else. I looked out the window placed high on the wall, up towards the clouds and the treetops. I smelled the leaves, wet from the rain. I smelled the smoke and wondered if I smelled death. I heard people talking in hushed voices, a woman's plangent cry. Out the door, I saw a teenaged girl holding her hand across her mouth as her eyes welled with tears, her face twisted with anguish at the realization of what had happened. Others, inured to the killing and death or simply too shocked and scared by what they found, unable or unwilling to cry, stood in small groups whispering among themselves.

We slipped out through the doorframe, turned and crossed the yard to the main house. The tile roof was burnt through on one side and smoke had smudged the white paint around the two windows on the façade. Small flowerbeds lined the walk up to the door; several people stood on the path but stepped aside as we came up. I glanced at the oldest man in the group. He wore a *plis* with a wool scarf wrapped around it to ward off the chill. I nodded to him, trying to offer him my condolences and to show him respect. With his right hand he touched his breast over his heart and nodded back. His eyes were full of tears and he clung to the elbow of an older woman, his wife I guessed, who held out her hand in a gesture of supplication. I reached out to her and touched her hand. I knew I could do no more.

But they wanted more. In their eyes I had come to make things all right. In their eyes I was America. I was the person, the people, the country who was going to make this all right. Mimi had said so.

"I'm sorry," I said, taking her hand in mine.

The woman held my hand for a moment and said something in Albanian, then turned and moved slowly away, gesturing towards the house and heaven, talking to no one and everyone. The other women in the group trailed after her. One took her hand and the other draped an arm around her shoulder as they walked slowly towards the drive. The old man turned back toward me momentarily. I tried to think of what I would find to say to my wife were we in a similar situation. There was nothing either of us could say, so I touched the sleeve of his jacket and went inside.

The door lay on the floor a few feet into the room, apparently kicked off its hinges. A young woman with a baby in her arms stood silhouetted in the frame of a window at the back of the house. She looked at me blankly and after a moment turned away. The walls, once probably white, were now charred bible black. Fire had burned a hole in the roof on the left side of the room. Beneath the remnants of the tile roof furniture and clothes lay ruined. A television sat upended in the center of the floor with a yawning hole in its screen.

In a bedroom on the left a mattress hung half on the floor and half on the bed. Its center had been slashed several times, and foam leached from the gashes. A dresser's drawers had been pulled out and ransacked; clothes hung from the drawers and lay scattered about on the floor. As I picked up a picture from off the floor, the shattered glass fell out from the frame. A teenage girl smiled vapidly from within— her make-up was garish, her dark hair blown and styled into a Texas shopping mall-sized thatch.

The fourth body was in the bedroom on the right. Less disfigured than the others, he lay face down with his arms by his sides and his left ankle crossed under the calf, his right leg forming a figure 4. Fire had completely engulfed the room but the body was more or less intact. Unlike the first two, the feet and hands remained, cracked and blackened but clearly recognizable. There may have been some scraps of clothing left on the body. I remember there were bullet holes in his back.

Rain fell through the holes in the roof and my notebook was getting wet. I kept scribbling, desperate to put something, anything, on the page that might explain what lay before me. People around me were speaking but I couldn't make out what they were saying. Albanian, German, English, the language didn't matter: I couldn't understand what people were saying. I saw them talking, I watched them carry on conversations, but I couldn't hear them. I looked at the body. The harder I tried to understand, the less I did understand. The rain, lapsing, fell onto my notebook, smearing the ink of the words that would never be good enough to explain what this was.

So I kept writing. I tried to describe the room. I tried to see the whole room, but I could only see the man lying on the floor. Something was wrong with the room. I could see it but I couldn't describe it. The room was screwed up; it wasn't all right. If it were all right I could describe it. If it were all right it wouldn't have a dead guy burnt up and lying in the middle of it with holes in his back and half covered in roof tiles and rain. Water dripped off my hat and ran down my face. I looked at my notebook. The paper was wet and I could read the words written on the other side of the page. Even backwards I could make them out: *burned, killed, destroyed*. My pen dragged across the wet page, tearing the paper. I knew I had to get the description of this house and this murder down onto the page but I couldn't. I couldn't describe the room. I couldn't understand why this man was here, why he was burned, why he was dead. I couldn't describe what I couldn't understand. I stood in the center of this room with rain dripping onto my face, feeling vacant and useless. I was an observer and yet I couldn't find the words to describe what lay all around me. I was the person who had come to make things all right and I stood feebly trying to document this horror. I was a bungler at best, a fraud at worst.

I was standing outside by the car. The rain had stopped momentarily. A team from the European Union's team of observers was in the yard. One of the officers, a German I think, was inspecting the car in the yard. He stood up and greeted me collegially—shook my hand and said something polite—then returned to his investigation.

Squatting next to the car door, he pronounced in English to no one in particular, but probably directed at me, "The two in there," nodding towards the smaller house, "died in this car. They were shot in the car, and after," he paused to search for the word and someone else offered, "rigor mortis?"

"Yes, after rigor mortis set in, someone moved them into the house. Then the houses were burned."

Several people were within earshot and his declaration coursed and pulsed electrically through the crowd as soon as it was translated into Albanian. I watched a few local journalists scribble into their notepads and remembered to do the same—two killed in car then moved to house #1, I wrote.

"I think," the German said looking over his shoulder at me, "they were shot somewhere else and brought here after some time."

I stood staring at the burned car as someone counted the bullet holes, "thirteen, fourteen, fifteen... "

I remember realizing that people were looking at me, waiting for me to do something. The German investigator had explained the order in which things had happened. The bodies in the small house lay wrenched into the positions in which they had died. They had been killed sitting in the car. Maybe they were burned in the car as well, but we didn't know that. He, and now we, figured that they died in the car somewhere else. Then their bodies and the car were brought to the compound where they were carried from the car into the house, obviously after rigor mortis had begun, and then the fires were set.

But unraveling the first riddle only introduced others. Why this compound? Who was the man in the bigger house, and why was he murdered? Who or what was the corpse in the small shed? Why couldn't I make sense of any of this?

I looked around at the site. I remember thinking I had seen everything. I didn't understand what had happened fully, but I had what I needed for a report. The European Union team would certainly do any further investigation. We were done. We walked to the truck and got in. We drove back to Podujevo and had a macchiato with our guide while we talked local politics.

Later that evening, my boss told me to write a factual, unemotional report about what we had seen. I did exactly that. It took about an hour. I remember turning it in and going to sit at the internet terminal with a beer to write an email. Behind me, Shaun, my boss, and Pat, the reports officer, were talking about the report and quietly—I assume they were trying not to be overheard—commenting about the understated tone of my report's description of such a grisly event. Pat asked Shaun if he thought I was, and this is the exact phrase, freaked out by what I had seen and needed some down time, or if I would be all right. Someone across the room said something loudly that drowned out their response.

A little while later, Morgan from the UN came by and we had a beer together.

"How are you doing?" she asked.

"I think I'm fine." I wasn't sure why she was asking—just making conversation or actually checking up on me. "It would be easy to be a little freaked out by what we saw up there today, though."

She frowned a bit, and then leaned a little closer. "Look, I've been talking to Shaun and Moon and they're worried about you. So don't say you're freaked out or they'll send you home." She paused briefly. "You want to stay, don't you?"

It was as much an affirmation as a question. And I did want to stay. I didn't want to be seen as weak or incompetent. I nodded. "Yes, I do want to stay."

"Okay." She finished her beer and got up to leave. "Ta," she said and turned away.

Shqiptar

WE WERE EXPECTING a bombing campaign to start at any moment. Milosevic had been typically recalcitrant and Madeleine Albright was being typically, well, Albright. Kosovo was tense; people were edgy. Early in the month my team went on mission to a village near Recane. It was a Serbian village, and we had received reports that some of the men there were armed and had been threatening nearby Albanian villagers. Hell, everyone was armed and threats were commonplace, but we decided to roll through the village and talk to some of the residents because we hadn't been out there in a while.

I was working with our translator Sanije and my Canadian colleague, Gavin. We were traveling, as always, in one of our fully armored Chevrolet suburbans outfitted with radios, two satellite telephones and some sort of super hush-hush tracking unit under the passenger seat so that people at the other end of the world would know where we were if we got into trouble. In theory, if we didn't update the code regularly or if we put in the special come-get-us-we're-in-trouble code, Special Forces guys from Stuttgart would fly in to rescue us. I don't think I knew the special code, and it probably would have taken way too long to figure it out *in extremis* anyway.

Gavin was a Newfoundlander, one of two Canadians sent to

augment the U.S. team. For whatever reason, we were working together in one of the U.S. vehicles rather than the Canadian Suburban—Canada One—and I was on mission with him instead of his usual partner and compatriot, a soldier named John. Sanije and I had worked together often.

The village was off the main road, just outside of Suva Reka. We had been through it a few weeks earlier, so we knew the way. Nonetheless, Gavin properly had his big map and a GPS out alternately sitting on the dash or on his lap.

It was a crisp autumn day, with a sunny and mostly clear sky. We were following a city bus down the street. When it stopped, four men stepped off. As the bus pulled away, Sanije said quietly, "These guys are Serbs." The four men walked towards our vehicle, one of them stepped up to my door and motioned that he wanted to talk to me.

We joked constantly that you could always tell the Serbian bad-guys, because they all wore hip-length, black leather jackets. Now I realized the truth behind this stereotype; sure enough, the guy standing at my door was wearing one. Our vehicles had three-inch thick windows that didn't roll down, so the only way to speak to someone outside or to pass a document was to open the door. Our standard procedure was that only the person driving, usually the mission commander, would open the door. I kept the power locks on for the rest of the vehicle, but unlocked my door and cracked it enough to speak to the man.

Unfortunately, this was enough for him to grab the doorframe and yank the door fully open. Just as I noticed that his three friends had taken up positions at each corner of the vehicle, this guy stuck his pistol up to my temple and started yelling at me in Serbian.

Okay, so let's review. We drive to a Serbian village where we know everyone is armed and the locals have been making threats against Albanians. The United States is clearly viewed as siding with the Kosovar Albanians, and NATO (aka the United States) has been threatening to bomb the hell out of Serbia. We have a 1:50,000 scale map and a GPS sitting on the dash of our fully armored vehicle that has big American flag magnets affixed to the doors. Then, I open the door to four guys in Serbo-Bob leather jackets. I suppose I should not have been at all surprised that one of them was holding a pistol to my head and screaming at me. But somehow, I was.

"Why have you come here? Are you going to bomb us?" The guy was yelling in Serbian and Sanije was translating very calmly from the back seat of the Suburban. He didn't wait for a response.

"I'm going to kill you right here and then we'll fuck this little *shqiptar*." Every time he reached a point in his rant that needed emphasis, he tapped the barrel of the weapon against my skull. He was talking, yelling actually, very fast and so this was happening every few seconds.

Of everything that was said that day, one word I remember very clearly is *shqiptar*. It's a derogatory term the Serbs used for Albanians and to hear him say it, almost spitting the word out of his mouth like it was something that tasted bad, gave me the sense that this guy wasn't rational. He was operating under a different set of rules, those set by the nationalist ideology that had already destroyed most of Yugoslavia and was fast on the way to burning Kosovo, too.

The guy was holding the pistol in his left hand. I remember thinking that since most people in the world are right handed (I'm a lefty, so I think about these things), he was likely less coordinated with his left hand than with his right.

With his right hand, he was pulling on the door handle of the back seat passenger door behind which Sanije was sitting, calmly (it seemed) translating his ranting, screaming threats.

Gavin, who spoke considerably more Serbian than I did, but probably only enough to get us into trouble, was trying earnestly to diffuse the situation by asking the guy questions, I think, and telling him over and over again that we were diplomats in his country with the approval of his government in Belgrade.

In times of crisis, I think we all fall back on our training and in some cases our upbringing. Since I hadn't been trained in how to react to someone holding a pistol up to my temple and screaming, I fell back on my Southern heritage. My mother always told me that it is considered rude to interrupt others who are speaking and that only one person should speak at a time. So I kept my mouth mostly shut except for the odd comment to ask Gavin to shut the fuck up or to Sanije to tell Gun-Boy something that was probably irrelevant.

"Unlock the doors," he demanded.

One of the guys in the gang stepped up to the truck and pulled on the other passenger doors. They were all locked, so he stepped back to his position a couple meters off the passenger side taillight. Gun-Boy didn't try to unlock the other doors. He either didn't understand the concept of power locks or really didn't care about getting into the vehicle. I suspect it was the former.

While all this was going on, the bus these clowns had gotten off had long ago pulled away down the road. We were alone.

Gun-Boy continued accusing us of being spies and of targeting the village for the NATO bombing campaign. Of course we weren't, but I made a mental note, briefly, that if we got away from there, I would make sure to let the NATO targeters know about this place.

I don't think I had time to think about this at the time, but it struck me later that Sanije never once sounded upset or afraid, never raised her voice much beyond what was necessary to convey the tone of what she was translating. All this while a handful of armed Serbian thugs were working to get her out of the vehicle.

Gavin meanwhile was still carrying on his discussion with Gun-Boy. I don't know how much Serbian Gavin actually spoke, but it sounded rather like Tarzan-Serbian at the time. Of course, I spoke about seven unassociated words of Serbian. All of those quite poorly.

I never turned my head away from facing the front, so as I looked out through the windshield, I saw that the bus these guys had come in on was returning. There was a turn about a kilometer up the road and I could see the bus making the turn and starting to come back towards us. I suppose it was just a local, public transport bus and had dropped and picked up passengers in Recane and was returning to Suva Reka.

We were still sitting in the middle of the road. I hadn't moved the truck since we pulled up behind the bus on its way in. It was a narrow road, paved, but just. This being farm country, there were ditches on both sides. Gun-Boy was standing in the bus's lane with my door wide open and his arm fully extended, so as it approached, he stepped half a step closer to the truck and moved to shift the pistol to his right hand so he could pull the door a bit closed with his left.

I didn't think about this at all— if I had, I likely wouldn't or couldn't have done it—but when Gun-Boy took his half step out of the door, I quickly reached out and jerked it closed. Thinking back, a number of really bad things might have happened. But what did happen is that Gun-Boy acted instinctively. He pulled his arm back to keep it from being caught in the door. The door slammed. I hit the power lock, and shifted into reverse, then stomped on the accelerator. I heard a loud thump as we jerked backwards and I hit one of the guys standing behind the truck hard enough to knock him down—away from the wheels luckily.

I was driving backwards on a narrow road, trying to go as fast as I could, when I heard a couple of pistol shots. About two hundred meters back up the road, there was a little culvert in the ditch where tractors could cross and get into the fields. I figured the weight classification of that culvert was probably less than a ton, certainly no more. And I was in a 5,000-pound vehicle. But, my only choice was to do a quick two-point turn or drive backwards all the way to the highway. I slowed a bit, cut the wheel quickly, stepped on the brake and popped the shifter into drive. In a few seconds we were heading as fast as the Suburban would carry us towards the highway.

It was probably only a mile or so out to the highway, then a right turn towards Bruqe Mountain. I was driving as fast as the vehicle would go up the hill when Gavin calmly said, "You can slow down now." I gradually did. I don't remember breathing heavily or feeling my heart racing, but I was obviously amped up.

We called in to our headquarters in Kosovo Polje and told them what had happened. I don't remember much conversation on the hour-long drive back to the office.

Once we got back, things seemed almost normal. The translators in the office mobbed Sanije to support her and hear what had happened. Gavin and I sat with our reports officer and our boss to debrief. I think Gavin wrote the report on that day's mission. I don't remember what it said but it was probably short.

It's hard to imagine all the things that might have gone wrong in that moment when I had grabbed for the door. I suppose Gun-Boy had been distracted by the bus passing just behind, him so he didn't immediately see my hand dart toward the door handle. Otherwise, what might he have done? It would have been easy to pop off a few rounds from his automatic inside the vehicle.

What if the guy behind the truck had been a step closer to the center of the vehicle? It's likely I would have badly injured or killed him.

Did they shoot at us or only into the air? I don't know. There weren't any holes in the vehicle that I could find afterwards.

It's easy to second-guess and speculate, to "what-if" that moment to death. The bottom line for me is that those guys were bullies and we had strayed onto their playground. They wanted to scare us a bit. For my part, they succeeded. I don't think they wanted to kill or even really hurt us. If they had wanted to, things would have turned out differently.

Skopje

W E HAD BEEN KEEPING a low profile with the press. The fact that the war was taking place in Europe rather than Central Africa made it easier for the major media outlets to cover it. The fact that, once again, Milosevic and Ambassador Holbrooke seemed to be facing off, made it more interesting. But our team was instructed not to give interviews or to encourage the press to follow us as we did our work.

For the most part this was fine. The reporters generally had better things to do, but occasionally, they would come around asking for a quote or an interview. A real USAID officer had arrived, and I turned over the humanitarian portfolio to him. But I picked up the role of press attaché for our team. The Embassy had a full-time press officer in Pristina, but we were beginning to operate as a bit of an independent organization finally, so I took on the role.

Mostly, what this meant was saying "no" to people. No, you can't have an interview. No I can't give you a quote. No, please don't follow us around. But one evening the team chief, Shaun, came to me and asked me to organize a press briefing and tour. I was to gather up as many of the international reporters as I could and get them to follow me around for the day.

I made some phone calls and let people know they could come

by the office in the morning and that they would have full, on-the-record, access, cameras invited to follow, whatever they wanted to see or film was OK. But it was only for the day and it was only with me.

The next morning there were probably a dozen media vehicles out front. CBS had sent a film crew and a reporter. *The New York Times* sent a photographer. The AP, and several European services were present. I walked out and explained that for the day we were "on-the-record," and then pointed out on my map where we were going. They could film, photograph, record, write whatever they needed. We rolled out of the gate a few minutes later, and our caravan was off.

Our first stop was Kishna Reka, an IDP camp up in the Berisha Mountains. There were probably around 3,000 IDPs up there, many of whom I knew by sight because we had made a habit of stopping in every few days when we could to check on them.

The road up was rocky and treacherous, but passable. Nonetheless we often parked about halfway up and walked the last kilometer into the area. When we reached the top, Allen Pizzey from CBS News was waiting.

"I wanted to get a shot of your vehicle winding up this hill," he said.

How the hell did you beat us up here, I wondered. "Oh, well..." I didn't know what to say. My partner, Rob, who was notoriously press-averse, volunteered to walk back down the hill and drive up to give the cameraman a chance to get what would actually be some B-Roll footage.

We wandered through the camp with Allen, Anne Thompson from the AP, and a handful of others. Throughout, I would have some sort of interaction with the IDPs and the reporters and photographers would crowd around. For me it was a pretty normal day in the camp.

It took a couple of hours to wander through the camp so that most of the reporters got enough for a story. Still, about half of them followed us to another village near Suva Reka where we were checking to see if some books had been delivered to a school, as we had arranged. An hour's drive, another hour wandering around the town to find out that, no, they had not been delivered.

By that time it was early afternoon and the press had lost interest. No worries, I thought, we had done our job. We had served as a distraction.

A few days earlier, eighteen women, children, and elderly members of a single family had been killed by Serbian police in a small village called Gornje Obrinje. The same day an MUP officer had murdered thirteen men in the village of Golubovac. But one young man had survived the Golubovac massacre. Selman Morina, witness, survivor of a war crime, was badly wounded in the leg and arm. We needed to get him out of the province.

Someone up the line, Holbrooke maybe, but I really don't know, had made a deal with the Serbs that would allow us to take him out to Skopje, Macedonia for medical treatment. I was the distraction that kept the press busy so Morina could be quietly ferried to Skopje.

Once they learned what had happened, what I had done, many of the reporters were pissed. But we kept Morina alive and got him in front of the war crimes tribunal investigators, and they got stories. CBS had a nice four or five-minute piece about an American diplomat trying to save lives in the mountains of Kosovo. The similar AP story, accompanied by a photograph, ran in newspapers around the world. My aunt in North Carolina sent a copy of the story from her local paper to my mom. A friend at an NGO sent me a copy of the story from Denmark. It ran in "Stars and Stripes."

But despite small successes, things weren't going very well. The negotiations between Holbrooke and Milosevic were failing because Milosevic thought the U.S. was bluffing about using force. NATO was authorized to strike targets in Serbia, but Milosevic still refused to halt his operations against civilians in Kosovo.

Washington asked us to put together a survey of damaged housing. Apparently someone wanted to be able to point to a number and say that the Serbian forces had damaged X percent of houses and destroyed Y percent. I was tasked to put this together. In fact, it would have been a daunting task for a cartographer, but I developed a relatively simple plan with an easy matrix that worked.

"Drive down the main roads of Kosovo," I told our teams.

"Whichever villages you can see from the roads, estimate how many houses fall into each of these categories: level one, no damage or lightly damaged, the structure would be habitable with window or door replacement; level two, major damage, a large hole in a wall or part of a roof missing; level three, roof off, burned."

This admittedly amateurish methodology allowed us to survey an estimated 20,000 homes. Of course, the damage varied widely with some villages suffering 10% level one damage and some with 90% level three. We sent the information to the embassy in Belgrade. The North Atlantic Council agreed on an Activation Order, one step closer to beginning combat operations against Serbia.

Our boss and his deputy developed an evacuation strategy that would send a team or two to Skopje each day until we were gradually all out of the country in the last hours before the NATO deadline. Some people on the team welcomed the opportunity to go for a couple days' rest in Skopje, while others wanted to be in the last truck to cross the border. I was in the latter camp.

But a few days after we had run our diversion on the reporters, I came back to the office after a mission to report that my truck was acting up. These big Suburbans had been collected from embassies all over the world and flown to Belgrade, then driven to Kosovo. They were behemoths, weighted down with steel plating and inches-thick polycarbonate windows. Mine had starting running poorly on the road back to Pristina.

I told our deputy, and he glanced at the boss. They said more or less in tandem, "Take it down to the motor pool in Skopje and drop it off for repair."

I asked if I would be allowed to come back that evening. Our deputy said, "Absolutely." I took off. When I arrived in Skopje, I learned that I had been assigned a room in the Hotel Aleksandar Palace and wouldn't be going back after all.

I was pissed at myself for being so gullible. I should have let someone else drive the truck down, someone who wanted to leave. I was afraid my war was over.

We spent a few days in Skopje, eating at new and different

restaurants, drinking a lot, and staring at the news on TV, watching for any sign. Just a day or two before I had been tricked into leaving Kosovo, the Deputy Chief of Mission in Belgrade called to tell me I had been promoted within the Foreign Service. This was a surprise since none of the work I was doing in Kosovo could have appeared in my file that went before the promotion panel. Nonetheless, I decided to throw a small party.

I invited all of my colleagues and a few of the reporters and NGO staff that had come out with us to join me at a restaurant. I threw a couple hundred dollars at the owner and told him to keep the food and wine coming. It lasted an hour or two but by then everyone else's wallets had come out, too.

I was pretty drunk and so were many of the others. NGO workers, reporters, soldiers, diplomats, are all similar in some ways—adventure seekers, highly competent, borderline intellectuals, drinkers. We drank until late in the evening; somehow we made it back to the hotel. The next morning we learned that Milosevic had blinked. We were going back in, but it was to be a vastly different mission.

Our little team would be replaced by a large international mission, to be run by the Organization for Security and Cooperation in Europe, the OSCE. That mission would be called the Kosovo Verification Mission, KVM. Their job would be to verify the withdrawal of the VJ (the Serbian Army) from Kosovo, and of the other elements of the agreement between Milosevic and Holbrooke.

The Duke of Dragobilje

A FEW DAYS AFTER THE October cease-fire had been declared, we began the process of verifying the withdrawal of Serbian Army units from Kosovo. Most of the fighting had stopped and only sporadic skirmishes continued. Outside the town of Malisevo, the Ministry of Interior police had occupied a gas station at an intersection leading south to the Pagarusha valley. The intersection was at a town called Dragobilje, which was completely empty save for a few KLA guys who watched the Serbs watch the town. The roughly five thousand regular inhabitants were now mostly living under plastic sheeting a few kilometers south in the Pagarusha Valley. I was talking with some IDPs there when my boss called me and told me to meet him in Dragobilje.

Dragobilje was an unlikely flashpoint in the high stakes game of Balkans politics. But as these things go, it was also somewhat typical of small wars. The phrase "isolated incidents of violence" is a favorite among government spokesmen trying to downplay the importance of burning villages and rampaging thugs. My counter to that, as someone more often than not living in these flashpoints was, "it's only isolated when it's not your village." Someone told me that on CNN Richard Holbrooke had called Dragobilje, "the most dangerous place in Europe." I never heard the quote, but even if it were true, I suspect he was thinking geo-politically and strategically, rather than tactically. But nonetheless, it was a dangerous place.

Our deputy was sitting in his truck talking on the radio when I arrived. Two KLA political committee leaders, Sokol Bashota and Fatmir Limaj (aka Chelik), and a handful of KLA fighters were also standing around in the courtyard of a lovely yellow brick house. "We're going to set up an office here to help keep these guys from shooting each other," Dean said. He, Chelik, Sokol, our translator, Sahit and I went into the house.

I had assumed I would be living in a burned out hulk of a house, sleeping on a cot at best with no heat—dramatic visions of Stalingrad or Sarajevo danced in my head. But the house, other than a broken lock on the door, was terrific. A wide tile-floored hallway led to the rear of the house. The kitchen and living room opened off to the left; there was a bath at the end of the hall; four bedrooms upstairs, one with a nice balcony looking off to the south. We stepped into the kitchen. There was a woodstove in the corner. A sink and stove took up the wall on the left. A small wooden table and three chairs sat under the window. A few glasses and plates were in the sink, clean. More plates and some pots and pans sat on a shelf above between the sink and stove. I quickly took note that the stove was gas and that there were two propane bottles. Well, we shouldn't starve, I thought.

Dean pulled a bottle of whisky out of his bag and poured a finger for each of us while we talked about the relative locations of the MUP and KLA units in and around the town. Sokol said the KLA had no intention of giving up the town, but neither would they attack the Serbs at the intersection. Dean finished off his whisky and headed for the door, leaving the bottle on the table. As he walked to his truck he spoke softly to me, "Set up a satphone and stay on the net as best you can. We'll try to get some electricity out here for you in the next few days." He paused as he got into the truck, "Don't get shot." I came to realize that when he had said "we" earlier, he was using the word in a corporate sense rather than the personal. I wasn't immediately sure how I felt about this. Dean was a Marine lieutenant colonel, a Force Recon special operator with lots of experience I would have welcomed. But he wasn't staying. I was leading a start-up, KDOM's first franchise.

After Dean left, my translator and I looked at each other and—seeing the sun starting to set—asked the KLA commander if we could get some firewood. The commander agreed, and within half an hour a tractor had delivered a pile of firewood to the drive and a couple of young KLA fighters were busily splitting the wood.

We left the compound and drove up the hill towards the gas station. As we pulled in, a couple of the Serbian Ministry of Interior troops came out to see who had arrived. We talked to the lieutenant and told him that we were living in a house in Dragobilje and would appreciate it if he wouldn't shoot at us (I was simply following the boss's instructions, as always). We pointed out to the lieutenant where our house was located. I got down behind one of his machine guns, noting that my house was clearly in the range of the weapons, and then asked if he would consider humoring me by moving the aiming stakes so that it would be taken out of their range fan. He and his sergeants laughed when my translator asked this. He suggested that I make sure that no KLA fighters (terrorists he called them) were walking around in my yard. We joined the MUP squad for coffee and slivovitz, and then trundled back down the hill to consider our situation.

Just to recap, I was now living in a house with no electricity or running water in late October in the Balkans. The Serbs had the high ground about 300 meters to the northwest, my house was clearly in their range fans, and they were drinking. For the first time the U.S. had opened an outpost between the warring factions. KLA fighters were all around me and they clearly considered my presence to be in their favor.

When we got back to the house we moved some firewood into the kitchen and started a fire. We found some oil lamps and lit them. I set up the satphone and made a quick call to the office to establish communications. We had a bit of a scare when I opened the kitchen window to see if the antenna would connect and an old man surprised us as he passed by the window walking around in the yard collecting kindling. Sahit brought in the sleeping bags and a box of MREs. The night passed with only occasional shooting, although at one point a few consecutive bursts of automatic weapons fire broke out. My American colleague—an Air Force tech sergeant—jabbed me hard in the ribs through my sleeping bag and sat upright, asking in a stage whisper, "Did you hear that?"

We called in to Pristina the next morning and told them about the small amount of firing in the area. They seemed unconcerned since there was regularly much more firing in the vicinity of the Hotel Herzegovina each night.

Over the next few days our schedule settled into a series of visits built around two objectives: convince the Serbs to leave, and build confidence in the local Kosovar Albanian population. We worked on the first by visiting the Serbs a couple times a day. We got to know the officer and a couple of the sergeants well enough that we were regularly invited for coffee or slivo.

We worked on the second issue by driving around the villages in the area, stopping to shop for food and sundries to make our life easier, and talking to people. We figured out which shops in the villages ringing the Pagarusha valley were still operating and who sold what. There was a great place for meat and another that could reliably be counted on for cases of beer. One shop in the valley proper had begun selling little sausage sandwiches.

Our little outpost was the first visible symbol of the implementation of Holbrooke's plan. So, we were regularly visited by reporters wanting quotes and video. I had a pocketful of approved quotes—talking points—that kept them sated temporarily. One evening Nic Robertson from CNN came by and asked if he could shoot a few minutes' interview with me. I asked my boss and we got permission from the Embassy in Belgrade.

Sitting and talking over a coffee or a beer with a reporter is one thing, but an on-camera interview is quite another. I was awful. I stuck to my talking points and got the information out, but I was shaking and felt like I was stammering the whole time. Nonetheless, CNN International ran clips from the piece every ten minutes and the whole piece at least hourly during the day. That evening I got a call from the press attaché at the Embassy who said I wasn't to do any more TV interviews. I assumed it was because I had screwed up, but he said I had done fine. In fact, everyone at the Embassy and in Washington was pleased that a Foreign Service officer was leading the news. He told me that Holbrooke had called and told him, "I don't know who Ron Capps is, but I don't want to see him on TV anymore." Years later, I had the chance to ask Ambassador Holbrooke about this, and he said he didn't remember it. Regardless, my days on CNN and in the newspapers, were over.

In Dragobilje, the KLA kept a few fighters in one house that was screened from the MUP at the gas station by other houses on a small hill. We would stop in to visit them every afternoon just to check in or to get a message to their leadership. The floor was covered with cheap carpet and blankets the fighters slept under. The place smelled of sweat, stale smoke, and dirty clothes. It was, in fact, more or less like any other combat outpost in any other war. We called it the Fraternity House.

On the fourth day of our routine, we dropped in on the Serbs and found a replacement team in place, but packing to leave. They were simply moving out of the gas station up to their larger headquarters two kilometers away in Malisevo, but they were leaving Dragobilje. At first, the lieutenant wasn't keen on talking to us, but after a few minutes, he loosened up a bit and began to talk to me. I pointed out that I hadn't known he had kept so many armored vehicles in the village—there were five armored vehicles along the road and two more moving nearby—he smiled as if to say, "That's not all you don't know." He told me they were simply moving up to Malisevo and might move back to the gas station in the next week or so. But it was clear they were leaving for good and were unhappy about it.

I asked the lieutenant whether there were any mines or other booby-traps in the building or surrounding area. This was a necessary precaution because, in the days immediately following the agreement and subsequent withdrawal, several people had been injured or killed by booby-traps and mines left by withdrawing Serbian forces. "We're not that kind of police," he said curtly. I could smell the liquor on his breath. It was about 8:30 in the morning.

By noon the MUP had left the town. We watched as they moved out of their positions. Within a few minutes of their departure, KLA fighters had moved into the area to check for stragglers or snipers. Within a few hours, a few young men from the town were back to check their houses. It seemed a victory when I called it in to the office.

But, that afternoon mines killed two KLA fighters. These had been placed in the field directly behind the gas station. The men were apparently walking across it, when they hit a daisy-chained series of mines, killing one fighter outright and leaving the other barely able to drag himself out of the field. He died in the street scarcely fifty meters away. His blood was still there when we drove back into town after our daily trip around the valley.

Someone had dropped some flowers on the spot where he had died. A young KLA fighter with a Kalashnikov stood more or less at attention a few feet away from the bloodstain. The Serb lieutenant's words echoed in my head as we passed two weeping girls who, having just returned to their village that afternoon, would be burying two of their neighbors the next morning. I would drive slowly around that spot for weeks afterwards.

That evening one of the KLA commanders confirmed to me that his unit had found several other booby traps in the area. One was a hand grenade fixed to the branch of a pear tree, set to go off if someone pulled a piece of fruit off the branch. Others were found in a large house overlooking the town just across the street from the gas station. Some were set into bunkers the Serbs had abandoned. Most of the booby traps were set in places where kids would instinctively go to play or explore. But none of them were positioned more than two hundred meters from the security of the gas station.

Over the next few days, many of the villagers returned to Dragobilje. Within a couple of weeks, I hoped, we would have families living in all the houses. However, this meant that now we had to find humanitarian assistance for them. Morgan from the UNHCR was my first target.

I called her and explained where I was living, what was going on, and how much assistance we needed. That afternoon, she dropped in for a visit. The next morning, Oxfam UK delivered small shelter kits consisting of plastic to cover windows, and a hammer and some nails to the local Mother Teresa Society representative. That was a start. The MTS house was just across from the Fraternity House, but I was surprised to see that none of the windows in the Frat house was covered by Oxfam plastic. Throughout my time in Kosovo, I don't believe I ever saw donated food or supplies for sale in the markets.

As we continued what we had dubbed our "hearts and minds campaign," we began to get to know a few of the villagers in each of the small communities. One of the objectives I had set was for us to be seen in every village in the valley at least every other day. We organized a schedule, and set up a simple rotation, sending us down the east side one day and up the west the next. Every couple of days we had to run into Pristina or Suva Reka for supplies and showers, and—truth be told—to give the rotating translators and observers a break from my cooking. After a few days, we fell into a regular pattern. On the road out of town to the south, towards the Pagarusha valley, a small store stood flush with the edge of the road, located far enough towards the edge of town that it had not been visible to the Serbs in the gas station. It remained sporadically open, and we would stop in for a talk once in a while—checking the pulse of the locals.

We stopped in for a chat late in our first week in the house. A couple of concrete steps led us up to a porch where a paltry few items were defiantly displayed. A tire, a sack of flour, and a case of beer sat, friendless, by the door. Inside, a counter with shelves behind it stood along the right wall and curved around the long back wall. A snooker table stood in the back of the room, covered by racks of beers. Batteries, cookies, soap, and canned milk collected dust on the shelves. With the entire town living under plastic sheeting in the valley to the south, business was slow.

There were usually a few men sitting around the store. They welcomed us in and offered us a beer. I sat on a crate and started asking them political questions. We talked about Rugova and the

LDK. One of the men said it was time for the Albanians to stop listening to only Rugova and to look at what the KLA had done. Another piped in sarcastically, "Yes, they got our families to move to Pagarusha while our houses sit empty in Dragobilje." I didn't know if I was supposed to laugh, but after a moment we all did anyway. One of the men wanted to know what we were going to be able to do, whether we could order the Serbs out of Dragobilje, and if we were armed. I always hated this question; being unarmed in Kosovo was like being naked. It was a culture of armed men where weapons were considered appropriate communion gifts. Nonetheless, we were always unarmed. But sitting there on that fall afternoon seemed as comfortable as if I were hanging out at my local with some friends. It was just some guys sitting around having a beer and talking politics.

Malisevo

AFTER THE OCTOBER AGREEMENT that pushed the VJ out of Kosovo, there were a handful of smaller, less visible agreements that had to be implemented in order to reduce the violence around the province. One of those was designed to simply reduce the opportunities for the MUP and KLA to stumble across each other in certain areas. This meant the MUP would tell us when they were going to patrol on certain main roads in the center of the province, and in exchange, we would get the KLA to stay off those roads during that period of time.

This worked reasonably well until it didn't. In early November, a MUP patrol stumbled across a handful of KLA fighters and the two groups had a shootout. Five KLA fighters were killed, which disrupted the sense of stability we had been working so hard to develop.

A few days later, two MUP reservists driving a delivery truck to the station in Malisevo were kidnapped just northeast of the town. Assuming the worst for the two, we spent the following days talking to KLA leaders and commanders to try to arrange their release. All day, we would drive around to meet with KLA leaders and, at each stop we were told the KLA didn't have the two men. At night we would return to the house and plot our mission for the next day.

A few nights into this routine, we were sitting in the house just after dinner, when we heard a big firefight break out to our north. The shooting went on for about twenty minutes. We were waiting for one of our other teams to arrive at the house and, knowing they were coming from Malisevo, started to get nervous. We spent about fifteen minutes trying to raise them on the radio. When they finally popped up on the net they asked us what the hell was going on. The team commander was relatively new to the area, so we figured out where they were and advised him on the best route to take to get to us. They roared in the gate about fifteen minutes later.

The team had been at a KLA unit headquarters meeting with the political committee. At about 8:30 they had tried to leave to come to our house. The KLA leaders urged them to stay for another beer and more food. This went on until the fighting broke out and the team realized they had been held in place to ensure they wouldn't be in Malisevo at 9:00, when the attack started. Although the fighting had stopped by the time they arrived, we figured it was best if they just spent the night in our house rather than drive back to the office in Suva Reka. The next morning, we all drove up to Malisevo.

The police station was a mess. It had been hit from three sides in a coordinated attack using small arms and RPGs. The spalling pattern of an RPG strike was visible just below the roofline on the southern side; another RPG had missed a window around the corner by inches. Bullet holes pocked the walls. Not a window remained unbroken. We pulled up out front and climbed the steps. A captain dressed in full battle gear came out to meet us. He explained his view of how the fighting had gone, and told us none of his soldiers had been killed. He showed us the damage to the building and estimated the number of KLA fighters at about a hundred in three groups. He pointed to three areas around the town and explained that the firing had come from those directions. We spent about half an hour with him and then drove around the town to have a better look.

The police station stood about a hundred meters northeast of the town's main crossroads. At the intersection we met an ICRC team in their vehicle and stopped to talk with them for a few minutes. They told us there were two bodies lying at the edge of the road a couple hundred meters to the southeast. We assumed the worst for the two MUP reservists.

We found the two men lying face down with their hands tied behind them. Both had several bullet holes in their backs. Blood had pooled in the gravel underneath each of the bodies. One was lying in a pool of mixed blood and urine; we assumed he had been the second to die.

We immediately tried to get the Red Cross team to collect the bodies and transport them to the morgue in Pristina. They wisely refused. The next few hours were entirely predictable. We walked back to the police station and informed the captain what we had found. He and a small group of others, all in full battle gear except the captain who had lost his frag vest and helmet, walked back to the site with us.

The captain identified the two men as the missing reservists, and instructed one of his troops to call Pristina. While we waited, several of the troops began a haphazard search of the surrounding area.

Within half an hour, other police units began arriving, some from nearby towns and some from Pristina. A news crew from RTS (Radio/Television Serbia) arrived as well. This was going to become a media event. My colleagues and I stood around or sat in the vehicles and waited with the MUP officers, watching and waiting for the judge to arrive to conduct the formal investigation.

After a few hours, one of the MUP who had been searching the surrounding area came back to the site with a young Albanian man in tow. The Albanian, probably about sixteen, looked scared. I suspect he was trying to look defiant, but he was failing. The police began talking to him, and informed us they considered him a witness rather than a suspect. He related an unlikely, but plausible story to the MUP captain and began obviously looking for ways to get out from under MUP control and into ours.

He said that he had been in his family's apartment late the previous evening collecting some of their goods when the fighting had broken out. He told the MUP that he'd watched from the window as a handful of KLA fighters dragged the two MUP reservists out of a four-wheel drive vehicle, pushed them onto their knees, and executed them. He said he knew who the trigger-man was and named Fatmir Limaj, my contact known as Chelik.

Fatmir was a well known KLA leader, once a brigade commander, later head of the KLA's military police and finally member of the political committee who would be named Deputy Defense Minister in the Provisional Government of Kosovo following the bombing campaign. He had studied law at the University of Pristina but dropped out to join the KLA.

The boy asked that he be allowed to return to the village where he and his family had moved when Malisevo was overrun. One of our teams volunteered to take him home long enough to see his mother and change clothes. We promised to return him by sunset. Once the team got him to the village, the boy recanted his entire story, and refused to return to Malisevo. One of our translators told us the boy had been looting another IDP's apartment when the fighting had broken out. He had no idea who had pulled the trigger on the MUP officers and had only mentioned Fatmir's name because he was the best-known KLA commander in the area. Limaj's home village, Banja, was about five kilometers southeast of Malisevo.

Over the next few days, the police quite properly raised a stink about our having "lost" the boy, and we were forced to go back to the village to convince him to come to Pristina for interrogation. We went back to the village and spoke with the boy's grandfather who agreed to let him go to Pristina with us as long as he (the grandfather) could accompany us. So off we went.

We arrived at the police superintendent's office in Pristina and took the boy up to see the lieutenant colonel conducting the investigation. A Serbian investigator who spoke perfect, unaccented Albanian conducted the interrogation. One of our translators whispered a translation of the questions and answers to me as we all sat around the table. The boy admitted that he had fabricated the story and was eventually released. The MUP Lieutenant Colonel gently chided us as we were leaving for having disrupted his investigation.

We stopped along the way back to the village and fed the boy and his grandfather. Then we brought them home. The tears and wails of his mother and sisters when he got out of our truck were sign enough that they couldn't believe that we had been able to bring him back. And, I have to admit, neither could I.

Not long afterwards, my time in Kosovo, already extended by several months, was curtailed. I was going home to Montreal. I didn't want to leave. I missed my wife, but I didn't miss the dull, workaday life of a Vice Consul in a border post. I talked to the Deputy Chief of Mission and to the management officers in Washington to get my assignment extended. I was told to go back to Montreal and they would get me back to Kosovo before Christmas.

My wife Maureen was actually covering my slot at the consulate. She had been through the consular course before one of our earlier tours—the Department is always looking for ways to put spouses to work overseas—so she was covering for me. I had convinced her to look for work with an NGO in Kosovo (assuming I would be there, too). So she was heading out in mid-December to work for Catholic Relief Service.

Back in Montreal, the consul general and the chief of the consular section weren't keen to see me go. It made for a very tense atmosphere in the office. Finally, days before Christmas, the Bureau of European Affairs struck a deal with the consulate to send an officer to the consulate on temporary duty so I could go back to Kosovo. It was, of course, an unnecessary expense for the Department, sending two officers TDY when only one was needed. But I was out of Montreal and back to the war. I flew out on Christmas Eve and landed in Belgrade on Christmas Day.

Racak

THE EUROPEAN UNION TEAM had already been up on the hill for an hour or so by the time we'd arrived. We had been blocked at every possible entry point from entering Racak, the town just below us. So we were all watching and waiting to see what would happen. The wind was cold and all of us were finding ways to stay out of it as much as we could, yet while still keeping an eye on the town.

Once in a while we could see someone dash between buildings or hear a round or two fired, but not much else. The EU guys said they had seen tanks and infantry fighting vehicles firing into the town earlier in the day. So, even though we couldn't see anything, we could tell something big was going on. Throughout the morning and on into the early afternoon, we would call back to Pristina, tell them what we knew, and ask for instructions. None came.

I had been to Racak before. The Serbs had come through in the fall and driven most of the civilians out, but a few had remained. One of the holdouts I'd spoken to then said three hundred people had stayed on. That number seemed awfully high to me at the time. But however many there were, the Serbian special police were attacking them that morning.

The Serbs were there because a nearby police station had been attacked by the KLA a few days earlier. Three policemen were killed, and the Serbs believed that this town was the base for the KLA unit that had conducted the attack. Some guys with Kalashnikovs attacked a police station, and the Serbs retaliated with tanks. Proportionality is one of the principal tenets to the law of land warfare.

We stayed for a couple of hours until we were convinced we weren't going to get anything. Dark came early and we were supposed to be back at the office before 4:00 p.m. On the way in, I called the embassy in Belgrade to tell them what had happened. We discussed whether or not I would go back the following day, but we never reached a final decision.

That night I had dinner with a French colleague on the OSCE political mission, who told me one of their teams and an AP film crew had gone into Racak a few hours after I had left. The team learned that Serbian police had arrested a couple dozen men from the town and taken them away, probably to Urosevac (the Albanians called this town Ferezaj). The police at Urosevac refused to say whether or not the men had been brought there. The team planned to go back the next morning.

The temperature in Kosovo during the month of January, 1999, did not rise above freezing. Every night I came home to find that I either had electricity or water, but never both at the same time. If I had water, the water heater would fill. If I had electricity the water would heat. So, the optimum sequence was water in the evening and electricity at night.

That night I had a full water heater but only partial electricity. The bedroom's electricity was working, so I turned on the tiny space heater, my only source of warmth. But the bathroom did not have electricity, so I knew I would have to heat some water on the gas stove in the morning and do my best to be clean for the day. Still, I rationalized, I was better off than most.

The phone woke me in the morning. It was about 6:30 and still dark outside, but I still felt a little guilty for being caught in my sleeping bag. I grabbed the phone and saw it was my OSCE friend calling.

"The Serbs killed forty people in Racak yesterday," she announced in lieu of "good morning."

I couldn't quite get my brain around that, so I said something like, "Huh?"

"Forty dead. All shot in the head and left in a ditch."

I had been in Kosovo for six months at that point and had witnessed and reported on some significant atrocities, but if this information was accurate it would be the biggest killing since the Jashari compound attack in Gornje Prekaz almost a year before.

"How do we know?" I asked.

She explained that the KLA spokesman had been calling around. I immediately felt left out and wondered why he hadn't called me. Just then, my phone beeped, alerting me that I had another call. Of course, it was him. In the middle of my conversation with him, the phone beeped again. It was the Watch in Washington calling to find out if the reports were true.

After I had rung off with the watch officer, I called my translator, Valon, and told him to meet me at the office. I asked him to check around with his contacts to see what we might learn. At the office I talked to my boss and to the embassy to find out what they wanted us to do. We all decided that one of us should go to Racak, and I seemed the logical person. So we got a vehicle, and Val called everyone we knew who might know something, staying on the phone until we reached the edge of Pristina where the cell network dropped off. This all took some time of course, and it was well into the morning before we got out of town.

Just past the edge of town, rolling through the pasturelands toward Lipljan, Val said, "There weren't any KLA in Racak."

"Do you know that or is that what the KLA are saying?" I asked.

"Don't you remember when we went there?" He was avoiding the question.

"Yep. But that was months ago."

"I'm sure the guys in Racak were all farmers." He sealed the deal. We joked around with each other almost constantly, but in a situation like this we were both pretty somber. He said it; I believed it. If he was right, dozens of farmers had been murdered in cold blood by Serbian special police.

It was probably 11:00 when we got to Racak. I spotted an OSCE verifier team and stopped to talk to them. We learned there were bodies lying on the high ground just ahead on the left, and that the head of the OSCE mission, American ambassador William Walker was on his way. One of the guys was a cop from the UK. He said it was pretty grisly stuff, and asked me to watch my step if I went up there since it was a crime scene. I could tell he would have liked to tell me to go fuck off somewhere and stay out of their way, but I guess he knew that I had as much right to be there as he did and, like him, I was just doing my job.

A clutch of local Kosovar Albanians huddled at the edge of a small gully running up a hill. I parked the vehicle at the edge of the road, and we began the slow walk up towards them. One of the men standing around said something to Val in Albanian. He didn't bother translating, so I assumed it was something about how worthless the U.S. and OSCE observers were. Given the circumstances, it was hard to argue.

About twenty meters up the trail, we started to find bodies—three men wearing work clothes and coats. Then we found one more. They all appeared to have been shot in the back of the head. We pressed on. I had my notebook out, and was taking notes on what we saw, counting the dead.

Atop the ridge we found more bodies. Most were face down in the dirt. The men were wearing inexpensive ski jackets and blue jeans, work coats and cotton trousers, work boots and cheap shoes, civilian clothes. There was so much blood: on clothes; staining the ground; stuck to the skin of the dead.

A young man, a teenaged boy actually, was standing just off to the side. He had blonde hair that was wildly unkempt. His clothes were dirty, and he looked like he hadn't bathed in days. He wore no gloves or hat, and his coat was thin. I thought at the time he must have been freezing, but he didn't seem to notice the cold. He was probably a hardy local farm boy who had been dragged into this war by virtue of his ethnicity and the hatred erupting between these two groups. Our eyes met for just a second, then he looked away. I turned my attention back to the corpses, and went back to work.

We were counting bodies and taking notes as we moved slowly around a pile of corpses, when Walker arrived. He was dressed in his signature blue ski jacket, and half a dozen OSCE verifiers were with him, plus some guys that were pretty clearly a security detail. Some photographers and people I recognized as journalists were tagging along, too. I had a jacket that was, coincidentally, the same color as his, and I remember being immediately self-conscious about it, lest someone think I was emulating him. He spotted me and acknowledged my presence with a nod, but we didn't speak. I suppose he was pleased that another American diplomat was there to bear witness and get the information into the American system.

Walker took up a lot of space. We stepped back to let him and his entourage move through. They stopped and conferred a couple of times before making their way back down to their vehicles. The OSCE operated in bright orange-painted vehicles that we called "pumpkin-mobiles." Walker gave a quick glance back up the hill. Someone, maybe his press attaché, said out loud that he had called a press conference that afternoon in Pristina. We watched them leave, and the hill was quiet again.

The UK cop and his partner came back to continue their investigation that we had interrupted. It was their gig, and I was happy to let them have it.

"I count twenty-three here, is that right?" I asked him quietly.

"Yeah, that's what we have." He was less surly. Maybe it was the impending visit of his boss that had him uptight before. "There's more in the town." He pointed his chin down the hill.

More? I thought. More? "OK, thanks. Is there anything we can do to help?"

"No, thanks. We'll muddle along," and he went right back to his grim task.

We were there for another quarter hour. I took a few minutes to soak it in and write down some atmospherics, mostly about the lack of smell—maybe it was too cold, I don't know—and the dirt, then we headed back down the trail. Back in the truck, we turned towards the village center and saw other OSCE and European KDOM teams in the town. One of the OSCE guys told us there were more bodies spread around the town and that family members were moving them to the Mosque.

We were just on our way to the Mosque, when a local man stopped us. He said he had something for us to see, and we followed him to where he showed us another corpse, mostly covered with a blanket. The man was staring at me as he pulled the blanket back. The body underneath was wearing a heavy tan coat with what might have been shearling lining and work pants, but there was only blood on the ground where the head should have been.

A woman was standing nearby holding a hand to her mouth. She wore a long skirt and white socks with the black plastic shoes many women wore out in the country. I thought, she's a farmer's wife in a farmer's town and she has a decapitated body in her front yard. I had to look away.

The guy took over as our guide. He walked us around to show us two other bodies in the town. While the men on the hill seemed to have been killed in a group, these victims had been executed individually. They were all wearing civilian clothes.

We drove over to the Mosque, parked and walked up to the door. There were a few men standing outside the door. We could see some bodies, wrapped in blankets, lying side by side on the floor just inside.

One of the men outside the Mosque wanted to tell us his story. He had an enormous mustache and was wearing a *plis*. His hands were thick and rough, a farmer's hands. We interviewed him for half an hour and got a reasonably clear idea of what had happened.

The Serbian police had attacked early that morning before sunrise, shooting up houses and dragging people out into the street. When he heard the shooting, he left the village and ran to the woods. His house was far enough away from the entrance to the village that he had time to get away. While he was talking, others joined us. Another man told me his son had run away carrying his pants and coat. He hadn't been seen since. I decided not to ask the man if he had been to the ridgeline.

As the men continued talking, I wrote down what they said. Women, girls and boys under age fifteen were allowed to leave or to hide in cellars. All the others, all the men of fighting age and older, were rounded up and taken away. Two of the men said the Serbs had used cannons and mortars in the assault—these might be the tanks the EU guys had reported. I didn't see any evidence of it, but I couldn't see the whole town or the woods just at the edge of town where the KLA would likely have set up their fighting positions.

We asked for specific details, like what the Serbs were wearing. One man said that most of the Serbs were wearing blue uniforms and some were in black and wearing balaclavas. These last were probably a special anti-terrorist unit. Most of the civilians didn't wait around to see what was happening.

The Serbs had stayed in Racak until just around sunset, then pulled back to allow observers and a film crew in. Sometime later, the people who had remained in the village began to emerge from their cellars to look for their missing family members. There were dozens of men missing, but no one had an accurate count.

One of the men gave me the names of many of the dead. He spoke quietly, reading the names from a small notebook he pulled out of his jacket pocket. He gave me names and ages. Some of the men were in their sixties; one was said to have been almost a hundred years old. That's too old to be a rebel fighter.

We were done. The OSCE teams would finish up. That was their job. We headed back to Pristina. It was a very quiet ride. I called the embassy in Belgrade and spoke to Jack Zetkulic, the Deputy Chief of Mission. He told me to call the Watch and to start writing a cable.

There was a pause in our conversation. "How are you doing?" he asked.

"I think I'm fine." Another pause.

"There's nothing you could have done," he said. "You know that, right?"

I knew then that there was more I could have done. I didn't try very hard to get into the town. I didn't try very hard to mobilize others. I had sat in my warm vehicle atop the hill for a couple hours, then left, maybe at about the time the twenty-three men were being murdered up on the ridge.

"I know."

Two days later the U.S. released signals intelligence intercepts of a phone conversation between a senior Serbian military commander in Racak speaking to the Prime Minister of Serbia in Belgrade discussing the number of dead and how to make it look as if they had been killed in fighting. There are also intercepts of the ground commander being told to "go in hard."

Within weeks, French journalists would claim the massacre was a hoax perpetrated by the KLA by putting fighters killed in combat into civilian clothes as a way to pressure the U.S. and NATO into attacking Serbia. They used slight discrepancies in stories filed by other journalists as their evidence. They lied. The findings in the forensics reports proved it.

Celebratory Gunfire

DURING THE LAST FEW WEEKS before the bombing campaign on Serbia had begun, while the peace talks were ongoing in Rambouillet, France, my phone would often ring in the middle of the night. This was almost always the State Department Operations Center staff calling to ask me some question in order to have something about Kosovo in the Secretary's Morning Brief.

In Kosovo, as in much of the Middle East, weapons aren't just for killing. They are appropriate gifts for communions. They are also used in celebrations. Football fans will often come out to the streets to fire off a few rounds after a Galatsaray win or a Red Star Beograd loss. This is the meaning of the phrase "celebratory gunfire." So sometimes at night, if I received a call from the Operations Center about reported firing in downtown Pristina, I would explain that it was just celebratory gunfire after a football match, then turn over and go back to sleep. If I were wrong, I could always file an amended report in the morning.

Once brutally cold January night, I was in bed, actually on the bed in my sleeping bag and under a heavy stack of blankets because there was no heat, when I heard the loud boom of an explosion across town. I waited a minute or two, lying still and waiting for something else to happen. I turned on the radio next to the bed that was set to the BBC, and within minutes, a report came on stating that a bomb had gone off in Pristina near a previously damaged Orthodox Church. Then my phone rang; the conversation went something like this:

"Hello?"

"Hi, is this Ron Capps? This is the State Department Operations Center."

"Yes, this is Ron."

"Hi, Ron. BBC is reporting that a bomb exploded in the center of Pristina, can you comfirm that?"

"I can confirm that I heard something that sounded like a bomb."

"Do you know where it exploded?"

"BBC says downtown near the Orthodox Cathedral."

"Uh huh, can you confirm that?"

"Not personally, but it sounded like it came from that direction."

"Have you gone downtown to investigate?"

Pause…

"Hello, Ron? Are you still there?"

"Yes, I'm still here."

"Oh, good. Have you gone downtown to investigate the bombing?"

"No."

"Oh. Well, will you call us when you do?"

"Yes. I will."

"Oh, good. So what time do you think that will be? We need to get the Secretary's Morning Report out in about half an hour."

"Oh, I don't think I'll disturb your work. I suspect I'll go down around 8:30 or 9."

"Oh. Well, we need to know what happened for the Secretary's Morning Report."

"Well, BBC says the bomb went off at the Orthodox Cathedral, so I would put that in the report."

"Oh, no. She'll want confirmation from KDOM."

"Well, she'll get that at about 9:30 or 10, once I've had a chance to go down there."

"Can't you go now?"

"No, you see, a bomb just went off down there."

"Right, that's why we want you to go."

"Right, and that's why I want to wait a few hours just in case another one is sitting there ready to go off."

"Oh."

"OK, good night."

Despite the bombings and the tension of waiting for the outcome of the peace talks, life went on in Pristina. The next night, or sometime that week, I was having a beer at a bar not far away. The bar was owned by a couple of Western European journalists and was called Tricky Dick's—reportedly after Richard Holbrooke. It was crowded and I was sitting and drinking with some friends when I overheard the BBC reporter sitting behind me say to her friend that she thought she was about to be "verified" by the handsome British Army officer assigned to the Kosovo Verification Mission sitting across from her.

Over the next few weeks, Tricky Dick's became less and less crowded. As the tensions between Serbia and NATO increased, as the peace talks in Rambouillet were failing, as Holbrooke and Milosevic waited for the other to blink, Pristina was gradually becoming more and more apprehensive. We were heading for war.

In late February, our time ran out. I was instructed to go back to Skopje. The Embassy staff in Belgrade were moving on to Budapest.

We had developed a little code among my NGO friends and contacts that would serve as a signal to them that the Americans were pulling out, and that they should do the same. Every evening, they would call me and ask where I was having dinner that night. If I said, "I'm going for Mexican," it meant I was pulling out. The only Mexican restaurant for hundreds of miles was in Skopje. That afternoon, I made a bunch of phone calls about my dinner plans.

I made a stop by the office of an international NGO team to say goodbye. My friend Zola and I were talking about the arc of the conflict and how bad things had gotten. Racak was a turning point in the conflict. The massacre there seemed to me to have been a point of no return, hardening the resolve of the NATO countries to stop Milosevic from committing further atrocities. Those forty-five murders had tipped the scales for me, too. I said something to the effect that I hoped the coming NATO bombing campaign flattened Belgrade. I suppose I said even worse things.

Zola looked at me and said, "You've lost your perspective. Not every Serb is guilty." I'm sure she went on, but that's what I remember specifically.

And of course, she was right. I had lost my perspective. I was working my ass off to find proof of war crimes, evidence that would cement the conviction of the leaders and actors in mass atrocities, ethnic cleansing, and murder.

She asked me how long I thought the bombing campaign would last.

"Three days, three weeks, or three months," I said. If President Clinton were to let the military bomb Belgrade and the Serbian military infrastructure immediately, it would be over in three days. If he held them back and only bombed specific military targets it would take three weeks. If he were very cautious and only went after units in Kosovo, it would be three months, maybe more.

I went to Skopje that night. A few days later the bombing campaign began. I remember watching the CNN reports in the hotel with colleagues, NGO workers and some reporters.

Hundreds of thousands of Kosovar Albanians began to flow across the border. My team was instructed to travel around Macedonia and Albania interviewing them to document their stories to send to the Tribunal. We interviewed hundreds of Kosovars about the experience of being driven out of Kosovo. Our reporting became part of the case against Milosevic at The Hague.

My third guess had been right. The bombing campaign lasted about three months.

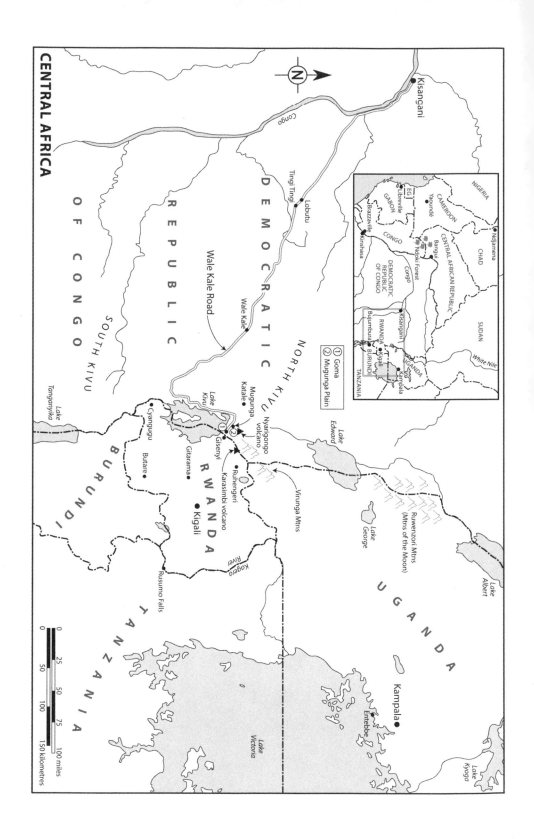

Central Africa

1995-1998 and 2000-2002

He has to live in the midst of the
incomprehensible, which is detestable.

JOSEPH CONRAD,
Heart of Darkness

No Good Deed Goes Unpunished

I WAS LIVING IN YAOUNDÉ, Cameroon in early 1996, working at the embassy there on my first Foreign Service assignment. Cameroon borders the Central African Republic, and both posts were considered sleepy little African backwaters at the time. I came to work one morning to learn that the capital of the Central African Republic, Bangui, was enveloped in a shooting war between the Central African army and the few troops remaining loyal to President Ange Felix Patasse, and that U.S. Marines were flying in to provide security at the embassy and evacuate Americans.

At the time I was stuck in the consular section of the embassy, involved in issuing visas and passports mostly. There were two Americans in the section and between the two of us, I was determined to be the one who went to Bangui to work rather than sitting in Yaoundé helping to get American citizen evacuees home or into hotels and such.

I packed my bag that night, and flew to Bangui on a Marine KC-130 aircraft the next evening. As we were loading the aircraft, a Marine handed me body armor to put on. "We took some fire flying in last night," the sergeant said. We took off around sunset and flew almost due east towards Bangui.

As usual, I knew pretty much fuck-all about the place I was flying into. I had grabbed a copy of the U.S. Government's Central African Republic: A Country Study at the embassy library and skimmed the basics. I learned things like the birth rate and the name of the national anthem *(La Renaissance)*, but otherwise, it was not much use.

Luckily, the flight was uneventful and I even napped a bit, lying on the ramp of the aircraft as it crept over the Central African forest. One of the Marine crew members woke me just before we began our descent into M'poko Airport. I strapped myself into one of the red nylon seats as the pilots did a kind of corkscrew maneuver down to the tarmac. I don't think anyone fired at us.

Once we were on the ground, there was a kind of mad scramble to figure out where to go. Often, on less modern airfields, there is a truck or jeep with a "Follow Me" sign that leads the aircraft to where the ground crews want the pilots to park. I don't know what happened that night, but the pilots parked about a kilometer or more from where the Americans were sited.

The passenger door slid open, and I jumped out with one of the Marine communications guys. He popped open a mini-satellite antenna, and within about thirty seconds I was on the phone with the embassy's Regional Security Officer (RSO) who was standing on the airfield 1,500 meters away, waiting for us to taxi over to his location.

The RSO and members of the Marine detachment on the ground had lined up the thirty or so passengers for the flight home, expecting to simply load them up and turn the plane around. My arrival had changed everything, of course. My job was to conduct an initial screening of everyone who wanted to get on the aircraft and have them complete a set of documents (by hand, in ink, in triplicate) including a promissory note through which the United States government could, if it chose, require payment for the flight out.

The existing ground team took this all in stride, and over the next two hours, I interviewed each passenger, checking passport details and having them complete the set of documents. Then we called the embassy in Bangui (again over a satellite connection), read off the list of names—spelling out each name—in a painfully slow process in order to get approval to load them on the aircraft. Only then could we load them up and ship them off to Yaoundé.

After that first load of mostly Americans and a few Cameroonians were off, the RSO loaded up onto a French Armored Personnel Carrier for a ride over to the American embassy. I stayed out at the airfield, and the Marine first sergeant and I sat down to hone the process a bit. As we were getting to know each other, he pulled a bottle of whisky—given to him by the French sergeant major the day before—out of his bag and offered me a paper cupful while he sipped out of his canteen cup.

The process: interview to determine status, completion of paper-work, approval of transport list by the embassy. This was to become our pattern, two or three times a day for ten or eleven days. One of the Marines was an administrative specialist, so the first sergeant assigned him to me, and the young lance corporal took over the majority of the documentation work.

That night, just before we went to sleep, there was a firefight on the perimeter of the airport. We could hear the report of the rifles and see red and green tracers—incoming and outgoing—for about fifteen minutes. Most of the Marines were eager to join the fight, but their French counterparts—most of the French colonies in Central and West Africa had been explored and placed under the military governance of French Marines—had things well in hand. Still, it was a chilling reminder that we were in the midst of a military mutiny.

A couple of times each day I would receive a message about a group of Americans in some remote location—these were usually missionaries, but there were also hunters, scientists, and Peace Corps volunteers spread around the country. When I got a message I would walk across the airfield in the 114-degree heat to the French military's air operations center and request their help in finding our people.

Each night, the air operations planners would spend long hours sketching out flight plans for the following day, working the complex equations of temperature, altitude, weight, and distance involved in every helicopter operation. Then I would arrive and ask them to go find seven American missionaries who really didn't want to leave their village, and who were probably safer out on the border with Chad or Sudan than they were at the airfield surrounded by an ongoing rebellion. The French non-commissioned officers would sigh heavily and glance at their meticulously planned schedule, then stoically begin to erase sorties in order to incorporate my request.

"Oui, Monsieur, nous les trouverons," was invariably the response: Yes, sir, we will find them.

In one such case, at about 3:00 in the afternoon, the hottest part of the hot day, a family of missionaries arrived and trundled over to the hangar: two parents and five kids, all with that clean-scrubbed, optimistic look that is universal to missionary families. The parents immediately set up a shortwave radio powered by a car battery—we were working and living in a ground vehicle garage—and made calls to other families still in the bush to say they had arrived safely. We handed them some MREs (Meals Ready to Eat—packaged military rations). The kids complained that we didn't have African food to serve them, but their complaints were good-natured. I processed them in after they had eaten. The kids stood in line quietly from tallest to shortest while I was checking their passports. Again, typical of missionaries in the bush, they were squared away. Everyone had their passport, everyone knew their blood type, was easy to work with. I'm not sure I remember their names but I always think of them as Matthew, Mark, Luke, John, and Abigail.

The parents told us that many of the other missionaries preferred to stay in place rather than evacuate to Bangui. They were actually going to be safer outside the city on the Sudanese or Congolese border, but I was supposed to encourage them to evacuate because that was the official U.S. government position. In some cases we were able to turn their information over to the Mission Aviation Fellowship (MAF) pilots and let them work out a pick-up and destination that worked for everyone.

The MAF guys were great. They flew around the continent dropping off missionaries, delivering food and other supplies to missions, and showing the "Jesus" film as part of their proselytizing mission. We referred to the MAF as the "Missionary Air Force."

All the while we were processing a few dozen passengers out each day, the French were processing hundreds a day. They had a very efficient system set up in the main airport building with computers and pretty French women filling contracted DC-10s and 747s for flights back to Paris (for the French) or Gabon (for the Africans).

And the French, of course, had good food and wine at their meals. We were eating (and feeding everyone who came through) MREs. I asked the French adjutants if we could eat in their facility, but they had to refuse, pointing out that they were already operating at about 300% capacity. They said they would get us some fruit if they could. We asked the Marine pilots to ferry some real food for us as well.

About halfway through our time there, the French embassy officer tasked with running development programs (called in their foreign service "Le Cooperant") came by to ask if we could transport some Catholic nuns to Yaoundé. "Of course, we can," I answered. Fifteen minutes later twenty-one nuns in grey habits arrived on foot at our front door. I initially thought no good deed goes unpunished. But they were wonderful. They filled out their own paperwork quickly and quietly, and then set about cleaning up the hangar and organizing the kids in games. The women had come to the CAR from all around the world. Some, I think, were from Vietnam and the former Soviet Union. I missed them after they flew out that evening.

I spoke regularly with the RSO at the embassy. He told me one day that there had been a running battle in front of the embassy the night before. It turns out that the building directly across the street was the warehouse for Bangui's brewery and both sides were fighting to control it. It seemed to change hands every couple of days as both sides replenished their beer stock. With a platoon of Marines guarding the American embassy, neither side seemed particularly interested in taking that fight on. Most of the damage to the embassy consisted of bullet holes in the outer perimeter fence—and those from rounds passing up and down the street rather than fired onto embassy grounds.

The U.S. had a Peace Corps mission in the CAR. The volunteers were scattered all around the country, and it took us a while to bring them all in. As they arrived, I would put them to work. They all spoke

French and could conduct interviews and complete forms as well as I could. One in particular stood out. When we distributed rations he asked, "Do you have anything vegetarian?" We did not. He shrugged and slipped just outside of the small circle around me. After everyone else had received the meals, he came back and quietly asked if he could leave the building for a few minutes.

"I have to say good-bye to my boyfriend," he said. Several of the Marines standing nearby blanched.

"Okay," I said, "but stay close or you'll miss the flight." He vanished.

The Marine first sergeant went around the hangar collecting cheese and a couple of apples for the vegetarian with the boyfriend. As the two young men—one American, one Central African—sat quietly on the curb holding hands, the first sergeant strode up to them and handed the volunteer his lunch. The Marine smiled a little as he came back to the hangar.

The first sergeant and I were about the same age—it turned out that we were born about a month apart—and had both grown up in military families before joining the service. We got along well and things ran beautifully, or at least as well as they could under the circumstances. I was glad I had chosen to deploy to Bangui rather than stay in Yaoundé.

A couple of days later, the French Cooperant came back and said that there were some Canadian children who needed consular services. The nearest Canadian embassy was in Yaoundé and, he asked, would they be able to fly on the American aircraft? As soon as I said yes, he walked to his pick-up and lifted the canvas flap covering the back. Six disheveled black children tumbled out of the vehicle and formed a rough line side-by-side. The Frenchman grinned and waved as he left.

We fed them and gave them water, then began to coax their story out of them. The eldest said they lived near Bangui but that their father was Canadian and their mother was visiting him in Canada, so he was taking care of the others. He was, I guessed, eleven or twelve, and there may or may not have been an uncle or auntie checking in on the kids. None of them had any form of identification, several were only half dressed, only a couple had shoes. One of them filled us in that soldiers had come to their house drunk after looting the brewery. There had been some shooting and the soldiers had stolen anything of value the family had.

One of the smaller kids looked at me in the middle of all of this and asked in French, "What is Canada like?"

"Very cold," I said, thinking there was no way these kids were going to leave the Equator and end up north of the 49th parallel. With no documentation to prove their case, I faced a dilemma. I wasn't supposed to board Central Africans—we couldn't encourage residents to leave to become refugees. But they said they were Canadians. I called the Canadian ambassador. He and my boss, the American ambassador, agreed that I could put the kids on the next flight and that the Canadian embassy would take charge of them at the other end. A few hours later when the kids walked up the ramp of the C-130, one of them was wearing a t-shirt about five sizes too big, emblazoned with "Devil Dog USMC Camp Lejeune N.C. "

About a week into our work, the Marines replaced the first sergeant with a first lieutenant. Things were winding down; we were only pushing one flight out per day. The Marines in Bangui were part of Second Battalion, Second Marine Regiment. They were embarked as the ground combat element of the 22nd Marine Expeditionary Unit (MEU). The MEU was simultaneously conducting operations in Liberia and Sierra Leone as part of Operation Assured Response (our mission was known as Operation Quick Response) and that operation involved ground combat. I suspect one of the Marine company commanders was missing his first sergeant during those combat operations, and asked to swap him out for the engineer lieutenant.

In point of fact, the Marines in Bangui were getting a little restless: you can only do so much PT during a day. We had processed out about four hundred fifty people from twenty-one different countries. Over the ten days we were operating in Bangui, the expatriate population of the country had dropped by 90%.

The lieutenant and I got along just as well as I had with the first sergeant. He followed me around a bit to get the lay of the land and then took on some of the additional tasks I had as a way of fighting off boredom.

Just before we were to re-deploy, a French brigadier—the ground commander—came by to visit. He apologized for not coming by sooner to pay his respects, but noted that he had been occupied with quelling the mutiny. He asked if there were anything we needed and I reiterated my request to eat in the dining facility. He nodded his assent, and that night we had our first hot meal in nearly two weeks.

At dinner, the French adjutants asked if they could come see me at eight pm. Of course, we said, yes. The lieutenant and I expected something was brewing, so we had set up a small table and some chairs out on the apron. The two captains came through the garage building we had lived and worked in for ten days out on the apron, and with the Southern Cross shining down on us, they pulled a bottle of chilled champagne and some plastic cups out of a musette bag. We popped the cork and toasted Franco-American cooperation.

They invited us to join them at the officer's club. I drank a fistful of beers, played some songs on a French flier's guitar, and, at the end of the night, we shut down the place with full-throated renditions of *La Marseillaise* and *The Star Spangled Banner*. It was a night I want to remember as long as I live.

The next morning the Marines and I packed out and trundled aboard the KC-130 that had been our lifeline for the previous ten days. I was smiling as the ramp closed. I was ready to be gone from the dirt and heat of a ground vehicle garage on M'Poko airfield, ready for a hot shower, ready for a long sleep in an air-conditioned room on clean sheets, ready to see my wife.

But just as the crew chief was closing the passenger door, a Land Cruiser pulled up and someone ran up to the aircraft. It was the RSO. He motioned me off the aircraft. I sagged. The Marines around me smiled and shook their heads. One of them, the admin Marine I had sat next to while we processed evacuees for ten days, leaned in towards me and said over the road of the engines, "BOHICA, Sir."

BOHICA: Bend Over, Here It Comes Again: the high hard

one, the mind-fuck. I wasn't leaving, but instead would be staying in Bangui, just moving over to the embassy. In my place, the Deputy Chief of Mission stepped onto the aircraft. She was wearing high heels and a dress, a beautiful silk scarf around her neck. She looked completely out of her element and extremely uncomfortable. One of the Marines hoisted her bag onto the plane. I waved goodbye to the Marines as the door slid closed.

The RSO and I knew each other well, so he got right to the point. Things weren't going smoothly at the embassy; the DCM and the ambassador were fighting, so the ambassador had ordered the DCM out. I would stay for a couple of days to help him sort a few things out. We watched the aircraft take off, called in 'wheels-up' to the embassy, and headed into Bangui proper from the airport.

At that time the airport at M'poko was a relatively new facility. As we pulled out of the gate and turned onto the highway, I noticed that the road was extremely wide and that there were aircraft landing markings on the pavement. I had seen this sort of thing before, on an alternate landing site for the Space Shuttle, so I immediately flashed on to that idea. Wow, I wondered, is Bangui an emergency landing site? Apparently not, the African sites were in Gabon, Senegal, and Morocco, I learned. When the newer M'Poko airport had been built in the 1980s, the old runway simply became the road to the terminal.

We reached one of the main intersections at the edge of the old city. At the side of the road, I saw a man walking down the street with the business half of a toilet balanced on his head. The RSO and I looked at each other. He said, "If your building doesn't have a French paratrooper standing outside the gate, all your stuff is gone." Apparently, "all your stuff" included toilets.

At the embassy the Marines had established an observation point and had set up a bunch of comms antennas on the roof. Inside the main building, Marines in full combat gear worked alongside the few remaining State Department officers. I met the ambassador; she thanked me for my work at the airport.

We went upstairs to meet the Marine major who was commanding the security team—I think they were from a Fleet Anti-

Terrorism Security Team (FAST), but I didn't ask. He quietly told me the embassy leadership was, in his words, a soup sandwich. This description, while perfectly clear to anyone who has served in the military, probably requires explanation to anyone else. Imagine trying to make a sandwich that you could eat with your hands out of two slices of bread and a ladle-full of soup, but without the ladle. You get the picture. The major confirmed what the RSO had said: that the ambassador and the DCM were at each others' throats, and that neither had seemed very competent or composed during the fighting. I was happy I had been out at the airport the whole time.

We wandered around the embassy compound for an hour or so, the RSO checking the perimeter, as I tagged along to get a feel for the place during daylight.

In the late afternoon the RSO and I drove over to the DCM's house to package up some of her shoes to ship out to her. Her house was in a pretty nice neighborhood, for Bangui. There were ficus trees in all the yards; tall, whitewashed walls surrounded the compounds and steel gates that for the most part remained in place and locked. A few French paratroopers were at each major intersection. We went inside and packed up a boxful of shoes—we might have packed out more stuff, too, but I only remember the shoes. Then we loaded them into the Land Cruiser, pulled out of the gate, and headed back to the embassy.

The route we took—which really was the only way to get where we were going—passed uncomfortably near the presidential palace. The mutiny had broken out because President Patasse had failed to pay most of the military, and his troops had rebelled. Patasse's Presidential Guard had remained loyal (and paid), and the French supported Patasse through the uprising while the surviving mutineers were paid. As we approached the palace, we heard Kalashnikovs firing ahead. Not too much, just a few rounds and a reply. The RSO turned quickly onto a side street, and we avoided whatever the skirmish was, but it seemed awfully silly to be out running around town in a thin-skinned vehicle to rescue some FSO's high heels.

I loaded onto another Marine flight a couple of days later and went back to Yaoundé. It was nice to be home. I went to a party at one of my colleagues' houses the first night back, but I was so exhausted I could only stay for half an hour.

Back in the office, things were incredibly boring in the consular section. Never mind, though. Within a week I came down with malaria and typhoid. For the record, this is a really effective weight-loss program—I think I shed about eighteen pounds in a week or so—but I don't really recommend it. Like I said, no good deed goes unpunished.

The Banyamulenge War

I N THE FALL OF 1996, I was called to active duty and sent to Uganda to work with the defense attaché there. There was a war across the border in Zaire in which Rwandan troops fighting alongside their Zairian ethnic brethren (the Banyamulenge) were battling the Zairian Army (known as *Les Forces Armées Zairoises*—the FAZ) and Rwandan Hutus living in Zairian refugee camps.

Many of the Hutus lived in a place called Mugunga, a few kilometers west of the border town, Goma. The thing is, the people on the Mugunga plain weren't all refugees. I tried to think of them as refugees, but it was difficult to do so. They had fled from Rwanda, at a rate of about ten to twelve thousand a day, and crossed the border into Zaire in mid-July 1994 after the Rwandan Patriotic Front rebels had finally captured Rwanda's capital, Kigali, and put a stop to the genocide.

They arrived with pots and jerry cans and with what food they could carry. Women with infants strapped onto their backs, older children walking barefoot and carrying whatever they could lift, a lucky few leading a goat or holding a chicken. Some came with their pangas, the machetes used to kill eight hundred thousand Tutsi and moderate Hutus in the hundred days after April 6 when President Juvénal Habyarimana's plane was shot down. They had committed genocide. They weren't refugees; they were *génocidaires*.

No one knows who shot down Habyarimana's plane; well, someone certainly knows, but I don't. You could make a plausible case for either side pulling the trigger. But either way, within hours after Habyarimana died, the Hutu Power militias had erected barricades and were roaming the streets killing Tutsi.

They had been well prepared by their political leadership. "The Tutsi are coming back to steal your land," the Hutu Power radio, Radio Libre des Milles Collines, announced. "Make lists of the nasty Tutsi," the Hutu Power leaders urged. "We are the *Interahamwe*, the people who struggle together." Soon the radio hissed, "Kill the *inyenzi*." To the *Interahamwe*, the Tutsi weren't even people, they were *inyenzi*, cockroaches, vermin to be exterminated.

Many of the Hutu women waited at home while their sons and husbands went out day after day to the barricades or around the towns and villages, then came home in the evening after having killed innocent Tutsi men, women, and children. When they started running out of Tutsi to kill, they killed other Hutus—someone wrote that at that point the Hutus without shoes were killing the Hutus who had shoes.

Often men and boys were killed while women and girls were raped, then told, "Now you will give birth to a Hutu baby." Bullets were expensive, but five thousand Francs Rwandaises could buy a bullet to the head instead of a machete. When the killers were too tired to kill, they would cut the Achilles' tendons of their Tutsi victims to preclude any escape, then return after a rest and a meal to finish them off.

The killing went on for a hundred days. The UN did not intervene. The European powers did not intervene. America did not intervene. In Gitarama and Ruhengeri, in Cyangugu and Butare, in the capital city of Kigali and in villages almost too small to have a name, Hutu killed Tutsi; Rwandan killed Rwandan. By the time the genocide was over, eight hundred thousand Tutsi and moderate Hutu were dead at the hands of the *Interahamwe*. It was the most efficient mass killing in history. Nearly a million people murdered in a hundred days. Not even Hitler managed that.

The 1994 genocide wasn't the first such outbreak of violence between the Rwanda Hutu and Tutsi. In 1959, just before the country's independence, Hutus killed Tutsi. One hundred and fifty thousand Tutsi were killed, and half a million were driven out of the country into refugee camps in Uganda, Tanganyika (now called Tanzania),and Zaire. In Uganda, many young Tutsi refugees became part of Yoweri Museveni's rebellions against Idi Amin and Milton Obote. When Museveni took power in 1986, his military chiefs of operations and intelligence were Rwandan Tutsis from the camps. Four years later they led the Rwandan Patriotic Front across the border into Rwanda in an attempt to overthrow the Hutu government. They fought the French-supported army, the *Forces Armées Rwandaises*—the FAR, to a stalemate, and were implementing a negotiated power-sharing agreement when Habyarimana's plane was shot down and the genocide ensued.

Since no one else was coming, the Rwanda Patriotic Front had to fight the Rwandan army and the *Interahamwe* alone. As the fighting ended, the RPF drove the *Interahamwe* and their families out of Rwanda into Zaire and Tanzania. The French finally showed up, authorized by the UN to create *Opération Turquoise*, and set up a safe area for the exodus of Hutu into Zaire. Bodies of genocide victims lined the roads and the fields, bloated in the equatorial sun. The *Interahamwe* dumped thousands of victims into the Kagera River at Rusumo Falls, blocking the river just as tens of thousands of Hutu were crossing the bridges over the falls into Tanzania. Eight hundred thousand killed; over one million fleeing.

But the killing didn't stop once the *Interahamwe* had left Rwanda. Zairian strongman Mobutu Sese Seko protected them and, despite an arms embargo and the fact that they were granted refugee status (which precludes being armed), weapons and munitions arrived. Many of the men in the camps had taken part in the genocide. Many of them continued to take part in violent attacks on Zairian Tutsi in the hills west of Lake Kivu, and even back into Rwanda to kill more Tutsi there. The Rwandans and their ethnic brethren the Banyamulenge began to fight back, moving north from Uvira, driving the army and the refugees from the camps ahead of them. That was in the summer of 1996. In September, the UN brokered a ceasefire.

But in October, the cease-fire collapsed when Goma was hit with mortar fire. The rounds came from the west, from Mugunga, from the refugee camps. Rebel alliance forces, mostly Zairian Banyamulenge and Rwandan Tutsi, moved up the main road from Goma toward Mugunga. Chaos ensued. Incredible brutality was commonplace as the Banyamulenge tried to move up the road but collided with hundreds of thousands of Hutu refugees. The *Interahamwe* pushed civilians forward to act as a shield to cover their escape. Thousands of civilians were killed on the road in the first hours. The war was back on.

When the cease-fire was first broken, rebel leader Laurent Kabila had closed the roads between Goma and Mugunga to all non-military traffic. Things quickly got desperate. There were too many people and not enough food or water or sanitation. Aid workers reported cholera. Some said that by keeping aid from reaching the refugees the rebel leader, Laurent Kabila, and his Rwandan backers were trying to cause "genocide by starvation." Was Kabila committing genocide by starvation by blocking food aid to the *génocidaires*? Such are the politics of aid.

The war in Zaire, later re-named the Democratic Republic of the Congo, really began in Rwanda in 1990 when the Rwandan Patriotic Front rebels crossed the border from Uganda in an attempt to overthrow the Hutu-led regime. The genocide in Rwanda in 1994 is a part of it. The Banyamulenge War is part of it. As this book goes to press in early 2014, the war still continues, with millions of people dead. Most of my work in Central Africa between 1996 and 2002 focused on this war and these people.

Count the Feet

L IFE AT THE HOTEL LAKE VICTORIA, *The Lake Vic*, is placid. I take morning coffee on the veranda with the BBC news on the radio. I've been here for three months reporting in support of the international military task force that has assembled in Entebbe. Each day I drive over to the new airport and talk to task force staff officers about what's going on in Eastern Zaire, then go talk with pilots, missionaries, humanitarian aid workers—anyone who has recently been in the area—in an effort to try to get a better, clearer picture of what is happening across the border.

The basic facts are that there is a war and a few hundred thousand people are missing. Rwandan authorities say two hundred thousand people crossed the border into Rwanda on one day in October alone. In the following days another two hundred thousand returned from Zaire. Rebel troops ostensibly led by Laurent Kabila cleared the plain at Mugunga, driving the other six or seven hundred thousand refugees north and west, fleeing into the Ndoki forest. Many moved along the Walekale road, a dirt track that winds five hundred kilometers to Kisangani, the center of the country, and indeed the center of the continent. It is very far and there is very little in between. The Banyamulenge are pursuing the *Interahamwe*, and we're trying to find them.

The international military task force was sent here in case the refugees needed protection. A few dozen soldiers were the advance party for what might have been a few thousand American and European troops sent to protect the refugees from the advancing rebels. One of the staff planners is a former classmate of mine. He will be the only one of us to become a general. He tells me the commander doesn't want to bring his force down from Germany and Italy.

"The politics are complex," he says. Zaire is part of the French sphere of influence, but the French won't act because they were criticized for helping the Hutus escape Rwanda in 1994.

I think it's more about Washington than Paris. "Clinton won't intervene to save the Hutus," I counter. "He didn't stop the genocide in 1994, why would he intervene now?" He shrugs.

The Canadians are technically in the lead, there is a Canadian lieutenant general here. But everyone knows the deal: if the U.S. won't go in, no one will.

Every other day or so, I go to the embassy in Kampala to write reports back to Washington. The embassy is a small, quiet outpost occupying space in the back of the British High Commission building. I meet the ambassador and his deputy, the defense attaché and chief of station. They are harried and are more interested in the internal situation in Uganda than the war across the border. Let the UN sort it out.

We're keen to move closer to the fighting, but my partner and I are told to shuttle between Entebbe and Kampala. The UN is evacuating its personnel from Goma and moving operations to Gisenyi, just across the Rwandan border. The American ambassador in Kigali doesn't want us there. So we stay at *The Lake Vic*.

The shelling at Goma and the break-up of the camps change everything. It seems to me we've now passed the point where a small task force could come in and protect the refugees. It's not clear what Washington will do with the task force. The advance party is based in the new airport terminal at Entebbe. Their offices are up on the second floor, near the World Food Program (WFP) logistics office.

The new terminal is nice. It's well appointed and clean—orderly. The old airport is just across the tarmac, though. You can walk over there and still see the pockmarked walls from the Israeli commando raid that freed the hostages from *Air France 139* in 1976. The Ugandan Air Force MIGs that had been crippled by the Israelis are still rusting nearby and will soon be covered in vines.

A couple of big U.S. and British military surveillance aircraft rest on the tarmac, their combat grey a striking contrast among the white UN cargo planes and the few incongruously small Twin Otters and Caravans that the missionary groups use to fly around Eastern Zaire.

It's hot during the day; Entebbe isn't far from the Equator. The task force is under what the military calls General Order Number One, which means they are not allowed to drink alcohol, have sex or even look at porn. It sucks to be them.

A message from Washington tells us to try to determine where the refugees are and where they are going. "That should be easy," my partner Jack says, rolling his eyes. We order beers and try to think of a plan. We order a few more before the night is done. The plan turns out to be pretty simple: continue doing what we're doing. We can't go anywhere else, so we've got no other way of gathering information.

I interview a pilot who flies for one of the missionary groups. He's an old guy who flew for the U.S Air Force in Korea and Vietnam. He tells me about seeing an Antonov land at a remote strip in North Kivu where men offloaded boxes of weapons and ammunition. The landing was north of the line where we think the Banyamulenge have reached, so these must be re-supply missions for the FAZ and the *Interahamwe*. He has a mission the following day to pick up some Catholic workers who were attacked by the retreating FAZ. I want to talk with them. He says he'll try.

The next day I interview the nun who worked at the parish that the FAZ had attacked and looted. She hobbles off the plane wearing a sheet of *panya* cloth wrapped around her waist and a man's shirt that is a couple sizes too large. She is limping off her left leg. When I get closer to her, I see she has a swollen cheek and lip. She tells me in French that she was cleaning the rectory when she heard noises. She went outside and saw two soldiers beating the priest. They wanted to know what money he had. Every time they would ask him about the money, he would ask them to pray for forgiveness. And each time they knocked him down, he would get back up. Finally one of them hit him in the face with a fist, and then again. When the priest finally broke down and told them about the cash box, one of the soldiers hit the priest in the side of the head with his rifle butt. The priest didn't get up. Then they turned to her.

One of the soldiers put a knife—a bayonet probably— up to her face, and forced her to the ground. She couldn't bring herself to tell me what happened next, but the MSF nurse said that three soldiers raped her, and one beat her before they left. The Banyamulenge arrived the following day. They took her and the priest—he survived—to the *Médecins Sans Frontières* physicians, who then got her out to Uganda.

One of the MSF team tells me that the people are severely traumatized by the fighting. "There is a great deal of fear," she says. The *Interahamwe* are telling their people the Americans are helping the Banyamulenge and will kill any of the Hutu they capture. They are driving the refugees ahead of them, away from the truth.

We spend a couple of days in Kampala at the embassy writing up what we've learned. We wander down the street past the National Museum, and I buy some soapstone coasters and other tchotchkes for gifts at the crafts market. Our favorite restaurant downtown is the Masala Chaat House. Whenever we can, we go there for lunch and eat the daily curry special, washed down with a glass of passion fruit juice. Afterwards, when I go for a run I can smell the curry coming out in my sweat.

We send our messages back to Washington and get feedback from our bosses. They like what we're reporting, but they want more and better. Demoralized, we drive back to *The Lake Vic*.

We have an idea where the front lines are. We still aren't sure about the refugees, although they can't be too far apart. The two US Navy P-3 surveillance aircraft, originally designed to hunt submarines in the open ocean, fly over the Walekale road and the forests to the north and west of Goma to take photographs. The pilots fly the plane at nineteen thousand feet above the treetops.

One of the pilots observes, "The top of the forest looks like broccoli." Their cameras can't see through it. "We should be able to see smoke from their cooking fires or something. Maybe they just aren't out there."

"They are," I tell him. They don't want to be found, and they don't have anything to cook until we can get food to them. So they don't make too many fires. They are living off the forest.

I speak by radio to a Catholic priest whose station is along the Walekale road. He says hundreds of thousands of people are moving west, pursued by the rebels and by Rwandan troops who have joined them. The people are in bad shape, he says. They are living off whatever they carried or can scrounge along the road. There isn't much water, only what they find in the forest or at wells near the small stations along the way. When the rebels catch up with groups of stragglers or a group of *Interahamwe* who stop and fight, there is no mercy.

We begin to hear whispered stories of mass graves in Kibumbo and Katale. I write more reports.

I'm invited to Thanksgiving dinner at the residence of one of the embassy staff. It's a nice house with bougainvillea and citrus trees; kids play in the grassy yard. There is turkey from South Africa and ham from Italy. There is good red wine from France and California. It's a typical Thanksgiving dinner except that it's about 85 degrees outside and there is no football on TV yet, because we're eight hours ahead of Eastern Standard Time.

A military colleague tells me the Canadian general is in Goma on an assessment mission. A friend on the UN staff tells me over a drink that there are forty thousand Hutus walking northwards along the edge of the lake in South Kivu. Today, the WFP is moving truckloads of BP-5s, high protein biscuits used for emergency food relief, down to the lake. I imagine eating compressed sawdust, and look over at the turkey dinner being assembled.

There is no clarity. Every day I try to find pilots or aid workers or journalists who actually have access to the east and who can help me find hundreds of thousands of people.

I interview another Congolese woman who is brought to Entebbe from North Kivu. She was from Lobutu, a town near the Ugandan border. She tells me that her husband had passed information to the Banyamulenge about the disposition of the FAZ and *Interahamwe* in their town. The FAZ intelligence service found out and came to their house. The FAZ officer ordered her husband bound, and began beating him and cutting him with a knife. Then he shot their son and killed him after the boy tried to help his father. The officer left after a couple hours, but the two soldiers stayed. They were eating the family's food and drinking all of the beer and liquor in the house while they tortured her husband. It took all night for them to grow weary of this, and he suffered a great deal, she said. The soldiers raped her in front of her husband as he sat tied to a chair, beaten and bleeding from dozens of cuts. The building next door housed a mechanic's shop and the soldiers eventually brought her husband over there and turned an acetylene torch on him. He died quickly. She escaped early in the morning when the soldiers were sleeping off their drunk. I send this information back to Washington in a report. The analysts ask, "But where are the refugees?"

In early December, two young missionary pilots tell me a large population of refugees is forming near a town called Tingi-Tingi. The World Food Program and High Commission for Refugees planners are organizing relief supplies.

I tell my classmate on the task force staff. "The general doesn't believe the reports," he says.

"It doesn't matter does it?" I ask. "Washington has decided not to do anything."

He shrugs. "Leave it for the UN; the boys are going home for Christmas."

I give the pilots a video camera and ask them to show me what they find in Tingi-Tingi. Two days later we have the proof. The video the pilots bring back shows crowds of people standing shoulder-to-shoulder, eight or ten deep along the edge of the road for eight hundred meters. We can see thousands more in the surrounding forest, and the pilots say the leaders told them there were twice as many hiding just out of sight. They are gaunt and haggard, their clothing mostly rags; some are naked or covering themselves with leaves. Some of the men are holding pangas and I cannot help but wonder if these are the same they had used during the genocide.

We do some basic math, then ask the World Food Program staff to run the numbers, too. We estimate that there are probably one hundred thousand people around Tingi-Tingi. I bring the video to the headquarters. But, the general isn't all that interested in watching it.

"What's on it?" he asks.

"Proof that these people exist, and the exact location where you can find them," I say.

"How many are there?" I notice that now at least he looks up from his other papers.

"We've counted about twenty-five thousand, and there are easily that number again in the forests that we can't see on the film. People on the ground told the pilots there were twice as many in the surrounding area. We think there are about a hundred thousand in the area."

"Hmphh."

"We feel good about the number. And the fact that there are so many there already, we think there will be more coming." I think I'm winning.

Then the bombshell drops. "Well, it's too late for us to do anything now. We're going home."

"General, we're talking about a hundred thousand people." I'm losing big. "They need help, and you have the power to help them."

"Hmphh..." Then, after a pause, "What's your methodology for counting?" he growls.

I've already lost, so I figure I might as well go out big. "We count the feet and divide by two."

There is dead silence for about two beats. Then sniggering from his staff. Then broad laughter erupts from everyone except for the general. He leaves the room.

As the general leaves, his chief of staff says, "It's a UN problem now. You've found them; we can all go home. Nice job."

Ten minutes later, Jack and I are standing atop the roof watching the sunset and raging against the folly of spending weeks looking for hundreds of thousands of people, finding them, and then taking no action. Our frustration and anger are sour. My government has failed to do the right thing.

I carry the tape to the UN. They already know about Tingi-Tingi. They already know the Task Force is leaving. I go to *The Lake Vic* and drink gin and tonics.

We've found over a hundred thousand people, but hundreds of thousands are still missing. Where are they? Dead along the way? Hiding deeper in the forest, convinced that the U.S. and UK surveillance aircraft are looking for them so we can kill them? The UN organizes a camp in Tingi-Tingi that eventually supports one hundred-sixty thousand people, but by February the rebels arrive, and the refugees and the *Interahamwe* are again forced to flee.

In the next week the team disbands. The task force goes back to Italy for Christmas. The defense attaché goes to Zimbabwe or Mozambique, somewhere in the south. Jack goes home to his family in Germany. I am asked to stay through the New Year to help finish up some reporting and shut down the office.

I still don't know what happened. I can't make the logic or the numbers work. Too many people are missing, too much remains unexplained. I learn I can catch a ride on a UN flight to Goma. I have a couple of days to kill and no one to tell me not to go. I pack a small bag and jump on the Antonov.

Prostates

GOMA IS BEAUTIFUL. I spend a few days right around Christmas running around with some NGO types and a reporter from Belgium. No one really has any clarity on what is happening around Zaire. The UN publishes a report every day through IRIN, the Integrated Regional Information Network, but it's a hodgepodge of data points interspersed with a factoid here and there about the cost of fuel and bus fare. Just after Christmas the rebels capture Bunia in the north, which gives them a major airfield for re-supply (and denies this to the FAZ). The war has moved on from Goma and Mugunga.

I try but I still can't make sense of what has happened beyond the basic facts. Maybe that's all there is. Maybe there isn't any sense to be made of this.

On my last night in Goma I go to dinner with some of the contacts I've developed. When it's time to pay for dinner, someone tallies up the bill for food and beers, counts heads at the table and determines that we each owe about sixteen million, tip not included. No one blinks. Sixteen million is reasonable for dinner with a couple extra beers. We each reach into the bags and backpacks we carry and begin to pull out bricks of dirty bills held together with rubber bands. A likely kilogram of money-bricks are stacked up at the center of the table among the empty Tembo and Primus bottles as we start to make our way out of the restaurant into the night.

Of course, this is the old money. No one really wants to take the new money here in Goma. Only the old Zaires are accepted here. New Zaires are used in the west, 1,500 kilometers away at the capital, Kinshasa. Since you never can tell which currency will be in vogue at any place at any time during the day, we carry U.S. dollars, French Francs, and old Zaires with us everywhere. We are walking foreign exchange bureaus.

Old Zaires are ragged and worn down from use by people whose lives are for the most part ragged and worn down. They live here at the neglected edge of the nation where the roads have crumbled away and electricity is rare. The Kalashnikov is the only dependable power. There is little law. To call the formal economy a shambles gives it too much viability.

New Zaires are clean and crisp with pictures of Mobutu Sese Seko on the front. It's the old Mobutu of course in his Field Marshal's uniform and black-framed glasses, not the current Mobutu who is frail and sick, undergoing treatment in France. He's dying of prostate cancer, so with typical Zairois humor people here refer to the New Zaires as "Prostates." You might actually hear someone ask if the price is in Zaires or Prostates. Even in the midst of this war and all of this suffering, people need to laugh.

"*Bon soir,*" call the restaurant staff as we head out. "*Bon soir,*" we echo, stepping from the concrete steps onto the dirt road where a half-dozen white land cruisers are parked higgledy-piggledy, protected by the teen-aged guardians we've engaged to ensure our trucks aren't vandalized. We pay them each five hundred thousand Zaires, about eighty-five cents at the current exchange rate.

On the drive back to the guesthouse we're stopped at two roadblocks. The Banyamulenge rebels have held the town for months. The FAZ are long gone. But the town is still tense. We give the boys, for that's what they are, packs of cigarettes and talk to them for a few minutes. I like to chat up the kids with guns a little. It's always dodgy dealing with a fifteen year-old carrying a Kalashnikov, especially one who is likely high and clearly admiring your watch. So I figure it can't hurt to be friendly.

We get to the guesthouse safely and turn in. But I can't sleep. I look at my watch: it's just past midnight. The fan turning over my head squeaks once on every rotation. I get up to turn it off. Just before I do, I look through the louvered window and see the guard in his chair. He is wrapped up in a heavy coat against the cool night air. He has a transistor radio on his lap, but it's turned off. He is sleeping heavily. I go back to bed and listen to dogs barking and someone snoring down the hall. I get up and turn the fan back on, but I still can't sleep. Maybe it's the altitude, almost a mile high. Maybe it's the Mefloquine, although I like the dreams the drugs bring on.

In the morning I meet a contact for a breakfast of baguette, Nescafé, and part of a papaya. We talk distractedly about our plans for the day. We're both supposed to leave Goma for Entebbe around noon, but we think that maybe we can get a couple of interviews in before we go.

I drink my Nescafé and look out across the town. We're just above Lake Kivu. Fishermen in pirogues paddle in after setting their lines. Kids are swimming next to the concrete pier. You can see the hills, the volcanoes and the relentless forest of palm, mahogany, ficus and podocarp that are the Virunga Mountains. A UN Antonov is on final approach to the airport. The eleven thousand foot runway once hosted jetliners arriving directly from Paris and Geneva. Tourists came to enjoy the perfect weather, the impossibly lovely lake, and to see the mountain gorillas that live on the slopes of the Nyarigongo and Karisimbi volcanoes. That was before.

I get out on a UN flight in the afternoon. On the trip north to Entebbe, I try to put down some notes for a longer report I need to write. But it's useless. Even after three months here I still don't think I know enough to say anything intelligent, so I decide to read more of my book. I re-learn that Mobutu's full name is Mobutu Sese Seko Nkuku Ngbendu Wa Za Banga, which means "The all-powerful warrior who, because of his endurance and inflexible will to win, goes from conquest to conquest, leaving fire in his wake." I end up dozing, and wake as we are descending. I think I dreamed about the ashes of

Zaire in Mobutu's wake.

I pass through customs, and an embassy driver meets me and takes me to *The Lake Vic*. I shower and make some phone calls, then meet some colleagues and friends to drink gin and tonics on the terrace at sunset. Some of the men are in jackets. There are a few women in dresses and heels. It's all quite civilized.

I stay in Uganda until just past the New Year. In the embassy on my last day I read reports of Serbian mercenaries training Zairian army forces near Kisangani. It truly is a World War.

I spend my last night on mission in a room at the American club. It's away from the city center, so it's quiet out. I get a beer and go out to the veranda with a book and a cigar. The forest seems close even though I am just at the edge of the city. Bats swoop over the mango trees in the dark. Things smell fecund, ripe. I can hear music playing from a bar down the valley.

I order a couple more beers and drink them, staring out across the valley. I think about the killings. I try not to think in numbers but it's impossible not to. So many dead. I can hear two women talking and laughing just outside the wall of the compound. They are safe here; the killings are over in this part of Uganda for now. There is a generator so we have electricity all night, and even though it isn't really hot at this altitude, I sleep with the air conditioner running to provide white noise. I sleep well.

The next day I leave Kampala on my last trip to Entebbe airport, this time to fly out to London. The driver passes a man riding a Chinese-made Flying Pigeon bicycle. He has a machete, a panga, tied to the handlebars by a rubber thong made from an inner tube. He's probably a gardener heading home for lunch, or a farmer who has been working his fields just on the edge of town. Pangas have lots of legitimate uses. I look up to see that we are on Mobutu Sese Seke Road, and remember that I have a few million old Zaires left in my bag.

By the spring, refugees have begun to arrive in Kisangani. In March, a French journalist writes about sitting in a bar at the edge of town and seeing one hundred thousand ghosts come walking out of the forest. The Banyamulenge are close behind them. UN human rights monitors and investigators from Human Rights Watch and Amnesty International find mass graves along the Walekale road and around the city of Kisangani.

Our Ndoki

T HE WAR IN ZAIRE wasn't the only fighting going on in the area. In early November I traveled out to the border area with a bunch of operators from the Army Special Forces unit in Germany. A colonel and a handful of his staff had come down to Uganda to meet with senior leaders of the Ugandan Peoples' Defense Force (UPDF), and one day we flew on a Soviet-made helicopter from the capital Kampala out west toward the Zairian border. One of the UPDF battalions was engaged in a fight against supporters of the deposed dictator, Idi Amin—a group called the West Nile Bank Front—and the SF colonel wanted to see the UPDF units in the field, so off we went.

The leader of The West Nile Bank Front was a guy named Juma Oris, who had been a minister in Amin's government. Once Amin had been overthrown, Oris and his lot began attacking civilians in northwest and western Uganda from bases in Sudan and Zaire.

Oris's rebels had been slipping into Uganda from Zaire, maybe making a stab at the improved road that ran from Fort Portal to Kampala as a high-speed avenue of approach, we thought, and this battalion was tasked with stopping them. This was a small war: a few hundred rebels trying to mobilize an insurgency against a standing government. President Museveni had been fighting a couple of these wars simultaneously at that time.

Up north, Museveni was also fighting an insurgency against the Acholi, part of which included Joseph Kony and his Lord's Resistance Army. Kony was the nut-job of nut-jobs. He claimed to be visited by no less than thirty different spirits—including Juma Oris, who was still alive. He captured and enslaved children, used rape as a weapon, cut off the feet of people he captured riding bicycles. Museveni's neighbor to the north, Sudan, supported and protected Kony, Oris, and pretty much anyone else who would take up arms against Museveni.

We were sitting in or right on the edge of a National Park just north of the Ruwenzori Mountains—the Mountains of the Moon and the source of the White Nile. We were a kilometer or two inside Uganda, and there was a whole bunch of stuff going on just a few klicks away. This area is only a few degrees south of the Equator, but the altitude keeps it cool. The hills are covered with dense, green forest and the roads are red laterite. On the ride out to the bivouac site from the landing zone, a rain shower popped up and, since we were sitting in the back of beat up Toyota pick-ups, left us all drenched and shivering in minutes.

We met the battalion commander and his staff, who briefed us on what they had been doing for the past few days and what they expected to do. The U.S. colonel had a few questions and then the real discussions got going.

We figured this would take a few hours, so one of the SF warrant officers and I jumped in a pick-up and spirited away towards Zaire. A couple klicks down the road, the little voice in my head started saying, *we're really not supposed to cross the border, you know.* I just nodded silently as we pushed forward, into Zaire. We were up in North Kivu province, just on the edge of the Ndoki forest—the continent-sized forest that runs from Cameroon across Central Africa to the edges of Zaire. *Ndoki* means black in Lingala, but it also means magic, as in black arts and black magic.

In just twenty minutes or so, we found what we were looking for: the Rwandan soldiers who weren't there. Officially, the Rwandans weren't in Zaire. I had heard that on the BBC a day or so earlier. But it was cool, because I wasn't there either. Officially, that is.

We quickly figured out who the Rwandan officer was. It actually wasn't very hard because they all dress alike: he was wearing dark green gumboots—like Wellies—his uniform pants stuffed into them, with a Makarov pistol stuck in the back of his belt against his spine and carrying a Motorola walkie-talkie. Plus he was about 6'5" tall.

The Rwandan tried very hard to convince us he was actually a Zairian Banyamulenge, but he wasn't a very good actor He couldn't speak French worth a shit because he had grown up in a refugee camp in Uganda, not Zaire. I couldn't speak French worth a shit, either, because I was born in a trailer park in rural Florida. But we both did our best.

The Rwandan did his best to cover his tracks, and I did my best to play along. I was taking notes in my little stenographer's notebook—this is what I kept in my belt snuggled up against my spine instead of a Makarov or a Beretta—while the Rwandan officer was explaining that his guys had just come out of combat, so they were tired. And they'd lost a soldier—a popular lieutenant—in the fighting, so they were pissed off.

He told us their standard operating procedure was to send a message to the unit commander they were facing to let him know that they were coming in three days. The following day, they would send another message saying they were going to destroy his unit and kill him in two days. On the last day, they'd send a final message offering to let the unit escape alive if they simply walked out of the town and disappeared. All the while, the Rwandans would have been conducting reconnaissance, maybe infiltrating the town with a few troops in civilian clothes, and recruiting locals.

By the third day, of course, probably half of the Zairian commander's troops had moved on. The remaining half would get busy with raping, stealing, and robbing the villagers. Then they would leave with the dead lying in the streets, the women raped and beaten, and houses, schools, and shops smoldering. After a few weeks of watching this sort of thing, we started referring to it as "the loot and scoot."

The following morning the Rwandans would walk into the town more or less unopposed. The Rwandan commander would call together any remaining civic leaders, teachers, priests, and so forth. He would tell them to go to work, and give them a salary—likely for the first time in months. Then they would move on to the next village where a similar series of messages and violence would occur.

I asked the commander what happened when the Zairians actually had to fight. By this time we had dropped the pretense of speaking in French. He smiled, and squatting down on his haunches, sketched out in the dust a battle plan for a double envelopment. This has to be one of the most difficult combat maneuvers in the arsenal. He said it was their preferred mode of attack. I asked about scouting and reconnaissance and he said they used local scouts and guides— adding that the Zairians hated their Army so much they would do almost anything to get them out of the area.

We talked for a while about combat support like mortars, artillery, armor, or aircraft. He said they occasionally had mortars but never anything bigger or more sophisticated like helicopters. When I asked what made his troops more successful, he explained that they trained hard and were professionals. I wrote that down and then asked if there was anything else. He paused for a moment, and then said "We're better because our Ndoki is stronger than their Ndoki." *Our magic is stronger than theirs.*

This is, of course, no different than some other military leader saying that his force had been successful on the battlefield because God favored their cause. But it's colorful and exotic, so I remembered it.

We only spent about an hour in Zaire that day. We scampered back across the border and made it to the Ugandan battalion's bivouac just in time for a dinner of goat and beer before we flew out to Kampala in the gathering dusk.

Oris's insurgency would survive for about another two years. It petered out just around the time that the First Congo War, as it was called, ended in 1997. The major fighting in that war came to a stop once Mobutu had fled. The rebel army, led by Rwandan general James Kabarebe, had marched all the way from Goma. They installed Laurent Kabila as president, and he promptly renamed the country the Democratic Republic of the Congo. Just as Museveni had relied on Fred Rwigema and Paul Kagame to run his army for him, Kabila relied heavily on his Rwandan advisors: James Kabarebe became chief of staff of the Congolese Army and stayed in that role until 1998.

I left the region in early 1997, not long after that trip out to the border. I went back to my job with the State Department in Cameroon and then to Montreal and Kosovo. But the Congo war spun up again in 1998 and spread more or less throughout the country, drawing in Zimbabwe, Chad, Sudan, Libya, Angola, and Namibia. A United Nations-brokered ceasefire took effect in 2000, and a small force of peacekeepers was authorized. I came back to Rwanda that spring for the State Department as the chief of the embassy's political section.

I was sitting at a hotel on the border of the Democratic Republic of the Congo and Rwanda—for the record, on the Rwandan side—cooling my heels while a delegation of Congressional staffers I was escorting was across the border in Goma, DRC. I didn't have a visa— or the permission of the American embassy in Kinshasa— to enter Congo, so I stayed in Rwanda. Of course, none of them had a visa either, but that's a different story. About half an hour after they'd crossed the border my phone rang. On the other end was a U.S. Army colonel in Washington DC. He was looking for his subordinate lieutenant colonel, the military escort for the delegation.

"He's with the delegation," I told him.

"Where are they?"

"I think they're in meetings," I replied, trying to cover for the guy.

"Did they cross the border?"

I decided I couldn't cover any more for the guy, especially since I'd met the colonel on the other end of the line and he was a good guy. "Yep." There was a brief pause.

"Would you ask him to call me when he comes back?"

"Absolutely."

"Thanks, man."

Click.

At that point, the war in the DRC was officially in a cease-fire, which was being monitored by a UN peacekeeping force. But it was complete bullshit. The peacekeepers couldn't keep the peace. There were too many rebel groups to name and troops from neighboring countries were scattered all around the DRC.

The Congolese people were, for the most part, exhausted from two generations of abuse and a generation of war. The Rwandans were in South Kivu prosecuting their war against the *Interahamwe*, the *génocidaires* from 1994, who were then banging around in eastern Congo calling themselves the FDLR (*Les Forces Démocratiques Pour La Libération du Rwanda*) and making regular attacks into Rwanda. The Ugandans were still running around in North Kivu, too.

The Rwandans infiltrated Congo because the Congolese Army was useless, and the UN Peacekeepers weren't capable of stopping the FDLR raids into Rwanda. They came over to protect their borders and kill a few *génocidaires*, then take home a little Columbo-Tantalite—a mineral that makes your cell phone work—for their trouble.

After a few hours, the staff delegation returned, all of them jazzed from the trip. They were all talking at once, gesturing and laughing, and there was a lot of backslapping. I passed the message to the Army lieutenant colonel, and he slipped away to call his boss.

The rest of us stayed out on the patio of the hotel, looking out over Lake Kivu. We had just ordered some beers when President Paul Kagame walked onto the patio. He strode up to the table where we were sitting—of course we all stood up—and threw his arms around one of the staffers. They'd known each other since the early days of Kagame's rule.

I hadn't been around Kagame very much, just a couple of brief meetings where I was a note-taker. He ordered a Coke, and we chatted a bit about the war, politics, his strategy for re-integrating Hutus returning from Congo, and probably a few other things. I was pretty much star-struck, I have to admit. Kagame had been Museveni's chief of intelligence during the Ugandan insurgency. Then, after Fred Rwigema was killed, he led the Rwandan Patriotic Front rebels in their fight against the Hutu-led Habyarimana regime, fighting to a draw before Habyarimana's plane was shot down. Then he led the RPF to a win over the *Interahamwe* in 1994. He had been running the country and fighting a war in Zaire/DR Congo ever since, including the Banyamulenge War that ended Mobutu's reign in 1997.

I don't think I took any notes. Kagame was serious, there wasn't a lot of joking. But he was also pretty forthcoming about the Rwandans' goals in DRC and the region. It was a really interesting conversation that lasted about fifteen minutes. Then just as abruptly as he arrived, he stood and shook all of our hands, and walked away. I'm pretty sure there were security guys all around, but I never saw them. He wasn't staffed or escorted at all—no note takers, no deputy ministers, no one else appeared to be with him. He just arrived, talked, and left.

Back in Kigali, a couple of weeks later, I was at a diplomatic reception, and I had a discussion with James Kabarebe, the chief of staff of the Rwandan Army. We eventually got around to talking about Congo and the time he had spent there: he was at one time the chief of staff of the Congolese Army. Four years earlier, he and his Army had walked across the vast nation in pursuit of Mobutu's troops, chasing them from the highlands of the east across the forested interior all the way to within twenty miles outside the capital. General Kabarebe told me a story about President Joseph Kabila—who walked across the country with them—which painted President Kabila in a not particularly attractive light, as a petty, selfish young man who hoarded food and stole beer from the troops. Then Kabarebe shrugged and waved his hand dismissively. He said, "The Congolese are not serious: they sing, they dance..." Of course, that's part of what people love about the Congolese.

Later that year, the defense attaché and I traveled up to northwestern Rwanda just after a major incursion by the FDLR. The Rwandan military had trapped a thousand or so FDLR fighters in a valley. About half were killed in the ensuing battle; the other half were captured. Our defense attaché had been on the edges of the fight, and his reporting was some of the best I'd ever seen. He was invited to come and interview the captured rebels, and he graciously invited me to come along.

The five hundred remaining fighters were being loosely held in a former college not far from where they had been captured. I say loosely held because we saw no fencing surrounding what amounted to a prisoner of war camp. There were no barriers to keep the prisoners inside and only about ten Rwandan soldiers and one officer present as guards. They weren't needed. The men stayed in the camp because they were supposed to. Rwandans have a strong sense of duty. It is something that can be both positive—people show up to do their civic duties when asked to—and negative—people show up to commit genocide when told to. Some of the men were even allowed to go to their home villages on pass to see the family members they had left behind when they fled in 1994; they all returned, and did so on schedule.

Any senior officers had been skimmed out of the group, and the men remaining were mostly poorly educated, low-ranking fighters. They spent their days in what could best be described as re-education classes, learning how the new Rwanda was different from the one they had left years before.

In the old Rwanda, every Rwandan carried an identity card that noted their ethnicity—primarily either Hutu or Tutsi. In the new Rwanda, the government's plan was to simply ignore ethnicity, to make it irrelevant in society. No more notations of ethnicity on identity cards, no more ethnic quotas in the schools, no more delineation between the Tutsi and the Hutu. Of course, I thought this was complete nonsense. The government is now Tutsi-dominated and will remain so until there is another major upheaval. But it sounded good, and was both forward-looking and hopeful. I read an essay once in which the author said Rwanda is a place where the past is just around the corner.

The defense attaché (DATT) and I walked around the camp

speaking occasionally with one of the men, mostly in French or sometimes with the help of the sole Rwandan Army officer in charge of the camp, translating from Kinyarwanda to English. At one point a man approached the DATT and asked if we were interested in knowing who had killed the American tourists in Bwindi. That attack, in March 1999, by one hundred and fifty *Interahamwe* against a small group of American, British, and New Zealander tourists, had left eight dead. When Rich nodded yes, the man began to point to individuals within the group of prisoners. A few years later, three of those men would apply for asylum in the U.S. after their cases were dropped following allegations of torture while in Rwandan custody. Only one would be convicted of murder and receive a long prison sentence.

One NGO has estimated that 5.4 million people died as a direct result of the Congo Wars. French researcher Gerard Prunier has called these wars Africa's World War. And most Americans never heard anything about them.

The team at the embassy worked exceptionally well together. It was, at least for the first year I was there, the best professional working relationship I've ever enjoyed. Our reporting was good, solid. We were telling the story of the war across the border, of the regular FDLR incursions into Rwanda, of the Rwandan's efforts to re-integrate the ex-FAR and the *Interahamwe* and their children and families back into the new Rwanda. Naively, I thought we were finally getting some traction on turning the world's attention to the war. That all changed one Tuesday afternoon, when just after 3:00 pm while I was in the office waiting for a USAID colleague to stop in for a meeting, I looked up at the TV just as CNN was reporting that a plane had flown into the World Trade Center in New York.

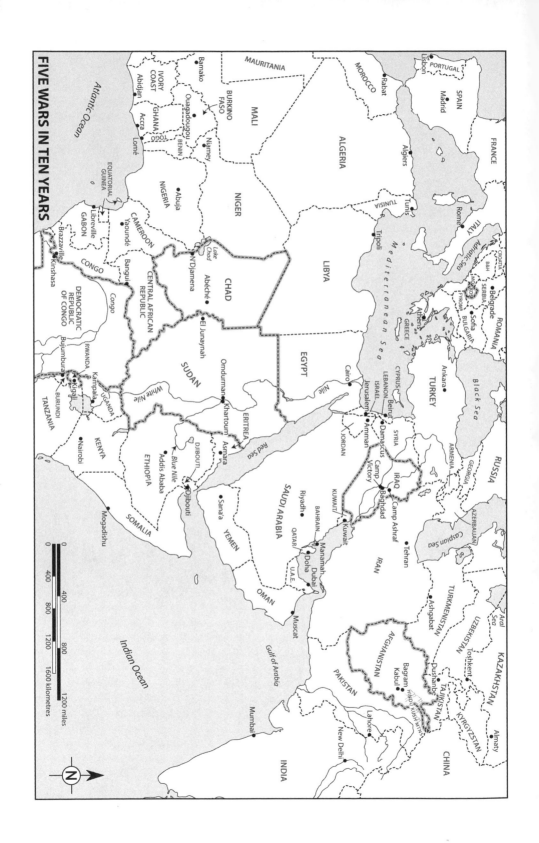

Afghanistan and Iraq

2002-2004

The man who knows himself weaker than
another is more alone in the heart of a
city than a man lost in the desert.

SIMONE WEIL
The Iliad or The Poem of Force

Hold the Javelinas: Bagram

JUST BEFORE THANKSGIVING, the puddle outside my tent is frozen in the morning. During the day, the weather is fine, but at night it gets cold. On Sunday afternoon I sit outside my tent in a T-shirt and shorts and sunglasses, enjoying a good book and a decent cigar. There is no breeze, and dust as thick as mashed potatoes is kicked up by the relentless flow of trucks, humvees, gators, and the scuffling of soldiers' boots. It hangs in the air and then settles on everything that stands still long enough.

I am still a little surprised to be in Afghanistan. Five months ago I was in Rwanda. When I left there, my orders were to go to Washington, learn to speak Serbo-Croatian, and go to Sarajevo as a political officer at the embassy. But one Saturday afternoon, I pulled an envelope out of the mailbox that changed all that. I had been mobilized to active duty for a year under Operation Enduring Freedom. Two months later I am in Afghanistan, a soldier again, sent to augment a regular Army unit that is short a field grade officer—I'm a major about to be promoted to lieutenant colonel—in my specialty.

My military occupation specialty code is 35F, Area Intelligence Officer. Officers with this specialty are called Case Officers, trained to conduct sensitive human intelligence (humint) operations—some people think of us as spies.

But I'm not conducting operations myself. My job in Afghanistan is to direct the actions of all the other human intelligence operators. I am called the CJ2X—the Director of Human and Counterintelligence Operations—for Coalition Joint Task Force 180, the U.S. military command in Afghanistan.

I have a hundred or so people working for me in specialties ranging from counterintelligence agent to interrogator, from explosive ordnance disposal technician to computer systems exploitation experts. Some of us live and work on the base with the XVIII Airborne Corps headquarters at Bagram, but my teams are spread around the country, and even across a few borders, so we travel some, too. A couple of weeks into the tour, I go outside the wire for the first time. Nothing too serious, just a trip up to Kabul to meet with our European counterparts to set up a combined operation we are planning to undertake about a month later. Just before we leave we brief the route with a map and talk about what we should do if we're attacked.

"Your first instinct in an ambush is to take your foot off of the accelerator—Don't!" My sergeant says. He continues, "Drive through the ambush, return fire, and speed through the kill zone."

In the back of my mind I am thinking, I'll stay in the boat while Jim wrestles the giant anaconda. Kabul is about one and a half hours away by land cruiser. It's been there for centuries and will certainly be there when there are no longer any ambushes. I can wait. But we don't.

We check the phone cards in our Thuraya phones—mobiles that connect to a satellite when there's no network available—and throw a case of water in the back. We load up in Toyota pick-ups with all our body armor and Kevlar helmets—battle rattle, so-called because it's hard to move quietly in this gear—and head out the gate.

The town of Bagram sits just outside the gate of the airbase. It's a funny thing, but it looks just like the area outside the smaller bases in Korea, where the US have been for fifty years. There are lots of small shops selling blankets and lanterns and cigarettes. A couple of teahouses (in Korea these would have been bars), and some bicycle repair shops. About a hundred meters down the first alley on the left, a shop still stands in disrepair several weeks after a UN land cruiser had hit a mine buried in the street in front of it. The kids in the street wave, then turn their hands palm up in the universal gesture of entreaty, which has changed, I'm told, in the few months since the Americans have been there in force. Previously, a UN worker with lots of time on the ground there said, the kids only waved. But, by 2002, they started to implore passing troops to give them something, anything. It's the same gesture the kids in Rwanda use, and the kids in Kosovo.

In minutes, even with us crawling through the snarl of Land Cruisers, Humvees, four-door pickups, and donkeys, Bagram dissolves and the countryside opens up. Scattered arbitrarily about the plains, lie the flotsam and jetsam of past wars—wars with the Soviets, between warlords, between the Northern Alliance and the Taliban: armored personnel carriers and infantry fighting vehicles, trucks, and tanks twisted and long-stripped of their tracks and weapons, rusted in place where they've died, or were killed in battle.

A couple of Soviet howitzers mark the entrance to the compound of the local warlord, Baba Jan. Just past his compound, the call comes over the radio: "lock and load." We each load a round into the firing chambers of our weapons. We then become much more alert. But things stay calm.

About half an hour out of Bagram, we see a group of de-miners clearing a field. All along the stretch of plains the edge of the road is marked with rocks painted red and white, indicating that one side of the area—the one on the red side of the rocks—has not yet been cleared of mines. In the field, ten meters from the road, stretch lines of hundreds of neat rows of painted, cantaloupe-sized rocks, unrolling beyond sight. For ten kilometers, we roll past this script from a previous war, its font a deadly, coded cipher to the uninitiated. The de-miners don't look up as we pass. They swing their detectors in arcs in front of them and concentrate on the tones in their headsets— beep beep beep means boom boom boom.

Just beyond the minefields, trenches are carved into the land. I try to visualize what they might look like from the air. Are they cut into lizard shapes or—for the Soviets—a giant bear? Do they form bizarre geometric patterns like crop circles, or just indecipherable scars on the land like a child's crayon scrawl on a wall? At random but strategic points along the trench lines, steel sheds were transformed into bunkers during the fighting. Most of these were attached to the backs of Soviet trucks. But gutted and windowless, the ones near the road have now become shelters for the Afghan Army troops manning checkpoints. In their mixed outfits—usually either a camouflage uniform top or pants mixed with civilian clothes—they wave as we roll past them towards Kabul.

The land is flat, rolling for kilometers out to the foothills of the Hindu Kush. Snow covers the high ridges, and as fall encroaches, we watch the snow line creep down the mountains. With each passing day the grey-brown of the mountains is covered a little more with snow, marking the inevitable arrival of winter. The land in the valleys is sand-colored: dusty, rocky and dry. It is as though Mother Nature had ordered up a second helping of Southern Arizona—hold the javelinas and the saguaro cactus.

There are no trees on the plains. Scrub bushes dot the landscape; they look hardy, but not nearly big enough to build with. Houses are made from mud bricks. Across the plains we can see dozens of collapsed and disintegrating houses. Roofs gone, walls crumbling. I can't determine if they were years or centuries old. Nearby, new compounds are under construction. A new war means new money for houses, undoubtedly. Mud bricks dry in the sun outside the walls of fortresses along the edge of the road and well into the valleys beyond.

Fortresses. Eureka! I've cracked the code on Afghanistan: they fight because it is a part of their lifestyle—they live in fortresses. They live in fortresses because they have been at war for centuries, and they've been at war for centuries because they live in fortresses. It's a self-licking ice-cream cone. I gradually regain my perspective and remember I don't know anything about this place or the people. I've had about two hours of conversation with Afghans and that was in the

Bagram Collection Point with senior Taliban leaders we're holding before transfer to Guantanamo.

Soon, Kabul looms in the distance. Well, actually, there isn't much looming, nothing above three or four stories tall. Much of the architecture is a Soviet-inspired, socialist, concrete farce. I wonder how uninspired the architects must have been by their work as we pass blocks of Bloc-inspired buildings. Small shops line the streets and traffic circles. Auto parts stores, tea stands, video rentals, cassette tapes and CDs for sale, music blaring, street food: we could be anywhere in the third world, but this is Afghanistan, home to the Taliban.

Just a few months before, there would have been no music. All the men would have been wearing long beards, and no women would have been visible unless escorted by a male member of their family. Today, a few women are on the streets. Many are still clad in the *burkha*—the head-to-toe drape of blue commanded by the Taliban. Some appear with only the headscarf. On the way into town we count the number of women without the *burkha*—seven that day, up from the previous week, I am told. Almost everyone on the streets is male. Many wear short beards; all have their heads covered. Traffic is chaotic, but nowhere near the level of a central African city.

We approach the walled compound of the American Embassy. Marines man the gates. A donkey cart has stopped in front of one of the gates just as a pod of embassy up-armored Suburbans roars up. Two Marines come out to try to get the cart driver to move. The recalcitrant donkey sits as the driver shouts and throws up his hands.

We pass through the traffic circle where the former president, Najibullah, was castrated and hanged. There are apparently no rules about right of way or human rights in the circle. When the guys in the vehicle ahead of us use their turn signal it is the only one, perhaps in the entire country, in use.

We arrive at our objective, the compound of the International Security and Assistance Force (ISAF). A football match is in play on the small pitch that serves as the helicopter landing-pad: the Italians vs. the Turks. We jump out of our trucks and meet our ISAF counterparts. A Danish major pulls me by the hand a few hundred yards further into the compound to the Italian canteen.

There, sitting on the counter is the largest espresso machine I have ever seen. It's beautiful not only for all its chrome and baked enamel and moving parts, but for what it represents: western culture and civilization in the midst of a deadly Asian war. I want to put my arms around it. We enjoy a lovely cappuccino and then tour the base. No one is wearing battle rattle or headgear. There is no saluting, only smiles and waves between the Italians, Danes, Swedes, and Turks. My international counterpart, a Turkish major, offers me a beer and some lunch. I wish I could accept the beer, but we are subject to General Order Number One: no alcohol in theater, among other strictures. And early on in my tour, I'm still following that rule.

We pass the laundry. Cappuccino, beer, international cuisine, a laundry... I'm envious of the small U.S. contingent working at the ISAF compound. I learn too that ISAF also has flush toilets.

We get down to business, exchange target data and set a time frame for the operation we want to conduct. Running intelligence operations—or any operation for that matter—with international counterparts is always harder than it needs to be. They generally don't share our obsession with secrecy and technically aren't allowed to be privy to any intelligence that could be of value. (The U.S. tends to over-classify its information in comparison to our allies.) But we find ways to operate together.

Because it is such a primitive environment, Afghanistan is a particularly humint-intensive theater. The Army is organized, in theory at least, to go anywhere the war is, and be effective. But theory and reality often collide. The military's intelligence assets are structured so that we can listen or watch almost anything or anyone, anywhere. The big guns in the intelligence community are signals intelligence (sigint) and imagery (imint). These two services are tasked to collect about ninety-five percent of the information required in order for commanders to makes decisions. Humint is supposed to gather the last five percent, the last bit that you simply can't get from a satellite or a drone, from listening to a phone or intercepting an email.

If we were operating against Saddam's forces, or against

another Soviet-styled and structured force this would be perfect. But Afghanistan isn't like that. The Taliban and the other insurgent groups aren't fighting that kind of war. Human intelligence, going to talk to people face-to-face, recruiting agents when necessary, that's how we are going to come to understand what was happening. Doing just that is my job.

The work is slow. It requires a great deal of planning, trial and error, and patience. This last bit is what makes commanders itchy. And an itchy commander can make life hell for a J2X and all the humint collectors in the theater.

My boss understands that these operations take time to set up and to produce. He'll take the heat for me when his boss—the three-star general running U.S. and coalition operations in Afghanistan—gets itchy. But nonetheless, it's a tough job. My predecessor was hospitalized twice for exhaustion during his tour.

I have a lot to learn and must do it under conditions akin to building an airplane while flying it. I actually tried to get out of the job at one point early on. I told the boss I wasn't up to it. "I'm just a reservist," I said. "I'm a good operator, but I've never done staff work, especially at this level." The colonel, a tall skinny guy from Kentucky, looked down at me and smiled. "You're what I've got. Come to me if you have problems and I'll try to help, but there just ain't anyone else." So I got to work.

One of the first things I do is simply get to know all of the teams under my control. The biggest and most visible to the leadership is the Bagram Collection Point (BCP), the place where captured Al Qaida or Taliban fighters, or insurgents allied with one of the other uncooperative groups like the Hezb e Islami-Gulbuddin (under the control of Gulbudin Hekmatyar), are taken and interrogated before either being released or sent to Guantanamo.

There are two teams at the BCP: the military police, who run the downstairs detention cells, and the military intelligence team, who run the interrogations and debriefings upstairs. The interrogators ostensibly report to me, but only in a dotted-line sort of way: I can, and am, supposed to direct their work in order to gain the most intelligence out of the interrogations they run. But, the fact is, I know so little about their work that, after a couple of weeks, the colonel I work for—who oversees all intelligence operations in theater— instructs his deputy to oversee the day-to-day intelligence operations at the BCP (I suspect he's taking a few things off my plate to make my work easier). I am happy to cede the task to my colleague.

I have a team of EOD (Explosive Ordnance Disposal) techs whose job it is to buy up weapons. Technically, we are paying for information that will lead to the capture of weapons, but if someone shows up with a truckful, we're happy to pay for them. The program is so successful that we run out of funds in about three months and have to ask for more from Central Command (CENTCOM). This is the most fun part of the job. We are always finding some wild-assed piece of hardware that I can bring in to the staff meeting for show-and-tell.

There are teams of counterintelligence agents in pockets around the country collecting information about the enemy forces, but also working very hard to protect the force. The leaders of these teams are generally super-competent, young, non-commissioned officers. I love working with these guys. On one trip we went into a small village up in the mountains. I don't think any outsiders had been there for a very long time. One of the old men in the village came up and started speaking Russian to one of my guys. It turned out that agent was a Russian linguist and translated for us: the old guy thought the Russians had come back. He didn't know much about what was happening beyond the ridge line.

I also have a team of Case Officers working on pretty cool operations around the country, a team of linguists reading and translating captured documents, a handful of guys taking captured phones and computers apart, and a small staff of analysts I share with another lieutenant colonel.

About three weeks after I arrive, I go over to the office, which is in a big tent we call the Circus Tent, and learn that one of the detainees at the BCP—an Afghan named Habibullah—has died overnight.

The BCP was a former machine shop for the airfield built by the

Soviets. It's been converted to a detention facility by adding some big cages inside, a few wooden walls, and a modicum of creature comforts like heat.

That morning, anyone with any connection to the BCP runs down there to try to help figure out what happened. There's an investigation, but before it's even really in full swing, another detainee—Dilawar— is dead. Two Afghans dead in U.S. custody within a week. Both men's deaths are judged to be homicides. (In 2004, over a year after I left Afghanistan, charges were brought against twenty-eight soldiers, both military intelligence and military police, in the two cases.)

This is my first month on the job. Things start to go downhill from here.

A Danger to Myself or Others

I N THE COLD PRE-DAWN I can hear generators running and vehicles moving on the other side of the base. But it is quiet inside my tent. None of the other soldiers I share the tent with is even snoring. I've been awake for a few hours, but stay in my sleeping bag, fighting the nearly overwhelming urge to run away. The Taliban have launched a couple of rockets toward the base during the week, so we are all a little on edge, but that isn't what's keeping me up. I am bundled into my sleeping bag, trying to control my racing heart, and trembling because the dead have come to talk with me.

They've been coming every night for a couple of weeks. The dead from Kosovo or Rwanda beckoning to me, pulling me from a warm, comforting sleep into a series of wretched, tormenting, wide-awake dreams. Tonight it's the dead from a farm near the town of Podujevo. Burned Bible-black, twisted into hideous, contorted shapes, they lie in a cold rain that falls through the burned-away roofs and pools on the dirty floor. "Do you remember us?" they ask. Most assuredly.

The night before, it was the dead from the village of Racak. Forty-five of them, shot in the back of the head and left to die in that rocky ditch on a frozen January morning in 1999. They've dropped by for a chat. "Why didn't you do more to save us?" they ask. Why, indeed. Night after night they appear on the big screen of my mind in oversaturated Technicolor, writhing and imploring.

Night after night, the murdered and mutilated come back. Each time, I am scared and ashamed. I know they aren't real. I know that they are only images in my head. But I fear them no less for knowing this. They terrify me for what they remind me of: the fighting I didn't stop; the lives I didn't save. They terrify me for what they represent: I can no longer stop them from taking control of my mind. I lie on my bed, trembling, eyes wide open, but still seeing the dead in front of me.

The trouble begins slowly, developing over time, and by the time I am fully aware of it, I am having graphic, violent dreams nightly. I wake from these dreams in a panic: shaking, heart racing, crying sometimes, always afraid to go back to sleep. I am losing control of my brain, of my mind. In time, I even start seeing these images when I'm awake. During the day I'm unable to concentrate. I sit at my desk or go to planning meetings for operations, shaking until I have to leave the tent to go outside and get control of myself.

I fear I've lost my mind. But, I am afraid to ask for help. I fear I will be ridiculed, considered weak and cowardly. In Army culture, especially in this elite unit filled with rangers and paratroopers, asking for help is a sign of weakness. My two Bronze Star Medals, my tours in Airborne and Special Operations units, none of these will matter. To ask for help will be seen as breaking.

But when I can no longer control the images in my head, when in the middle of the day I am forced to hide, shaking and crying in a concrete bunker, railing against the noise and the images, when I realize that to continue to deny this would endanger soldiers I was sent to Afghanistan to lead, I finally do ask for help.

I stop my friend Ed, a doctor, on his way into the Circus Tent. I tell him I'm not sleeping, having trouble concentrating, that I am trembling noticeably. On more than one occasion, I've lost track of what day it was. I try to be coherent and explain what's wrong with me in simple terms without being overly emotional, but just talking to someone I think might be sympathetic brings all my anxieties and shame to the surface.

I ramble on about the dreams and the images that are stuck in my head from Kosovo and Congo and Rwanda. I attempt to explain why I'm not able to sleep and why my hands shake, and admit that it's because I'm afraid I'm not getting my job done that I have come forward to ask for advice. I look at the ground and mumble something about thinking I'm pretty sure I ought to talk to someone, although, of course, I don't want to waste anyone's time, and how I'm pretty sure I am probably all right, but since this is maybe starting to affect my work, I figure it's a good idea to at least bring it up, but I really don't want to bother anyone, and so forth, on and on. Ed listens carefully and says he could get someone to talk to me. He adds that these days, of course, the leadership is much more understanding about mental health issues but, oh by the way, he asks, what level security clearance do I have? Because going to the psychiatrist might be grounds for the security guys to pull my clearance.

Shit. The idea of losing my clearance hadn't occurred to me. I hold a Top Secret clearance with access to Special Compartmented Information. If I don't have this clearance, I can't do the work. Being unemployed because I'm a nutcase had never crossed my mind. All of a sudden, I face an enormous dilemma: ask for help, or keep my job.

Images of my wife looking sadly at me through the reinforced glass of Sheppard-Pratt's non-violent-but-loony wing flash in my head. I imagine friends gathered at a bar, lamenting how close I was to retirement—"if he had only been able to hold out a little longer..."— as they shake their heads in unison and order another round.

I look at Ed. He offers to make me an appointment with the psychiatrist and asks what day is good for me. I think about that day's schedule and say, "Well, Mondays are bad because we have so many meetings," trying to downplay how screwed up I feel. "Ok, I think he should be able to see you this afternoon," he says. "I'll email you with the time." From my stunned expression, I must look to him like he said, "Gort, Klaatu Borada Nikto," because he lightly takes my elbow and asks if that was all, and then asks me if I feel I am a danger to myself or anyone else. There are lots of weapons around and I have a 9mm pistol and about twenty rounds on my hip, but I hate carrying the damned thing so much it never crossed my mind that I might use it. "No," I say, "I'm not dangerous."

I go inside the tent and walk past the senior leaders towards the back where I work. I look at the briefing schedule and have the sudden epiphany that it is Sunday, not Monday. My stomach rolls. I realize I am completely screwed. I walk to my desk and shudder at the idea, once seemingly impossible, but now somehow horrifyingly real, that I might not be able to work. I need a security clearance to do my job, and who would trust me with a clearance in this condition? I wonder what kind of job I could qualify for: lawn guy, hell no, they work way too hard; ticket clerk at a porno theater, that's rich; maybe distributing those flyers about discount Chinese food to peoples' mailboxes in dodgy neighborhoods, I wonder what that pays?

I suppose I've always been a little out of step with the rest of the parade. I've never been talented enough to get away with any real eccentricities. I never truly had the self-confidence to be a real individual. I'm not intellectually deep enough to be avant-garde. I've always just been a little out of step with the other dancers, like a punk rocker trying to two-step. But it scares me to think that I might be crazy, that I might be forced out of service and become unemployed.

I'll probably be forced to wear some jumper with a big "L" for "Loony" on the chest or to bear a stain, visible to the whole world. People in the neighborhood will get some sort of notification from the police that I have moved in. Or not, since I certainly won't be able to keep the new house. How will I make those payments if I am unemployed?

I go see the doctor that afternoon. Apparently, the word of my appointment has preceded me. His young receptionist, a specialist, warily eyes me—the nut-bag officer—as I walk in, and bids me to sit. His nurse, a full colonel in the Army Nurse Corps, quietly says I should wait to speak to the doctor because only he can write prescriptions for medication. Oh great, I think to myself, I'm so screwed up they can already tell I need to be medicated. I sit in a chair and look at the television.

Larry King is allowing some faded ingénue to use his show as a vehicle for her attempted comeback, and he's explaining to his devoted viewers how important she is, and that she's a major star, whatever her name is. As I survey the room, I'm surprised to see several straitjackets, just sitting there in the open, folded neatly at the bottom of a bookcase next to the TV. Suddenly, my hands start shaking, and I feel like I've been hollowed out by some alien life form. "Oh shit," I say out loud, and wrap my arms across my chest to stop them from shaking. So, when the doctor comes out to get me, I'm sitting in a chair trembling and rocking slowly forward and back, staring at those straitjackets while Larry King takes a caller from Long Island.

In the back of the tent, behind some "walls" made out of blankets clothes-pinned to 550 cord strung from stanchions, I sit on a folding chair while he perches on a cot a couple feet away. I start rambling, explaining why I need to talk and repeating much of what I had told Ed earlier. The doctor watches me and listens earnestly as I describe the picture shows and the shaking, the wrenched guts and the fear. I talk for about ten minutes, I guess, explaining what I had seen and been a part of in Kosovo and Congo, and about how I have been unable to get past the images flashing in my mind and keeping me awake at night. As I talk, my fear and self-loathing spills out, and I start to cry.

He listens and asks a few questions. Then he says, "The first thing I want you to know is that I can help you." He seems earnest. I've been warned that he isn't very "Army." I suppose that in the end neither am I. He tells me I am suffering from Post-Traumatic Stress Disorder and Depression. Each is a part of the other, and they feed off each other. He tells me I need medication.

We discuss options: medication, therapy, privacy, security clearances. He says he will ask his bosses what the system would have to say about someone with my level security clearance being crazy— ok, those are my words not his. He explains the different types of medications he could offer me, their benefits and their side effects. He talks about Prozac, "it's been around for twenty years;" Paxil, "can't miss a day or quit cold turkey;" Zoloft, "side effect: soft stools;

but cheap for the Veterans Administration;" Selexa, "two forms: one active, one inactive;" Lexapro, "low sexual side effects; stops night sweats;" Xanax, "rapid acting sedative: like two shots of tequila in a pill—very addictive;" Propanidol, "a beta-blocker" Xeprexa, "makes you hungry and fat;" and Syraquil, "major tranquilizer and anti-psychotic."

I'm to come back in a week and he'll know what my options are; then we can start taking meds. In the meantime, he tells me to talk to myself, but not in public and not out loud. "Tell yourself you're OK and that you're doing the best you can. Stop beating yourself up," he says. Then he asks if I see myself as a danger to myself or to anyone else. Even though it's the second time that day I've been asked that question, I feel my gut wrench, and I cross my arms in front of me and rock until the shaking stops. Right then, I know intellectually what I've known emotionally for days: I am fucked up.

While this seems a positive first step— and the fact that he didn't want to put me immediately in a straitjacket was a slight comfort—I am also a little put out because now that I know I'm nuts, now that it's official, I want him to make me better immediately. Although I figure I'm not so bad and can make it another week, I still want a safety net. I want to know that the pictures will go away and the shaking will stop and the fear will subside. I leave the office scared and a little unsatisfied.

I return to the Circus Tent and compose a message to my wife. I say I've been to see the shrink and I tell her what he told me. I add that we're waiting to see if I will be able to keep my job before we decide on a course of action. I tell her he wants me to take medication and go to therapy—Happy School I call it. Then I go for a run and feel a little better.

A few days later I'm sitting at breakfast, not having a particularly good day. My hands are shaking and I've been awake most of the night. I probably look like hell, because when I glance up from my cereal at one point, I notice the good doctor sitting a few tables away trying not to stare at me. I slink out of the room and out into the sunlight. Following his instructions, I have begun documenting and cataloguing my days and nights according to how I feel. I design a simple scale: *All Right; Vaguely Not All Right; Seriously Not All Right.* This particular day I am *Vaguely Not All Right.*

At some point that week, I ask our security officer questions about how mental health treatment might affect one's clearance, not mentioning any names of course, and hoping that she isn't particularly intuitive. She says that certain medications are acceptable, and certain medications aren't—those being principally the anti-psychotics— but that it is critical that the patient immediately inform the service commander and the security officer that he or she is under treatment.

The decision I'm facing seems pretty stark: take the meds, go to treatment and risk my job, or skip it and risk my guys' lives. It sucks, but it is what it is. There aren't any other options. No *deus ex machina* will descend from the rafters and solve this because this is not a Greek tragedy. It is my own puny, personal catastrophe, and no god will come down to explain to me why things are just so magnificently screwed up inside my head, or why I am forced to sit fecklessly by as these horrible, repulsive pictures fester in my mind and shackle my thoughts and dreams—while all the while the world goes rolling merrily by, and everyone is just so chirpy and buoyant.

Man, I am up to here with chirpy. Don't these people know about the ones who were murdered? What about the ones who were burned, raped, humiliated, tortured? No, I guess they don't remember, the Chirpy Bastards. Is it just me who feels this way? Maybe the Chirpy Bastards do know about the killings and burnings and rapes and everyone else in the whole world can just process this stuff better than I can.

And now I have the wonderful option of taking medication that can make me feel better so I can do my job, but—and this is the Catch-22 of this generation's war—if I take the medication I can lose my security clearance and I'll lose my job and my house. Nice goddamn choice: crazy or homeless. I decide to take the medication, but keep it secret for a while.

The week passes with no major episodes. On Sunday morning I

wake feeling *Vaguely Not All Right*. I make it through the shower and shaving part with no major disasters. I go to breakfast, sit alone, and read an article in *The New Yorker* with my cereal and peaches. I have two glasses of orange juice in an attempt to beat the cold I've been fighting for a few days. I make it to work and sit behind my computer to read email. It's pretty quiet in the office. Maybe most of the people have gone to get something to eat. Then things start going wrong.

Seriously Not All Right

I'M IN THE MIDDLE OF A WAR and my brain is broken. I go to work, and after I've been at my desk for about half an hour, while I am transferring some files to Guantanamo over the Internet, I notice that my hands are shaking and my breathing has shallowed and quickened. My heart sprints. I feel *Vaguely Not All Right*, but I've had a cold, and figure I'm just a little feverish. But things around me are losing their clarity. I haven't lost track of what is happening, it's just fuzzy, and things are asynchronous, loopy. It's like I'm moving in waltz time while the rest of the world is in common time.

My arms are numb but I can still type. I feel like someone is tightening a metal band around my ribcage. The guy at the desk next to me asks a question at the same time Microsoft sends in a message informing me that the system has no more memory and I need to close some windows. So I say *ohforchrissake* to the laptop, and mumble something in response to my colleague so he'll think I'm listening, and I close off some of the windows so the program will execute and the files will transfer and the whining at the other end of the system will cease.

So, while I'm sorting this out, I'm dealing with my own little glitch; my brain is not functioning well. Just as the computer system has a fault in it, I seem to have one as well. I still can't feel my arms, but I watch my hands shake, and the guy next to me is reading an article to me off the Internet, and he's laughing and I don't think it's funny but I nod my head so he'll think I'm listening while I'm staring at my hands shaking, and I can't get enough air so I take a really deep breath. I start to cough, and someone at the other end of the room calls me a vector for disease and everyone laughs and, again, I nod my head so everyone will know I'm listening, and so everyone will think *I'm All Right.* But it's pretty clear that *I'm Not All Right* because I can't breathe and I can't feel my arms and I'm banging my knees together like I'm a one-man band.

Only there's no music, just static, and something keeps trying to come onto the big screen in the Drive-In that is my mind, but it won't come on so the screen is gray and I want to be nonchalant about it and blithely go about my day, but I'm scared and I'm shaking and I just want whatever it is that's out there to COME OUT AND SHOW YOURSELF, YOU GUTLESS FUCK, because I'm starting to hyperventilate. I can only breathe with the front part of my chest and I'm rocking back and forth in the chair like I'm listening to the goddamn Velvet Underground and Lou is singing "Heroin."

I cross my legs so they'll stop banging into each other, but I can't stop rocking so I cross my arms and curl over them into my lap because I'm feeling like I'm in a sack and it's tightening around me and squeezing me. And I can't see anything around me clearly because it has all gone to haze like I'm in the middle of a rainforest.

I know I'm really in the shit this time and wonder just what brought this on. I try to focus my eyes but when I take a peek around, the picture in my head looks like some vaseline-lensed, art school mockery of a David Hamilton photo from 1973, so I try to concentrate on something close in and tangible like the museum postcards I've put up around my desk to add some color to this monochromatic wasteland I work in.

I look at the Picasso postcard above my desk, and the woman's head is cleft in half and part of it is a phallus and even though she looks relatively content in her dream, I think I need to look at something, well, different. So I look at a Thomas Hart Benton postcard and the sky looks like a Hendrix song with clouds bent into flying tempura dinosaurs. And I think, wow, I need some different pictures up on my desk.

I am pretty damn sure that I am only a couple blinks away from rolling onto the floor and curling up in a ball, but I remember that there are some new guys in the office and they would most likely totally freak out if on their first day the boss started rolling on the floor and baying at the moon. So, I think now would be a bad time to roll on the floor, you know, because I'm supposed to be in charge of this circus, and if the Chirpy Bastards have to drag me out of here wrapped in a fucking straitjacket, foaming at the mouth and babbling about streetlights emitting death rays, that would be bad.

I try to stop my legs from shaking and I try to stop my arms from shaking and I try to stop rocking back and forth and back and forth. I look up and see that the files have finally transferred to those whiny bastards in Florida, so maybe they'll shut up.

Whatever it is that is scaring me half to goddamn death hasn't yet emerged from the coming attractions file, and I don't know how I know this but I do: I know for absolutely goddamn certain that whatever it is that's out there is coming. I start feeling the fight-or-flight nerves start to tingle, and I think avoidance might be a good strategy here.

I press down on my knees and make myself stand up and get up from my desk and I actually stagger a bit as I take a step, but the floor is just a tarp thrown over some rocks anyway, so it's uneven as hell and no one notices. I walk out of the office onto the main floor and then decide to go outside because the main floor is filled with Chirpy Bastards. I get outside and I lean against one of the trucks and I look up at the sky and it's beautiful and blue and there's not a cloud in it. I try just to breathe a little. I've got my hands stuffed into my pockets so no one will see them shaking and I just know I look like death cold out of the refrigerator, but no one seems to notice. I am almost cheered by this until it hits me that I must always look like this, and they all must certainly know that I'm *Seriously Not All Right.*

On the way back inside I try to figure out if they all know. I nod to

Jeff and he seems fine if a little fuzzy. Then, Boris asks how I'm doing and tells me a funny one he pulled on the supply guys and, you know, it is funny. I laugh a little, and when I turn away I go to get a cup of coffee, which I'm actually able to get into the cup without spilling it all over the place, and I think that's pretty good.

I turn around and start to head towards my desk and I see Heather, and she tells me—in what turns out to be a complete non sequitur—that Jon Bon Jovi wears women's jeans and, you know, that's pretty funny, too. So I laugh, and I make it out on to the main floor to tell one of the other colonels that I transferred the files to headquarters so the whiny bastards can shut up and now we're off the hook.

He's pretty happy because they've been complaining to him as well. And I should be happy, but I'm still not feeling particularly chirpy, so I go back to my desk and sit down and try to do something to get back to somewhere approximating *All Right* or at least to somewhere *Not Horribly Fucked Up* which is, I remember, an entirely new category on the scale. But I feel empty like I've been hollowed out with a spoon. I can't feel my hands, and my legs are still shaking so I put my hands onto the keyboard and try to make myself try to answer some emails.

But, of course, the first one is about sending people out to do dangerous stuff among the Taliban, and I think now might not be a good time to make those kinds of decisions. I figure I can gain some time by sending an email to my deputy, Heather, and asking her, what do you think about this?

She answers me in about a minute with her recommendations, and at least they are the same thing I was thinking. I feel like maybe I'm not as *Seriously Not All Right* as I think I am. I need to answer the guys in the field so they can at least get on with their lives and work. So, I answer the email and I tell them what to do and it makes sense and I think, OK, I can at least get my job done.

I take a deep breath and try to calm down. I think I can start to feel my hands again, so I stretch my arms over my head and open my eyes really wide and lean back for a minute and breathe out. The guy who sits beside me is away from his desk for a few minutes so he's not prattling nonsense in my ear, and I think I'm getting some perspective back. I take a chance and look at the rest of the shop to see if they're all staring at me or avoiding looking at me because they know that I am *Seriously Not All Right*. I look over my shoulder and even though things are still a little blurry, everyone seems to be going about their work just fine. With this, I figure I must not have scared anyone but me with my outing to Loopy World, so I shake out my arms trying to get the blood flowing to my hands and I see they're still shaking, but I feel somewhere to just the right of *Vaguely Not All Right* again.

It's like I have a hangover from being *Seriously Not All Right*. My eyes feel like I've been wandering in the desert without sleep for about three days. I have been barely breathing for so long that I have been starving my brain of oxygen. So I yawn and take a sip of coffee. At least I can tell how bad the coffee really tastes.

I take another breath and put my headphones on and dial up some Gillian Welch, because I figure I can get through some two-part harmonies. I concentrate on slowing down my breathing and telling myself that I'm ok even if I'm clearly *Vaguely Not All Right*.

Then the song comes on, and she's singing and playing beautifully, and way in the background there's this electric guitar ripping out some distortion through a tiny little speaker, that the producer put there because it's needed and it's just right and I realize that just right now it's a metaphor for how I feel because I feel like there's real stuff going on around me but I can't get at it. I keep getting distracted by this distortion that's sometimes in the background and sometimes comes up into the foreground, turning the real world upside down.

I hear the harmonies as the guitar player plays a contrapuntal lead line balancing a few bars of waltz time against common time—which, again, I feel is a perfect metaphor for my state of being—and the guy pulls it off beautifully and it fits so I take this to be a sign, and I figure maybe I'm going to be ok. I realize I have to make sense out of the distortion and counterpoint in my head because there is some seriously bad juju running around in there right now and I want to shake this thing and get back to something approaching *All Right*.

I concentrate on the music and try to make sense of it and let it wash over the fear, and I wring my hands and notice one of my thumbnails is ripped and bleeding on the leg of my uniform pants. I concentrate on that for a minute and I can't remember when or how that happened and so now my hands are shaking a little less, but I still feel scared.

I stretch one more time and sit up straight and think: ok, at the end of the day I'm still here. I'm getting along. I'm getting my work done and I haven't starting wearing a tin-foil hat and expounding on the lessons I've learned while talking to the satellites. Yeah, my hands are shaky and I'm only about one step up from a quivering pile of goo, but I'm hanging on, goddamnit, and this is not going to break me.

So I'm off to Happy School and my first dose of Prozac.

Here Be Monsters

A FEW WEEKS AFTER STARTING my passage through Prozacistan, the doctor and I discuss where to go with analysis, or more precisely, whether or not to go on with analysis. A week of OK days have displaced feeling *Vaguely Not All Right,* and it's been a couple of weeks since I was last *Seriously Not All Right,* so I wonder what comes next. I am feeling noticeably better. I'm starting to recognize the face in the mirror as my own; I'm starting to remember who I am, and I'm starting to remember what feeling OK feels like. I am trying to decide if I want to enter analysis. Basically, the question is, do I want to leave well enough alone now that the world is in color again, or do I want to dig around and see what I can uncover?

Even though I have been feeling better recently, in the morning, when everyone else in the tent gets up and goes to the shower and on to work, I stay in the sleeping bag a few extra minutes. I'm awake, and I usually have been for a couple hours or so. But I stay in bed, not yet ready to go merrily about my day. If I'm alone, I don't have to be chirpy, and I can sort out just how *Not All Right* I am before I have to face anyone else.

And I still haven't developed a taste for dining with the Chirpy Bastards—but that's nothing new or unusual, I tell myself. It's probably not evidence of some weird avoidance strategy, but rather just my normal feelings of inadequacy manifesting itself in a worry that I will appear needy and weak if I tag along with the crowd. And I get more reading done that way. Anyway, those guys go to dinner too early. I want to eat later, whether or not I'm already hungry.

I figure it can't hurt to talk about some of this mess. I'm curious and somewhat anxious to sort this out. Recovering my sanity and understanding this "glitch" of mine has become an intellectual pursuit as well as an attempt (no matter how feeble) to live an examined life, to look beyond the petty contrivances of day to day existence, beyond just going to work and feeding and bathing myself. I think it might be good to try to understand some of this, rather than just accept the "Popeye" view of the world, that *I am what I am and that's all that I am.* Especially when what I am some days is *Seriously Not All Right.*

But, on the other hand, do I really want to talk about this mess? Not having the snuff porn shots appear at irregular intervals in my mind is a pleasant change. That alone might be enough. I've apparently done well at compartmentalizing this stuff, but being in Afghanistan, dragged back into the military I left nine years ago, has rattled me to some degree. That much is clear. I picture these memories stuffed into boxes and jars, hidden under the bed and behind the winter clothes in the closet of my psyche, and I see some Tim Burton-esque gremlins scampering up and gleefully shaking and rattling these strongboxes labeled *Danger!,* until the lids slip off just enough so the sinister little nasties can escape, or cracking the seals on specimen jars marked Abnormal to let some of the goo spill out.

But it doesn't just spill, it splashes out and stains the carpet and then crawls up the wallpaper and spreads onto the ceiling, only at that point it's not a ceiling anymore, it's the night sky, and there is a kaleidoscope of constellations up there shining down on me. But the stars don't form any regular patterns I recognize; they're scattershot in odd and unrecognizable shapes. There is no Orion with a belt and sword, no Big Dipper with its constant line to the North Star to guide me. The designs aren't exactly random, but I can't make out the silhouettes or connect the dots. They hang over me in a nebula of anxiety and desperation and fear, still lingering up there as constant reminders that I don't have control over my own mind. And that I don't know precisely what caused this, or why these things have come to haunt me.

The thing is, really, other than my mind, there's not a lot about myself of which I can be proud. I'm neither handsome nor a good athlete. I have a kind of funky body that's soft in the middle. I'm losing my hair and my eyes are kind of close together. I am not a good dancer. I would like to be an intellectual, but I'm not. I'm just pretty smart. But, the issue for me—the thing that really scares me and sends me running for help—is that I am not in control of my mind. I am afraid I'm losing my mind. I can't control when the pictures come, and I can't make them go away either. I can't keep my hands from shaking. I can't make myself OK. I'm not OK. I have a fault somewhere and, man, that bugs me.

It bugs me because my mind is the one thing of my own that I have always been able to rely on. Now it is capricious, disloyal. If I try to lean on it like a bookcase in a comfortable den, the shelf gives way, and I fall into darkness. My mind has become fickle and frail, and I can no longer trust it. I feel as though I have placed all my trust in someone, given my heart willingly and truly, only to be deceived and betrayed. I can no longer browse through memories as if I'm looking for a snack in a familiar pantry because there are yawning crevasses between the floorboards. I no longer want to remember. I no longer want reverie. I no longer want a history. I fear the past because now, in the present, it has become horrible and uncontrollable. I have departed from a normal existence and entered a life of relentless dread.

So, at first, I figure it's a good idea to talk about some of this with a psychiatrist. But, now, I wonder if I have a sufficiently high tolerance for honest introspection. I mean real honesty. I suspect I am incapable of being really honest with myself. So I ask myself why can't I just snap the lids back on the boxes and jars? I mean, it's not like I'm wearing the tin foil hat, yet. My mind isn't in "material breach." But neither is it in "full compliance."

So I go on. But to what end? Do I try to fix the problems or just keep faking it, acting like I'm all right? That's what I'm doing every day when people blithely ask, "How are you?" What would they do if I said, "Well, now that you ask, I'm a complete mess. I have these visions of dead people in my head and I can't feel my hands sometimes. And you know, I think pretty soon I'm going to collapse into a pile of quivering goo. But enough about me, how are you?" What would they say?

Of course I'm not going to say that. No one really wants to know how you feel. So I say, "All right, you?" and keep moving, wringing my hands and staring at the ground, hoping to hell no one speaks to me or sits with me at breakfast expecting me to make polite conversation.

In the end, my curiosity remains unsated, and I find myself starting to believe that there is a chance that, by coming to grips with these memories and whatever it is that's driving them to the surface, I may be able to navigate the Lost Quarter of my mind.

So I find myself stalking the aisles for a guidebook, for a map. But, there is no map for this sort of thing, is there? If there is, it's probably one of those 13th century scrolls with emptiness at the middle of continents, with coastlines only vaguely defined, and sections of the unexplored seas emblazoned with "Here Be Monsters."

Or if not a map, can I at least have a guide? Is that what the good doctor is for? Is he to be my Tonto? We talked about psychiatry as both art and a science. He's apparently been able to fix mostly the errors in my brain functions, the science part of this problem. I wonder if he can get me through the errors in my mind, the art part. The flashbacks have mostly subsided, but the anxiety is still there. I'm still afraid of what may come and what it might mean to me. And just what is it I would be looking for? It's hard to find answers if you don't know the questions.

It's as if I'm one of those characters in a Hitchcock film who relentlessly chase MacGuffins, because even if everyone in the theater knows I'm doing it and can see the whatever-it-is coming over the horizon, I can't. And while I know that movies only work because our brain allows our eyes to see the single images presented up on the screen so quickly that we can block out the frames, and because we willingly suspend disbelief to allow ourselves to believe that the people on the screen are real and that they can move and talk and smile and love, and although I know that those images are no more real than the characters in a movie, I can't seem to convince my brain of this fact.

And there's more: given that these memories have whipped my ass into submission before, why the hell would I want to take them on a second or third time? Is it hubris to think I can tame them? They're just memories, right? Just some stuff I saw. Or is there really something under the bed?

The End of An Unruly Garden

AFTER I COMPLETED MY TOUR with XVIII Airborne Corps, I was assigned as the Army attaché at the embassy. So I packed up my stuff and moved to Kabul. There, living with a scrap of privacy—solo in a converted shipping container rather than in a tent shared with seven others—and the freedom to get off the compound to eat at a restaurant once in a while, I started to feel more alive, more human. I began to think I was approaching *All Right*. So I found myself missing a day or two of medication accidentally, then letting it go for a week, until one day I was sitting in a café watching my hand shake violently enough to scatter corn flakes from my spoon; I was shaking and rocking with a head full of anger and fear and embarrassment. I skulked out of the café and back to my trailer to gulp down a green and white.

I emailed the good doctor, who replied from Colorado or Oregon or some place back home, already finished with his tour and back in private practice, with the instructions to get back on the medication and the cautionary advice not to visit his replacement who, he said, was not as helpful to officers with high level security clearances.

I did as instructed. But, I started to wonder if I was being robbed of something. I was working at a pretty high level while I was at the airbase in Bagram, between episodes anyway. My mind, as dysfunctional as it was, was an unruly garden of creativity. That garden had now been mowed and tamed by Prozac. Although the clever drug diffused the explosions of ugliness in my head, I felt like it cut my creativity in half. I wondered if the relief from fear and anxiety, and having steady hands was worth losing my insight over. I no longer felt that I was out of control, but I felt diminished, and my creativity endangered.

My work at the embassy was interesting; attaché tours almost always are. We had a small shop of three. My boss was an Air Force colonel who had been recalled from retirement to come out to Kabul for a year. He had flown everything from the O-2A Skymaster as a forward air controller in Vietnam to B-52s and KC-10s. He'd completed his career flying C-12s as an attaché in India and South Africa. He had been in place for six or eight months already when I arrived, so he was well integrated into both the diplomatic and attaché corps. We also had an operations manager, a Vietnam veteran and retired Special Forces master sergeant.

Just down the hall, an Army major general was charged with the security cooperation mission—basically building and training the Afghan National Army. So our tasks were limited to representation and reporting. Representation meant that the colonel and I made the rounds of official events, sometimes tasked to show up in a uniform simply as decoration, but sometimes with an actual substantive mission. The reporting mission was pretty standard stuff: write back to Washington about what we saw and could figure out about the political-military situation in Kabul and beyond. I had the freedom to get off the embassy grounds when I needed to, and an assigned vehicle that belonged to the office, so I did.

Kabul is an old city. It grew up around the banks of the Kabul River around two-thousand years ago, and parts of it look like they've survived since then. The old market is still down by the river and possibly just as much a warren of alleys as it was five hundred years ago. It was a great place to go to take the temperature of the city—to walk around and get a feel for how safe things felt or what people were talking about. I went down one afternoon with a female colleague from the embassy. She was wearing a top that didn't fully cover her shoulders and upper back, and as we walked along, men threw pebbles at her. We turned and went quickly back to the truck. The old ways remained strong.

Maps of the city were hard to find when I was there, and I ended up just learning my way around the town by rote. The streets had names but there weren't lots of street signs, so you just did your best. Most of the street names were pretty simple and colorful. My favorite rug merchant was on Chicken Street. The Gandamack Lodge was on Passport Road.

There was an explosion of ethnic restaurants in the spring of 2003. At least two Chinese restaurants and a Thai place opened within weeks of each other. At the Thai restaurant you could go sit under the trees with lanterns lighting the grounds and eat pretty terrific food. It seemed very far from the restrictions of the airfield at Bagram and even farther from a firebase on the Pakistan border where some of my former soldiers were working. It was, in fact, pretty civilized.

Of course, Afghanistan was an Islamic republic, so alcohol was officially banned. This made it slightly more difficult to find alcohol, but only slightly. Any foreigner, more or less, could get access to it in some form. There were "official" outlets like the NATO commissary out at the airport where all forms of alcohol were available at all hours. And embassy events almost always featured booze unless the guest of honor was an Afghan. There were also bars, again both official and clandestine.

One of the quasi-official bars was in a hotel downtown. Security guards at the door made sure no one without an international passport got in. The hotel wasn't particularly nice, but no one seemed to mind. The elevator held maybe three people at a time, so there was always a line to go up or down. When doors opened at the top, the walls of the place were covered with frosted mirrors, and a disco ball spun from the ceiling. It was ghastly. I think I went once, maybe twice. It simply wasn't a place I needed to be.

The vibe was really weird, too. It was almost always filled with contract security guys—overly-testosteroned and probably steroidedup guys who were contracted by firms to provide security at a site or as part of a personal security detail. In the very early days of the war, people like Afghan President Karzai had close protection details provided by the U.S. military. Initially, Karzai's was a group of SEALs. One of the SEAL officers almost had to take a bullet for Karzai, and the team got him out of a couple of pretty serious attacks. But as the war went on, and at about the same time I was moving up to Kabul from Bagram, the security details were being turned over to contractors: some good, some less good, all dangerous.

Many of these contractors were former U.S. or NATO special operators who had chosen not to make the military a career. They were provided with lots of weapons and vehicles, and allowed to run amok in the streets of Kabul. The upshot of this was a sort of arms race amongst Afghan and international officials. If Karzai's protective detail had a truck with a .50 cal at the front and one with a Mark 19 automatic 40mm grenade launcher at the rear, then by God, the Minister of Defense's detail had to have the same thing, and the Minister of the Interior, and the Ambassador from Uzbekistan, and so on, whoever could afford it, ad infinitum.

Their gunned-up Humvees and up-armored Suburbans would careen through the streets as fast as possible, over-running sidewalks and barreling through stop lights with .50 cals swiveling threateningly side to side. As if the traffic in Kabul wasn't already bad enough, these convoys made everything worse.

And the contractors didn't seem to be particularly well screened or controlled either, at least in the early days of the war. Up in that hotel bar one night, two guys were arguing over the affections of an international woman—who wasn't interested in either of them—and a gunfight erupted in the bathroom. It was like the Old West, only with automatic weapons and steroids.

Across town, there was a dive on the station compound called The Talibar. Once you got past the contractor muscle out front and made your way onto the compound proper, the bar was inside, hidden away downstairs. It wasn't lovely. But what it lacked in charm it made up for with raw noise and the utter absence of creature comforts. The walls were covered with weapons collected and, one assumed, rendered harmless, then bolted to the walls. At least the beer was cold. The inarguable high point of a visit to The Talibar was a young, dark-haired American woman who worked behind the bar once in a while. She probably made a fortune in tips. In a place where most women were covered in the *burkha*, she served beers wearing skin-tight jeans and a wife-beater t-shirt with no bra.

One thing about working in different war zones is that you often see the same people—the usual suspects. I met several former colleagues in The Talibar, a list that included someone who had trained me as a Case Officer a dozen years earlier, to embassy and station colleagues I had known from Africa and Kosovo.

One friend from Kosovo, Carlotta Gall, (who for the record I did not meet in The Talibar) was reporting for *The New York Times* from Kabul. Carlotta's father, Sandy Gall, was a news reporter who had long experience in Afghanistan, and Carlotta herself had snuck across the border disguised as a man during the Soviet occupation. Her house was just around the corner from the embassy, and I used to drop in regularly for dinner or drinks with her and other reporters.

Another journalist, cameraman Peter Jouvenal, established a guesthouse with a restaurant and clandestine bar he called the Gandamack Lodge. In the evenings, you could go there and enjoy a cool drink while sitting on carpets Peter was said to have nicked from one of Saddam's palaces during the invasion of Iraq. Peter told me one night that the lodge occupied a house that formerly belonged to one of Osama bin Laden's wives. Who knows?

I guess the point is that life in Kabul was active and interesting, and very much unlike that of the troops fighting on combat outposts in the provinces or out on the Pakistan border. We were regularly reminded of the war when 120mm rockets hit nearby, or when a busload of German soldiers driving to the airport for the flight home, their tour complete, was blown up by a suicide bomber. But it was a good transition for me back in the direction of the Foreign Service.

I left Afghanistan in September 2003 and was released from active duty in the Army. After I got home, I went back to my civilian job at

State. When I signed back in, I was warned that if I didn't have an assignment quickly, I would be sent to Iraq.

I landed in a dreary office job moving paper through the bureaucracy of the European bureau, on the desk that covered France. My first task was to draft a note from the Secretary of State to the American ambassador in Paris declining an invitation to an event. It took about three tries to get something through the system. My first attempt was too breezy, my second too dour. Each time, the message came back with a snippy little note attached from the seventh floor staff, earning me looks of disdain from my colleagues. Sadly, that was more or less the high point of the job.

I clearly wasn't cut out for the tedium of a Washington assignment. "I'm a field officer," I said. But just back from the war and, with no real transition, I was stuck in a desk job feeling like Goldilocks just trying to draft an RSVP for the Secretary of State—it's too hot, now it's too cold; enough already. So when a friend who worked in the Middle East bureau stopped in to offer the opportunity for a State Department assignment dealing with terrorists in Iraq, I jumped at the chance.

Just under six months after I'd left Afghanistan, I landed in Iraq.

The Northern Alliance

IT WAS SCARY AS HELL if you thought about it, so I decided not to think about it. An aviator I knew half a lifetime before had told me that there is a comfort zone for helicopter pilots of at least a thousand feet over the power lines and treetops. At that altitude, the pilot had time to work out problems that might pop up before slamming into the ground. We were in a Blackhawk about a hundred and fifty feet off the deck going what I figured was just as fast as the aircraft would go. In the dark. It was a great ride, and I decided to enjoy it as if I were at a theme park.

The handful of passengers were leaving Camp Victory in Baghdad for what the press officers would have had to call an undisclosed location. It was still pretty early in the Iraq War, less than a year after the initial invasion. We were part of the advance party for a larger mission coming in to debrief members of a group designated as a Foreign Terrorist Organization. We had flown in piecemeal on commercial airlines from Washington through various hubs in Europe to Kuwait. The Kuwaitis, still ever so thankful to the U.S. for kicking Saddam out of their country in 1991, confiscated a bottle of single malt scotch from me at the airport. Bastards. We hung around Kuwait—which rivals Djibouti for the worst place on earth—for a couple days, drawing equipment and sitting through briefings before we pushed for Baghdad in a C-130.

One of our team members was enough of a senior official that he was designated a VIP, and we had a couple of colonels assigned directly from Combined Joint Task Force-7 headquarters as minders, so we got priority over a few other flights that were previously scheduled. Our Blackhawk and gunship escort took off from Camp Victory at about midnight.

Somewhere out over the desert, probably not far outside of Baghdad proper, the gunners test-fired their weapons. I was wearing a set of headphones; I could hear what the crew were saying over the ICS. So I knew what was coming. Still, only a few hours in-country and on our first night flight in Iraq, I jumped a bit when the two M240s on our aircraft and the gunship's 30mm chain gun fired. The guns served as a reminder that this really wasn't a theme park and, perhaps more importantly, that because I was in Iraq as a Foreign Service officer rather than a soldier, I was unarmed.

We arrived around 2:00 am, I think. After a very short meeting with senior staff of the camp, mostly in deference to our boss, we were trundled off to a tent and told when to show up for chow in the morning.

At daybreak, we took a walk around. The base was pretty spartan. A few cinderblock buildings made up the headquarters. Some huge fuel and water bladders lay scattered about, looking like giant waterbeds sitting out in the sun. The Army Reserve troops guarding the detainees slept in tents.

As the advance party, our small team's task was to determine if we could actually do what we had been sent to do. After a half-day of briefings and tours, we huddled and gave the thumbs up to the rest of the team to join us.

Within a day or two the others arrived, and we set out to organize ourselves for the mission. The task at hand was relatively simple: interview over three-thousand people about their past, what their intentions were towards the U.S., and what they wanted to do in the future. No prob.

The base was so small, not even the Kellogg, Brown and Root

(KBR) contractors would come and work there, so we had Army cooks making hot rations twice a day and MREs, or another pre-packaged meal, referred to as a "Jimmy Dean" for lunch.

We lived in tents, officially called Tent, General Purpose, Medium, and known as GP-Medium. They were green canvas duck, 32 feet long and 16 feet wide, 12 feet tall in the center and just under six feet tall at the walls, held up by wooden poles and tied down with ropes and wooden stakes. If you were lucky on this base, your tent had a liner. We weren't lucky. So when it was hot, there was only one layer of insulation. When it was cold there was only one layer of insulation.

There were no addresses or street signs to orient on, so people took to decorating the wooden doors of their tents with Magic Marker art and giving the tent a name that would serve as an address. Everyone in our tent had served in Afghanistan previously, so we became the Northern Alliance. The women across the path called theirs the Tent of the Rising Sun. Just down the block was the Sand Trap.

Because we would be in proximity to a large group of people whom the USG considered terrorists, we decided to use pseudonyms. I chose Andy. To this day, I still don't remember the real names for most of the people on that team.

The work, while weird, wasn't hard. Each morning we would have a short meeting and then most of the team would load up on buses wearing Kevlar helmets and fragmentation vests—not the current issue vest with the heavy SAPI (Small Arms Protective Insert) plates designed to stop a 7.62 round, but the old Kevlar vests that wouldn't stop a bee-sting—for the ride over to the area where we worked. I didn't share in this joy for the first few weeks. Our boss had me working as a liaison between all the different USG agencies on the base. Mostly just hanging around the headquarters in case something came up.

Usually, this allowed me the chance to attend briefings rife with Powerpoint slides, and drink lots of coffee with representatives of any organization in the U.S. government that had even a potential interest in the information our team was gathering. Sometimes in the afternoons I would grab a humvee and one of the other liaison officers and go exploring. There were weapons and ammunitions caches, both large and small, all around the area. If you were interested, you could pick up anything from a Kalashnikov or an RPG to a main battle tank or a howitzer.

The official motto of the staff officer is, *Livin' The Dream*. Even though the jobs are not what anyone joined the military (or the Foreign Service) to do, lots of senior officers get stuck in these positions and most suffer the indignities of preparing briefings, monitoring ongoing situations that other officers are leading, and generally making things happen behind the lines, with quiet resignation and with as much humor as possible. But after a while, I grew bored sitting on the staff, so I asked to join the rest of the team in the daily grind.

We interviewed all day. After work we would grab showers as we could, and then wait for meals. Some of the guys had brought a golf club or two, and had begun to hit balls off the earthen berms around the camp. For some reason this highly annoyed the military team, who instructed our guys to stop. So they started playing Frisbee golf through the camp. I'm sure this annoyed the military guys just as much, but there was little to be done about it. Personally, I read and wrote mostly. There was a small tent set aside as a "library" where boxes of books were unceremoniously dumped. I probably went through a dozen books a month.

I wrote a couple of short stories. I modeled characters in the stories on members of my team, taking both physical and emotional traits from the people walking around the camp and applying them to the people walking around in my stories. One story was about an Agency officer who made a professional decision that got his NGO-worker girlfriend killed. At story's end he put a bullet in his brain. Cheery stuff.

One of our team had brought a guitar with him, which I would borrow sometimes in the evenings. Several of us would sit around in the cool evening air, drinking whisky and passing the guitar around. I sent my mom a picture of myself in that setting. I figured it would calm her nerves since the news coming out of Iraq was pretty bad. I suspect every other American in Iraq had a harder, more dangerous, deadlier tour than I did.

In hindsight, heading off to Iraq so soon after returning from Afghanistan—with all of my problems there—might not have been the smartest idea. But, it turned out that the easy nature of most of the Iraq deployment served as a good ramp down from Afghanistan. If I had done something similar, taking a lower adrenaline job like I had in Iraq as an interim assignment rather than dropping immediately into a desk job in the European bureau, I might have actually been able to tolerate the tedious work in Washington. But probably not.

A few weeks into our stay, Moqtada al Sadr starting acting up. His Madhi Army were a belligerent group of insurgents who mostly lived in and around Baghdad, but they were also active on the road between our camp and the biggest U.S. base in the area, Balad Air Base. In my role as the liaison to every possible government agency, I attended a staff briefing for the soldiers on Al Sadr and his supporters.

The Army Reserve troops that manned our base were technically prison guards, so their assignment to guard the terrorists we were debriefing seemed logical. But the battalion commander was out of her depth. At the end of this briefing, she was taking questions.

As is always the case, the sergeants in the room asked the most pertinent questions: "What are our rules of engagement? How do we identify these guys? Do we shoot on sight?"

There was an ugly pause while the battalion commander looked stricken. She stammered some nonsense about following SOPs— Standard Operating Procedures. Her operations officer stood up to bail her out. But he was only slightly more effective. The staff clearly hadn't thought this through, and was too embarrassed to admit they didn't know. On the way out of the briefing, the senior sergeants formed a circle and began to develop a set of operational procedures on the fly. These are the kinds of staff failures that get people killed. Even in combat arms units this stuff happens, but happens less. This combat support unit wasn't prepared for this type of operation, so I decided that, unless instructed to leave the base, I would stay inside the bubble.

Still, I didn't feel safe. I sort of longed for a weapon. So on one of my drives around the camps, I stopped at a cache of small arms I knew about—one filled with Kalashnikovs, RPGs, and lots of ammunition. I found a Kalashnikov that was in reasonable condition and a couple of magazines' worth of ammunition to call my own. I borrowed a cleaning kit from one of the NCOs on the staff and got the weapon operational, and stashed it in my locker, just in case.

Not long after, we had a very non-specific threat against the base—we were to be rocketed sometime during a 24-hour period. It turned out that the camp was under the control of a brigade of the 1st Infantry Division and the brigade commander had been a cavalry troop commander I'd served under when I was a lieutenant in Germany. The guy was a very competent officer, despite being a bit of a martinet and a prig. His staff sent down the force protection posture for the post during this period, instructing us to wear body armor and Kevlar helmets at all times when we weren't inside hardened buildings.

The battalion staff interpreted this to mean that anyone inside the cinderblock buildings could operate as normal, but anyone in the tents had to wear their battle rattle 24 hours a day. The folly of this was manifest since none of the cinderblock buildings could in any way have been considered hardened, but the battalion staff simply didn't want to wear their combat gear so they interpreted the order in their favor. Further, in order to fully comply with the order, everyone would have had to wear helmets and body armor in the showers.

After the 24-hour period had passed, every base in the area stood down except ours. When I asked over at the battalion staff why we hadn't, the officer I asked told me, "Because brigade says so." In fact, it was exactly the opposite: Brigade headquarters had apparently forgotten to send the "stand down" message to this isolated little outpost. This battalion hadn't adapted to the new reality of being in a real war. They were still operating in the peacetime past, afraid of questioning or ignoring stupid instructions, unable to understand what was important in combat. The staff was probably as dangerous to us as were the terrorists their units were guarding.

Late in our stay I received an email from a friend at my reserve unit back in DC. The military, and really all of America, was still reeling in the wake of the Abu Ghraib debacle. The guys involved in the picture taking that broke the scandal were reserve MPs from West Virginia. But the pictures only exposed a deeper problem in the area of detainee operations, and that problem included elements of the intelligence community. So anyone with a human intelligence background was waiting for the phone to ring because so many military officers in a small community were under investigation or being relieved. My buddy emailed to say that my name had moved up on the list of reservists to be mobilized, and that I was likely heading to Iraq. The irony of learning I was headed to Iraq while I was sitting in Iraq was delicious, but quickly soured.

After a few rounds of give and take over the fact that I already WAS in Iraq—albeit for the Department of State—I learned I had a couple of options. One was to volunteer for mobilization, at which point they would offer me some choices. The other options were considerably less palatable, so I volunteered. The choices they offered me were: (1) go to Mauritania and open the embassy's Defense Attaché office. (2) go to Eastern Congo and run around out there in the midst of the ongoing war. (3) go to Sudan. I chose Sudan.

I went back to my desk job at State in Washington and broke the news to my boss, but left out the part about volunteering. It took a few weeks to get orders and to get on my way, but less than four months after leaving Iraq, I was headed for Sudan.

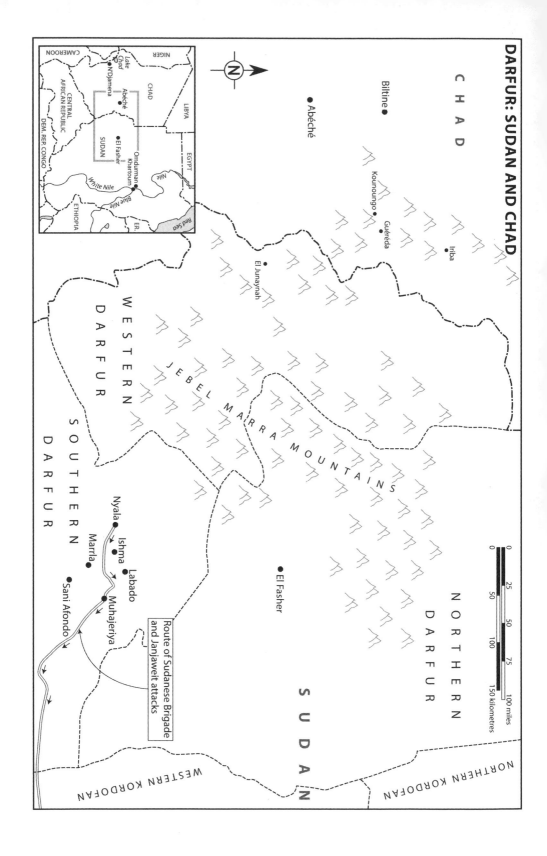

Darfur

2004-2007

If I start acting stupid, I'll shoot myself.

WARREN ZEVON,
I'll Sleep When I'm Dead.

A Trick of the Geographers

I HAD ARRIVED FROM WASHINGTON via London and Addis Ababa, but ran into some trouble getting a visa. Just before I was to deploy, Secretary of State Colin Powell had called what was happening in Darfur by its rightful name: genocide. The government in Khartoum shut off communications with the U.S. military and put a hold on visas for military officials coming to Sudan. Someone in the office at the Defense Intelligence Agency—the agency that oversees the work of defense attachés—thought I might have less trouble getting a visa in London, so I spent two weeks there waiting.

I got a nice room in the same hotel Eisenhower's staff had used in the months leading up to the D-Day Invasion. Every day I would call over to the American embassy to check in—they wanted nothing to do with me—and then I would call over to the Sudanese embassy to inquire about my visa. "No, not today," was always the response. For the rest of the day, my time was my own. I visited lots of museums and took long walks around the city. One night in the Red Bar of the hotel, I had a conversation with a group of American tourists from Texas. They were big George Bush supporters who still believed that the chemical weapons ruse that Bush and Cheney had used to get the U.S. into the Iraq War there was the truth. Several stormed out when I tried to disabuse them of that lie.

After two weeks in London, headquarters decided to send me to Addis Ababa. It wasn't any cheaper, but it was likely more defensible to my office director at DIA to have an officer cooling his heels in Addis than in London. So off I went.

I signed into the Defense Attaché office and began trying to be helpful. In some countries an extra set of trained hands around the office is a boon; in others, sometimes the best thing one can do is simply stay out of the way. Addis was in the latter category. I did my best to be helpful, and otherwise kept a low profile. After three weeks of this, the attaché walked in from a meeting and tossed my passport with a valid Sudanese visa on the table. The next day I was on a plane for Khartoum.

It's the heat, really. It hits like a wave. That's the first thing you noticed. No worse, I suppose, than Phoenix in the summer, but it was bloody hot. I arrived in October, just at the end of the rains. I landed at forty minutes past two in the morning. The temperature was 94 degrees in the city, considerably hotter on the airfield.

Khartoum sits at the confluence of the Blue and White Niles. The White Nile flows northwards from Lake Victoria in Uganda, through the Sudd, a leviathan of a swamp, rambling from the forests into the savannas and finally into the desert. The Blue Nile falls from the Ethiopian highlands, bringing with it the rich volcanic soils that for centuries have made Egyptian civilization possible. It was a trick of the geographers to give the rivers colorful names. For they are neither blue nor white, they are tan and grey. But they are lush, sumptuous gods in a place of want; they flow ever northward, carrying with them the true stuff of life. And where they meet is Khartoum and Omdurman.

Omdurman sits on the west side of the Nile, just past the confluence. Khartoum sits on the point of land between the White Nile flowing directly north, and the Blue Nile, which turns westward to join it. The oldest part of Khartoum faces north, watching the rivers flow past, looking toward Egypt a thousand miles away.

The old colonial buildings still stand facing the Blue Nile. Cannons left from the days of Gordon and Kitchener line the drive in front of the presidential palace. On the north side of the Blue Nile, upriver from the palace, a rusting hulk, half-sunk in the mud, is said to be one of Kitchener's steamers. Two hours north, at the sixth cataract, another rusty scrap is believed to be one of Gordon's gunboats. Who knows?

The new city is built around the airfield, which sits smack in the center of the two main north-south roads. I lived on the east side of the airfield in a neighborhood called Riyadh, hemmed in by the Blue Nile and the dozens of Soviet-made, UN-chartered Ilyushins and Antonovs that formed the backbone of the relief effort for Darfur. The din of their take-offs and landings was near constant, and in addition to simply providing background noise, it served as a reminder of why I had come, more or less.

I arrived during Ramadan, so at first I didn't get much of an idea what the city was truly like. The Eid al Fitr would come in ten days or so, and then I'd see the city come alive. But it was a fine time to learn the streets, with people staying in as much as possible during the fast. No restaurants were open during the day. They would start to come to life at sunset as people gathered for *iftar*, the breaking of the fast, and would remain open long into the night. When I first arrived, I ate at a roadside kebab stand and had a wonderful sizzling plate of beef with tomatoes and onions. In the embassy, we had a Lebanese restauranteur and several Sudanese cooks who made lunch for us at just slightly less than exorbitant rates. The hummus was good, but it could have used a touch more garlic.

On the streets, small three wheeled "Tuk-Tuks" served as taxis. I suspect their name is onomatopoeic for the clatter they made with their two-stroke engines. They are ubiquitous. New arrivals, myself included, invariably commented on how charming or cute or interesting they are. After one day of driving however, they became the bane of your existence and it was everyone's departure fantasy to crush one under the wheels of an SUV on the way to the airport. We didn't actually let people drive to the airport on their way out for just that reason.

Walking in the street was also a popular sport, rather like that 1980's video game "Frogger." Pedestrians would try to make it across five lanes of space in which cars jockeyed for position without regard for lane markers, at speeds rivaling NASCAR tracks. It was amusing at first, but like the Tuk-Tuks, it grated on one's nerves after a while and, as we learned as children—or at least as undergraduates—invariably, it's all fun and games until someone gets hurt. And someone always got hurt.

I lived for a while in a three-bedroom apartment on the ground floor of a three-story house. There was a small green space in the front into which I installed plastic lawn furniture and where I enjoyed breakfast or an evening libation—any time in between it was too hot to be outside. At eight o'clock every evening, the Imams began their verbal dueling from the minarets of the mosques in the neighborhood. During the plainsong portion, it sounded like polyphonic and polyrhythmic Gregorian chant. I regularly sat outside in the evenings for a post-prandial cigar to enjoy the music.

The courtyard performed its ancient function well: it secluded me from the world outside. Since I had no television or Internet connection, I would sit with my radio and try to pick up day-old Deutsche Welle news or Arabic channels. BBC did a broadcast, too, but only an hour a day or so in English, and I could never seem to connect with it. So I was somewhat news-starved. But what little news I did get was not good.

The cease-fire in Darfur wasn't holding. We were planning our first trip there. The situation seemed to be worsening despite the increasing number of peacekeepers—which remained ridiculously small. Perhaps, we speculated, it needed to get worse before it could get better. I learned this from Milosevic: if an insurgency and the government's response can be kept at a low simmer, the international community won't respond. A response requires an inciting incident, something like what happened at Racak in Kosovo.

In Darfur, there were hundreds of thousands dead and millions displaced and barely hanging on. Villagers displaced by the Janjaweit militias were now being forced by government troops to return to their homes—even though these had been destroyed. Janjaweit were wearing Government of Sudan police uniforms. A new rebel group had popped up, equipped and backed by neighboring Chad. And that wasn't the only war in the country.

In the south, where the war had been going on for a generation, both sides in the conflict were continuing to jockey for position in the waning days before the peace treaty was due to be signed. Both sides complained the other was profiting from maneuvering during the cease-fire. It wasn't really much of a cease-fire, and the fighting went on in Africa's longest civil war.

Sudan is one-third the size of the United States. Darfur alone is larger than Iraq; South Sudan is larger than France. The conflicts we were trying to stop were just as enormous, and there was little agreement on how to solve them. Religion was an issue, but not the issue. The Muslim leaders from the north paid Christians and other Muslims in the south to fight Christians who wanted equal or at least better treatment and more services from the government. Muslims killed Muslims in Darfur over ownership and control of scarce resources like water and food for cattle. Smack in the middle of the country were the oil fields that both the north and south claimed, and which funded the wars.

When, three generations earlier, two tribes would have fought with spears and moved on horses or camels, they were now racing around in Toyotas and carrying Kalashnikovs and machine guns. So it was a faster, more violent, and far bloodier fight.

The world intruded in both positive and negative ways. While diplomats worked to negotiate peace, soldiers from other African countries came as peacekeepers, and the humanitarian aid workers moved tens of thousands of tons of food weekly and built camps for the displaced; the fighting bands, like gangs, took on noms de guerre—one group called themselves Tora Bora.

In Khartoum, this escalation of foreign aid could be seen in the proliferation of Antonovs and Ilyushins at the airfield and of Toyota Land Cruisers on the streets. The usual suspects: soldiers, diplomats, aid workers made their homes there, clogging the stores and streets.

The bar at the British embassy was packed on Friday nights. The members of the British diplomatic corps, as always, were smartly attired; everyone else, it seemed, had shopped at the same REI outlet, with some adding a bit of local color for dash.

I was a newcomer. The wars had been going on forever, it seemed. The ghosts of Gordon and Kitchener haunted the city. The Sudanese People's Liberation Movement and Army were a generation into their negotiations with the government. Millions, yes, millions were dead because of the war in the south, and we were watching another war spin up in the west. Only a couple hundred thousand or so were dead so far in Darfur. And I was joining a team tasked to keep that number from growing.

Three Mohammeds

THE FIRST MOHAMMED was driving me to the airport, or what passed for an airport out there. It was a truly harrowing experience. It wasn't just that he was driving way too fast for the conditions, which he was. Or that he hit every pothole in the road, although he did. And it wasn't just that he didn't really watch the road ahead of him, for he certainly didn't. He did and didn't do the things I thought he should and shouldn't do because there wasn't any choice but to hit potholes since the dirt track on which he was driving was more or less one big pothole, and because there was about a zero percent chance he would hit another vehicle out there in middle-of-fucking-nowhere Darfur. And he drove really fast because, even though we were well within what the rebels called the "liberated area," you just never knew when you'd stumble across a few Janjaweit or some government soldiers. So off we went, our little convoy, on what could only be called a road in the vaguest sense, accompanied by a couple of dozen young, armed men who warily eyed the scrub and rocks around us looking for other young, armed men who wanted to kill them. Mohammed broke up the monotony of the drive by yelling in horribly broken English, which was a hundred percent better than my Arabic.

On that particular day he was simply carrying on a running commentary about the area we were driving through, pointing out the ragged trails that led to muddy watering holes for the herds and places where the rebels had previously engaged Janjaweit or government troops. Over the previous few days that he had served as my driver and protector, he told me how the Janjaweit had come to his village a hundred miles or so south of there, and killed his family while he was away tending their camels. He meticulously described what the scene had looked like when he returned home: his mother and sister raped, beaten, and forced to watch while the Arabs killed his father and little brother; the house burned, all their goods and the rest of their livestock stolen.

It seemed to me he really needed to tell the story, to get it out of his system. I'm sure the seven or eight guys sitting in and on the back of the Toyota pick-up truck we were riding in had all heard it before, and equally certain that most of them had a similar story about some of their family being raped or killed or worse by the Janjaweit. It was all too familiar to them, and by that time to me.

By this time, I had been traveling around Darfur for a couple of months, seeing for myself the burned villages, the bodies, and the graves. I had watched the Janjaweit attack, plunder, and burn a village, looting the houses just before they torched them, and then riding away on their camels with their loot. I'd been into the displaced persons camps and heard the stories from the women and older men. But out in the field, with the young men, these stories became somehow more intense, more real. The young fighters would only tell them to me one on one (through a translator). Otherwise, they didn't talk about those things in public. The women in the camps who were brought forward by the NGO managers to talk to the congressional delegations, the Umdas, and other elders who represented their villages and clans, could and did tell the stories on cue. They began to sound rehearsed and canned, especially after the women had been in the camps for a year or more.

They told me they grew weary of the politicians visiting the camps, promising to do something about the Government in Khartoum and the Janjaweit in Darfur, and then rushing back to the airport in their air-conditioned Suburbans for the ride home while dousing their hands with anti-bacterial scrub.

So I paid attention when Mohammed started telling me what happened. My friend Mara notes that one of the basic human needs is the ability to shape and to share your story and to have it be honored. She's right, of course. Everyone has a story and, I guess, many people want their story to be unique and uniquely theirs. But, in a group where everyone had a similar story to tell and no one was shocked, maybe no one wanted to hear about someone else's pain.

We were on our way to the airfield, which really was just an identifiable point of land between two dry stream beds, called wadis, where helicopters could land, so that I could leave while the senior rebel commanders deliberated over what I'd asked them to do. I wouldn't know what they would decide for a few days. By that time, Mohammed and some of the other guys with me might be dead, killed in fighting with the Janjaweit or with the government's troops.

The helicopter landed more or less on time. It was an old Soviet-made military aircraft painted white with the letters AMIS (for African Union Mission in Sudan), painted in black about four feet tall on each side. The white paint scheme was supposed to mean "don't shoot" to the rebels, the Janjaweit militias, and the Government troops—the three main parties to the conflict—but a couple of these aircraft had taken hits through the fuselage. A few weeks earlier, we had received some pictures of Sudanese government attack helicopters painted white.

The pilots of our helicopter were Russians and sort of lethargic while at the same time keen to get out of the hot zone. So they lazily encouraged me to quickly get on the aircraft. I went through the ritual departure acts of touching my right hand to my heart and then reaching out to touch the left shoulder and leaning in chest to chest with Jedou Issa Thagir, the rebels' Chief of Military Staff. Mohammed was just a driver so, despite the fact that he had been more or less glued to my hip for the past few days, he shyly dawdled by his vehicle while Jedou walked with me up to the helicopter.

I told Jedou that it was important that the rebels stand down and not incite the Sudanese army brigade that was laagered about five miles away. I explained, again, that the rebels had a responsibility to the civilians under their care not to provoke a government attack, particularly one that they could not defeat, and which would have resulted in yet more burned villages and more displaced and dead civilians. This was, at its core, the argument I'd been making for three days with the SLA leadership. As the translator relayed back what I'd said, Jedou smiled. I couldn't see his eyes because he wore sunglasses twenty-four hours a day, so I didn't really have a sense of whether he intended to accept my advice or not. I waved to Mohammed as I climbed into the aircraft. He turned his head away from the dirt and pebbles in the rotor wash as the Russians and I lifted off.

On the way out, I turned on my iPod and found some music. I got a good view of the village of Muhajeriyah out the port windows of the aircraft. Its sandy streets and mud-brick buildings were full of life: women in colorful *panya* dresses with their heads covered and, more often than not, a child on their back, worked their way through the wooden and plastic-tarped stalls in the market, shopping for food and sundries; young, often only half-clothed, children were playing in groups with improvised toys made from sticks and wire, apparently with no supervision needed; young men in flip-flops and turbans led wiry, hungry-looking cattle to watering holes. The survival of that village, and potentially all of those people, was at risk. I thought about the times in the prior weeks when we had chances to stop the fighting. We got one right and one wrong.

A few months earlier, in mid-December, I had been traveling with the African Union Cease-Fire Commission, led by Nigerian Major General Festus Okonkwo, a U.S.-trained and UN-seasoned peacekeeper, which included officers from the Sudanese Army, the two main rebel forces, Chadian military mediators, a few other African officers assigned to the commission, and me. During the first two weeks of December, a Sudanese army brigade with a few dozen Janjaweit militiamen had razed the villages of Suleya, Sani Afondo, Adwa, Ishma, Umm Zaifa, and Marrla. These were small, non-Arab tribal villages along the track from Nyala, the capital of South Darfur, to the east into Kordofan and on to the Nile and Khartoum. The few dozen houses in each village were made of sun-dried mud bricks formed in a circle with a roof of thatched sticks. The bricks didn't burn but the roofs, baked in the Sudanese desert sun, torched quite well. Each of the villages had a small market where merchants sold batteries and razor blades and tinned or powdered milk to people living hand-to-mouth.

The Sudanese army served more or less as a support structure for the Janjaweit militias, allowing them to enter the villages, loot, rape and burn, taking their booty away on their camels and horses while the regular army troops remained just outside in overwatch in case the rebels came out to fight or in the rare case the villagers put up substantial resistance.

The Sudanese brigade commander, Brigadier El Hajj Mohammed—the second Mohammed in this story—told us his instructions were to clear the road "all the way to Khartoum," and that they had come from "the highest authorities in Khartoum." He added that he had all the weapons in the Sudanese Army at his disposal, and that he intended to crush any resistance in his way. Jedou, my driver Mohammed, and a few hundred of their closest friends in the SLA and the Justice and Equality Movement (JEM), were in the Brigadier's way, as were the few thousand civilians that lived in Labado, along with some NGO workers.

Later that day, Mohammed Beshir—the third Mohammed—one of the local JEM commanders, gave the African Union monitors an ultimatum: have the Government of Khartoum pull its forces back from their positions within 24 hours or the JEM and SLA troops would attack them. The monitors took their message back to the headquarters in El Fasher. It's not clear to me what happened then, whether the staff notified their civilian leaders in Khartoum or Addis Ababa of the ultimatum or not, but according to rebel leaders I spoke with, the AU took no action to dissuade the rebels from attacking nor, to my knowledge, to encourage the Sudanese army to withdraw.

Two days later, the JEM and SLA rebels attacked the Sudanese brigade unsuccessfully. The Sudanese troops, with the Janjaweit militia integrated into their formation, counter-attacked with mortars, recoilless rifles, and heavy machine guns. The Sudanese air force flew their Soviet-made, MI-24 Hind attack helicopters in support of the attack, using a road into Labado from the northeast as a navigation aid. Zaghawa tribesmen and their families who had been previously displaced and had settled under plastic shelters along the side of the road were the target of rockets filled with thousands of tiny fleshettes, basically nails fired from a cannon. The rebels were routed, and, along with the civilians from Labado, withdrew to the next village to the east, Muhajeriyah.

The following day, we arrived to do our investigation. The town of Labado had been mostly burned and looted, its five wells destroyed. Market stalls in Labado were more substantial with steel doors and sheet metal roofs. They had all been looted. A small building at the edge of town where the SLA had been flying the old, tri-colored Sudanese flag in defiance of the Islamist regime in Khartoum, was burned out. Food stocks that were not looted were burned or sullied. Walking alongside the road to the northeast, where the previously displaced Zaghawa tribesmen and their families had camped in their shelters of sticks and plastic, I found parts of at least twenty aerial rockets that could only have been fired from the Government's attack helicopters, and lots of fleshettes that had come from those rockets. Notably, the rocket debris and fleshettes weren't near the road, where rebel vehicles would have been fleeing, but just fifty meters or so off to the northwest, where the displaced villagers had set up their shelters. The Sudanese were clearly specifically targeting civilians. The Red Cross estimated that two hundred and fifty civilians had been wounded, and the SLA spokesman in Muhajeriyah claimed that sixty-three had been killed. The survivors fled in several directions, though mostly to the east towards Muhajeriyah.

About one hundred people, mostly women and children, had returned to the village. They milled around a *zeriba*, a fence of thorn bushes, just at the southern edge of the destroyed village with their donkeys and goats and a few camels, sitting on blankets with what meager goods they had salvaged. Several young men were in the village proper, scavenging from the shops that the Janjaweit hadn't completely looted. There weren't any rebel fighters visible. They were probably a few kilometers away, licking their wounds. It struck me at the time that the rebel commanders were as responsible for the deaths of the civilians as were the Sudanese commanders and the Janjaweit. It also struck me later that the AU leadership were equally at fault for not using the forces at their command to stop the fighting, which was in their mandate.

A few days later, we faced a similar situation outside of Muhajeriyah. I had spent two days with the rebel commanders in the field, trying to get them to understand that they bore responsibility for the destruction of Labado and the deaths of the civilians because they had attacked the Sudanese army. That may not have been precisely accurate because the Sudanese might have attacked Labado anyway, but for my purposes—which were to get the SLA and JEM to back away at the same time we were asking the Sudanese to do so—it was accurate enough. My boss in Khartoum told me that the Sudanese had agreed to pull the brigade outside Muhajeriyah back, and also the one that was operating thirty kilometers to the north, rampaging through Duma, Hamada and Sani Afondo, if the rebels would withdraw from Labado and Muhajeriyah, and the African Union would position peacekeepers in the towns. There were two problems: getting the African Union to instruct the field commander to put peacekeepers in the two villages, and convincing the rebels to withdraw. Jedou and the other rebel commanders told me they believed they could defeat the Sudanese army. Further, they were unconvinced the Sudanese army would withdraw simply because the Americans had asked them to.

So, I spent a couple of days with Jedou and his intelligence chief, Hassan Salah, moving around the liberated areas in their Toyotas, eating their food and sleeping on the ground, talking to them about pulling their troops back. Then I returned to El Fasher and talked with the Nigerian major general and his Rwandan brigadier deputy. The general told me he was awaiting instructions from AU headquarters in Addis Ababa. The deputy said they could not deploy a force unless they were ordered to, and that no orders had come in yet. There were also handfuls of excuses: we don't have tents, we don't have field rations or kitchens, and so on. Some of these were true and some were not.

At that point I did something uncharacteristic: I broke the chain of command and called a friend in Washington, who had access to senior decision makers at State and the African Union. "They are stalling, and people are going to die," I said. My friend promised to take action by having a senior official, the Deputy Secretary of State or the Assistant Secretary for African Affairs, call the AU Chairman or another senior official there to ask for an intervention.

I don't know what happened after that in Washington and Addis Ababa, but the following morning the peacekeeping mission's chief of staff told me a platoon of Nigerian peacekeepers from the nearest camp, Sector 2 headquarters in Nyala, would deploy to Muhajeriyah within three days. I told the SLA and JEM representatives on the Cease Fire Commission the news and asked them to relay the message to the commanders in the field. The peacekeepers and a small team of contractors who would build a camp for them arrived in a few days. They settled onto a field that had served as a dumping ground for dead animals that would likely flood in the rainy season, offloading a pile of supplies under a tree, and began their work. Muhajeriyah survived due to the intervention of the AMIS peacekeepers.

But that was then. In the intervening months, I had worked with the rebels on a number of issues and I had come to know many of the field commanders. I think they came to trust that I would speak the truth to them, and would relay their requests and positions directly to our embassy in Khartoum and onward to Washington. A week earlier, the SLA representative on the Cease Fire Commission had invited me to come back to the Liberated Areas in the South and visit the command at Shearia. I called my boss and told him I was going out to the field for a week or so, and why, adding that I would call to check in daily.

When we arrived in Shearia, I learned that the rebels planned to re-occupy Muhajeriyah and hold a major military parade in the town to mark the initial phase of what they believed would be an expansion of the liberated areas and eventual victory over the government in

Khartoum. They believed that the United States would support them because I was there. Maybe they viewed me as the vanguard of a U.S. military intervention force. I believed the Sudanese military would bomb the town if the rebels held the parade.

So, I had spent the previous few days explaining that the cavalry wasn't coming. I said that the United States was decisively engaged in Afghanistan and Iraq and wouldn't be invading another predominantly Muslim country any time in the near future, particularly one on the African continent. I explained that, while the Khartoum government had powerful enemies on Capitol Hill and at USAID, its cooperation with the CIA on counter-terrorism, Department of Defense reticence to further over-extend its forces, and Chinese support in the United Nations Security Council gave Sudanese President Omar al Bashir and his cronies cover.

The rebel commanders agreed that it was unlikely that the United States would invade Sudan, but then countered with the idea of launching a few cruise missiles against Khartoum and against Sudanese military targets in Darfur much as we did in Bosnia and Serbia. After all, they added hopefully, the U.S. had a history of launching cruise missiles against Khartoum. (President Clinton had ordered the launch of cruise missiles against the Al Shifra pharmaceutical factory, a purported chemical weapons manufacturing facility, in North Khartoum in 1998.)

They held a small parade to show me their collection of weaponry. A couple of dozen vehicles bristling with anti-aircraft guns, mortars, and heavy machine guns, each with eight or ten young fighters clinging to the back, rolled by us in the blazing Darfur sun, raising clouds of choking dust that hung in the still air. It was an impressive display of weaponry until you considered that the Sudanese government had jet fighters, attack helicopters, and Antonov bombers.

In one long talk with rebel leaders, one of their senior operations planners suggested that some CIA support in the form of weapons and a few Special Forces trainers and operators would be sufficient for the rebels to defeat the Janjaweit and destroy the Sudanese Air Force. After that, he said, the Sudanese government would settle with terms acceptable to the rebels because the army had no stomach to fight. Legend was that the operations chief, Juma Haggar, had fought with the Chadian army against the Libyans during the Toyota War and been trained by Iraqi troops who had fought in the war with Iran. This seemed impossible to me since he had probably been born in 1980, and the Toyota War took place in 1987. He was, nonetheless, well acquainted with U.S. weapons and, as the military commander of the Minawi wing of the SLA, he was certainly acquainted with the Sudanese army.

Still, the chance of a U.S.-led military intervention was close to zero. So, as the helicopter lifted off from outside Muhajeriyah, I was thinking about the first Mohammed coming home from tending the camels to find his father and brother dead, mother and sister raped and beaten, their home looted and burned. The war was very personal for him and for the other rebels. They were the targets of the Janjaweit and government attacks. Their families had been killed or driven from their land and into camps. The government troops were mostly unhappy and ineffective conscripts. But they enjoyed the technological advantage of attack helicopters and Antonov bombers. They had the force of the state with its intelligence apparatus and the oil money behind it. The government recruited the Janjaweit by seducing the tribal leaders with money or political position or promises of land. And despite victories on each side, neither side could win outright, and a negotiated solution while the fighting was ongoing seemed unlikely. But the AU force wasn't up to the task of stopping the fighting, so on it went.

Later that night, back in El Fasher, I got a call from one of the rebel officers on the staff of the Cease Fire Commission. He said that the rebels had decided to postpone occupation of Muhajeriyah and the military parade, and had re-deployed their forces across Darfur's liberated areas. No major attacks were planned unless the government troops were to enter the liberated areas. I called my boss in Khartoum to tell him we apparently had earned a small respite for those civilians who would have been in the way.

An Empty Auditorium

"One of the few advantages that soldiers experience in having a desert for their theater of war is that the auditorium is empty."

Excerpt from a communiqué issued by British Army General Headquarters. Cairo, June 1940

O NE THING ABOUT THE WAR in Darfur was that, from a distance, it often appeared to be in remission. So little news got out from open sources like the press and non-governmental organizations that it could appear to be moving towards peace. Then, suddenly, some village would be attacked by one side or the other and the word would get out, and we were off and running again.

The pattern of the war in Darfur was determined by the fact that the government sought to destroy the villages and infrastructure of the non-Arab population. Cattle and camels were killed, starved, and stolen. Villages and farms were burned, farmland and wells poisoned. In my view, the government's plan was to drive out or destroy as many non-Arabs as possible and turn their lands over to Arab nomads.

But this wasn't particularly clear to most of the world, because the war was being fought at what we called the "edge of the empire." Also, the government in Khartoum were experts at controlling information: they denied visas for press, arrested reporters who snuck in from Chad, and made it clear to NGOs operating in the country that any reporting about crimes committed by the government would result in their expulsion.

Nonetheless, news got out from public sources—the BBC had a stringer or two in Khartoum, and dauntless free-lancers like Katharine Houreld and Reuters journalist Opheera McDoom strayed into Darfur when they could; organizations like Human Rights Watch and Refugees International occasionally got a team into Darfur, and stayed in contact with local Darfurian human rights organizations. The war captured the imaginations of tens of thousands of college students in the U.S., who formed groups like Save Darfur, and eventually became nationally and even internationally recognized for their efforts to inform and mobilize government and non-government action in support of the Darfurians.

In 1938, Neville Chamberlain had held a series of meetings with Adolph Hitler in which Hitler declared his intention to annex the Sudetenland (known to the hundreds of thousands of Czech citizens as Czechoslovakia). When Chamberlain emerged from the meetings, he faced the European press and announced that Britain would do nothing to stop Hitler. He called Czechoslovakia "a far away country of which we know little."

The fact that the country of Czechoslavakia no longer exists is not directly attributable to Chamberlain's insensitivity, but one could play that "six degrees of separation" blame game, and not wind up far from Mr. Chamberlain's door. I often felt as if Chamberlain's ghost were haunting the halls of state in Washington when I was trying to get something done in Darfur.

But first, a parlor trick.

If you have a map of Africa, get it out. Then take a piece of string a few inches long; floss will do. Put your finger on the map on the border between Chad and Sudan—depending on the level of detail on your map anywhere near El Geneina, Sudan or Abeche, Chad will be fine.

Now, hold one end of the piece of the string under that fingertip, and pull the other end out to the east-northeast towards the Red Sea; then move your hand north to the Gulf of Sidra (near Libya on the Mediterranean), then southwest to the Bight of Bonny (near Nigeria in the Atlantic). This piece of land under your fingertip is the furthest on the African continent from the blue water.

Far. Long. Hot. Dry.

In Washington and in New York, just before I left for my second tour in Darfur, I briefed some planners and policy makers. I showed them the little thing with the string and the map, then added some basic planning guidelines: from where you are to Darfur is a very long way; once you arrive, there is nothing, so bring everything you need with you.

I told them that, no matter what they planned, it would be considerably harder than they thought to accomplish that goal. They smiled at such effrontery. They didn't believe me. They looked at me like they wanted to send me on my way with a polite pat on the head. Smugness is unbecoming in military planners.

It turns out that all that planning that team was engaged in was unnecessary because the team's mission was stymied by politics. The Sudanese repeatedly seemed to diplomatically trounce the U.S. and our partners, so the military planners had no way to determine who was right.

But back to the Chamberlain quote, I find it tough to swallow that Chamberlain truly knew very little of Czechoslovakia in 1936. His observation was less that Czechoslovakia was a place about which we knew little, but more to the point, it was a place about which we cared little. We, and I speak of the western European powers, cared so little, we gave Czechoslovakia to Hitler without asking the Czechs what they thought. This was called appeasement.

In 1936, the British Empire included Sudan and Darfur; the French empire included what is now Chad. Because of this, we knew of Sudan and Darfur and the Sultanates of the Fur and Massalit, of the Tunjur and Ouaddai. Because of Burton, Speke, Gordon and Kitchener, we knew Wadi Halfa, Omdurman and Khartoum. Because of Commandants Lamy and Marchand we knew Kousseri, Ndjamena and Fashoda. Officers of the Sudan Political Service, including Sir Wilfred Thesiger, explored and lightly governed Darfur through the period of the Condominium and up until Sudan's independence in 1956. French administrators and French marines governed French Equatorial Africa until 1960.

But what we once know we often forget. The level of deep knowledge on Darfur within the Departments of State and Defense was low (particularly among field officers) when I arrived in 2004. Part of my job was to raise that level of knowledge, especially of the situation as it was at that time. As has often happened in my career, that process began with my own education. Just as had been the case in Kosovo, when the call came to go to Darfur, I didn't know the place existed and had to look it up. Once I was on the ground, however, the learning curve was steep and treacherous. But I was less afraid of failing than I had been in Kosovo.

Things were never really slow in Darfur. Even when the fighting forces stood down, there were investigations to run with the Cease-Fire Commission, travel to camps, reports to write, and so on. Because Darfur was in the news so much, senior U.S. government officials were regularly dropping in, too.

On the seventh floor of the State Department, the senior leaders divvy up the world's trouble spots and crises. Certain tasks belong specifically to the Secretary while others are given to the deputy or one of the six undersecretaries. Darfur belonged to Robert Zoellick, the Deputy Secretary of State.

Zoellick had previously been the undersecretary for economic affairs and the deputy chief of staff at the White House. He came out to Darfur a number of times while I was there. He was interested, asked good questions, and appeared to have done his homework beforehand (This isn't always true of senior leaders visiting the field). One of his staffers told me Zoellick had asked for twenty-five separate papers from the desk officers before the trip, and had committed much of the information to memory.

When I first met him, I was stuffed into the area behind the seat of a Land Cruiser—referred to as the wayback. The U.S. chief of mission, a senior USAID officer, a diplomatic security officer, and a driver rounded out the carful. We drove from the African Union camp out to one of the refugee camps nearby. By the time we arrived, Zoellick had pretty fully debriefed me. I didn't think much of it at the time. He saw me, for all I knew, as just another Army officer in the field. We showed him around the area, got him into a couple of meetings and sent him on his way.

A couple of weeks later, he quoted me in testimony on Capitol Hill.

Suddenly, both the U.S. and Sudanese governments were considerably more interested in what I had to say and where I went. Every trip I took out of El Fasher, the Sudanese government security wanted to check my travel authorization. During one particularly testy period in the relationship, the U.S. had restricted Sudanese diplomats' travel to within twenty-five miles from their embassy. Reciprocity demanded the Sudanese do the same, so when I flew back into the country after a few days in Nairobi, I received a stamp in my passport that was meant to restrict me to the immediate Khartoum area. This made for interesting discussions a thousand miles away in Darfur.

But I did get to travel and do my work. I spent time at most of the African Union peacekeepers' camps, learning the region and meeting as many rebel commanders as I could. I created an Excel file of data on the rebels that included names, ethnicity, sub-clans, factional loyalties, and contact information. I also created a list of Janjaweit leaders. These combined lists ran to over 250 names and they were of great interest to the intelligence analysts back in Washington.

Early in the fighting near Muhajeriyah, three Sudanese development workers went missing. They worked for an American non-governmental organization called ADRA—Adventist Development and Relief Agency—as well drillers, traveling to refugee camps and areas where there were large numbers of displaced persons, drilling wells and giving people access to clean water. They arrived outside of Labado a day or two before the fighting began, and were told to wait on the east side of the village under the protection of the SLA and the JEM rebels.

Then the fighting began. After the Sudanese troops and Janjaweit had taken control of the village, the men and their truck were missing.

ADRA leaders understandably wanted the African Union and the U.S. government to help find them. Over the next few weeks, I spent a fair amount of time talking to senior rebel leaders about the men. Both groups, the SLA and the JEM, denied holding them. I talked with a senior UN official, Mike McDonagh, and we compared notes. His research and investigation had turned up much more than mine had. He was sure the JEM were holding the men. One afternoon, weeks and weeks into their captivity, I received a call that the men had been released, thanks to a bit of nudging from some Italian military operators. McDonagh told me later that one relatively low-ranking JEM commander had captured the men and was afraid of his bosses' retribution, so he repeatedly denied holding them. After almost three months, the men were flown home to Khartoum in a UN aircraft. I don't think the truck was ever returned.

I called the embassy to give them the news. I explained to my boss that it was UN action that got the men released. A few weeks later I received a nice note from the Deputy Secretary of State thanking me for my "tireless efforts resulting in the release" of the three men. It seemed to me that things were going so poorly from Washington's point of view that our leaders wanted to dote on any small success. Nonetheless, it was nice to receive the note from Zoellick.

A few weeks later, my wife called to say my mom was going into the hospital for surgery and the doctors wanted me to come home. I flew out within the week. The Army released me from active duty, and I signed back into the State Department. I was assigned to be the Special Assistant to the Assistant Secretary for African Affairs, but the woman who had hired me was leaving, and her replacement didn't want me to serve as her special assistant, so I was allowed to take a substantial amount of leave. I spent two months sitting in a hospital room with my mom. She slipped into a coma and died on the first day of summer, 2005.

I drove home to Washington the next day, a Wednesday, to get a suit to wear to her funeral. On Thursday, I had a lunch meeting at the White House with Zoellick and then drove back to Virginia Beach for the funeral on Friday.

On Monday I was back in the office at the State Department. To say I wasn't well adjusted would be a colossal understatement. I settled into a job in the office that managed our policy with Sudan from Washington and was assigned an office that had been designed as a copier room.

Each day I rode the Washington Metro to work, and attended meetings on Sudan policy or read reports about the continuing violence. Within weeks I relapsed. I had panic attacks on the train. I hid behind the door in my office ignoring phone calls and emails. My hands shook uncontrollably. I wasn't sleeping. I wasn't medicating.

Every morning on the train, sitting with my bag on my lap, I would shake uncontrollably, in terror for my life, afraid of some unknown something, some invisible, ethereal vapor   an imminent attack that no one else seemed to realize was coming.

Sometimes I would have to leave the train, just get up and out of the car at some random stop because I was unable to control the crippling fear of an unknown something stalking me. I would rush out of the car and up onto the street in a panic, heart racing, eyes darting left, right, left, scanning the close and middle distance for some threat. Dashing about like a scared little rabbit, first left, then right, then back-tracking, hands and arms trembling and my breath coming in gasps. Through all of this, I would be dodging pedestrians on their way to work at rush hour, blithely oblivious to my desperation, my fear, my folly.

At work things were no better. In meetings I stared mostly at the table until I was asked a direct question. Then I would answer quietly, I think, and wish the meeting would end so I could go back to my office and hide behind the door. One of my supervisors called me on it one day. A management officer on our team waiting to take over his own office in another bureau called me into his office one morning as I walked down the corridor. He simply said that he'd noticed I had been a little shaky and wanted to make sure I knew he was around if I needed to talk or needed any help. I probably told him thanks, but I was fine or some such bullshit.

Soon after I came to work in the Sudan Programs Office, I was tasked to serve as an advisor to a United Nations team developing training for the African Union peacekeepers. I suspect people thought this would be nice and safe: travel up to the UN headquarters a couple of times and talk to the UN officials about the African Union staff. Instead, the team leader, a British cavalry colonel, recruited me, and I spent the next few months flying between Washington, Addis Ababa, Nairobi, and El Fasher.

Uncle Wiggily in Darfur

E L FASHER WAS A ONE-CAMEL TOWN. There were a few miles of paved road and only one or two buildings taller than one-story. There's an airport and the regional military headquarters, but at its core it was the hub of a neglected, distant province in a country where power and influence were distributed in direct relation to proximity to the national capital.

There were only or one or two restaurants to speak of. The largest and best known of these—it had three plastic tables and a handful of chairs—sat at the principal intersection in the town proper, near the small pond that had served to attract caravans for millennia and remained a source of both life and death, providing water to drink and mosquitoes to spread malaria.

The restaurant served grilled chicken. There may have been other dishes, but we stuck with the chicken. We would get chicken and pommes frites, a bottle of cold water and lots of napkins before the place closed just before the call to evening prayers. It was more or less the only game in town, so we went there a few times a week when we grew weary of the contracted kitchen food at the African Union peacekeeping mission headquarters.

Because I had spent nine months based out of El Fasher in the previous year, I was the local guide for the team of UN officials I had taken up with. One evening, after dinner, I was driving back from the restaurant to our guesthouse when my colleagues asked me to show them a bit more of the town. I decided to drive by the animal market. It was simply a field next to the road out towards the south of town where buyers and sellers of camels and goats, sheep, cattle, and horses could find each other.

I parked the truck near the edge of the field, upwind, if I judged correctly. The stink was inhumane. The dust and scurf were mixed with the shit of innumerable animals that had been festering in the sun for a generation. Fecal matter blowing in the air gets on your hands and face and lips and in your eyes and is ingested through the soft tissue in every exposed orifice of your body. The next thing you know you're spending half your day in the toilet and the other half begging the doc to try something new to make the puking and shitting stop. We all carried small bottles of hand sanitizer and used it liberally. Not always to good effect, though.

While my colleagues wandered through the market, laughing and posing next to and atop camels, I stood a bit apart, watching a smallish, grey-bearded man in a stained *thawb* sitting splay-legged on a woven mat under a scruffy tree. The man was cutting, stripping, and stitching small pieces of leather into pouches of varying sizes, and then stuffing small pieces of paper, folded or rolled, into the pouches. I'd been looking for this guy for months and had finally stumbled onto him. He was the *hijab* man.

Among Arabs, the word *hijab* refers specifically to the veil or scarf observant Muslim women wear, or more broadly to a modest style of dress. But in Darfur, the rebels call the leather talismans they wore *hijabs*. Further west, in western Chad and beyond, they are called Gris-Gris. In the U.S. and UK, people carry a rabbit's foot or wear their lucky socks for the same reason.

In Darfur all the rebels wore *hijabs*. I had been told all Sudanese do. Many rebels wore them by the dozen, strung on cords around their shoulders. They usually contained folded paper on which were written Koranic verses, although I knew at least two rebels that carried bullets that had been extracted from their bodies inside *hijabs* and others who kept bones, ashes, herbs and other shamanic offerings in theirs. Some rebel drivers kept dozens lying on the dashboards of their Toyotas as a blessing for their vehicle, and I had even seen them hanging around the necks of camels, donkeys, and goats.

A rebel commander named Mubarek had given me a small one as a gift during the Sudanese Liberation Army election conference in Haskanita. When I explained that I was an infidel, he said it didn't matter. "God and Allah are the same," he said, smiling, "it is we who choose to worship them differently."

I carried that one in my small backpack. I kept a bag with me almost all the time filled with notebooks, pens, a hat, sunglasses and sunscreen, hand sanitizer and a packet of toilet paper—essentials all. I also carried a book. You never knew when you would be stuck somewhere waiting for someone or something over an interminable period of time. I had learned long before to carry something with me to read and pass the time. This was not my first rodeo.

Since I nearly always was seriously deficient in my knowledge of the history and politics of any area I worked, I usually carried some sort of history book. But after spending almost a year previously in Darfur, I had decided upon my return to alternate my education with some literature. At that point I had in my bag one of each: W.T. Massey's *The Desert Campaigns* was my history, and *Nine Stories* by J.D. Salinger was my literature.

Massey, a correspondent with the Egyptian Expeditionary Force, was an early adapter to the embed process. His book was pretty good if a bit dated—he wrote it in 1918. He said in the introduction that he decided to write the book because someone told him that he should leave the desert and go to Europe to see what real war was.

Like Massey, I had been in wars in Europe and in the desert. They were both violent, terrible examples of creative inhumanity and testaments to political folly. At least in Europe the press showed up to cover the war and you could get whisky.

The Salinger book contained nine short stories including "Pretty Mouth and Green Eyes," "Just Before the War with the Eskimos," and "De Daumier-Smith's Blue Period." In retrospect, the Salinger stories weren't such a good choice.

"A Perfect Day for Banana Fish" was also in the collection. At its end, a veteran pulls out an Ortgies calibre 7.65 automatic and shoots himself through the right temple. "For Esme—With Love and Squalor" was also in the book. It details the descent into near madness of an American soldier in the Second World War. As screwed up as I was, maybe something a bit lighter would have been smarter.

I was standing at the edge of the animal market, looking at the guy who would make my own *hijab*. I had to decide what would go inside. I'm not religiously observant, so Koran, Old Testament or New, none of that seemed relevant—nor were any of those close to hand. I decided to put some scrap of literature inside. By chance alone, J.D. Salinger would be my protector.

I gave a quick glance over to the field to locate my colleagues, and then walked closer and took up a spot in the shade of his tree. The *hijab* man looked up at me and then quickly back down to his work. I reached into my bag and pulled out *Nine Stories*. The spine was broken already, so I didn't feel badly about yanking out a couple of pages from near the front, probably out of "Uncle Wiggily in Connecticut."

I folded them into a small, tight square and passed them to the man sitting under the tree. He unfolded them, glanced at the script, which he presumably couldn't read, then huffily re-folded them and stuffed them into the small, square pouch made of camel leather he had been stitching. He pulled a small strip of leather through the folded eye he had left at the top, tied that off, swabbed a daub of glue onto the flap, closed and sealed the flap, and handed it to me. I paid and we were done. I stuffed the *hijab* into my bag and met my colleagues at the truck.

I was in El Fasher in support of a United Nations mission to organize and run a training exercise for the African Union peacekeeper staff. I was the scenario writer. The three scenarios I had written were roughly like this: (a) a humanitarian emergency develops into a security crisis, deal with it; (b) a security crisis develops into a humanitarian catastrophe and includes significant press interest and bad weather, deal with it; (c) the kitchen sink of problems arrive sequentially, deal with all of them. The AMIS staff had an officer on the UN team who had helped with the details of the scenarios. He had the plots and knew the solutions. He also gave these to his colleagues on the AMIS staff. They still failed.

Personally, I was failing, too. I was falling apart, in some ways worse than I had in Afghanistan. I was deep into a bad PTSD episode. I was drinking myself into a stupor every night—in an Islamic republic where alcohol was banned—and I was carrying on a clandestine affair with a UN official. The genocide was actually diminishing, but we had no way of knowing that at the time. What I saw around me was 300,000 dead and 2.5 million displaced.

I had no real safety net to catch me, nor anything during the day to hold me together. I had very few actual responsibilities. Since the scenarios were already written, I was mostly along for the ride with the UN team. Despite this, I was managing pretty well until one really bad day.

The woman with whom I had been having an affair for a couple of months asked me what would happen after our work together ended. We had been at it for a few weeks, first in Nairobi, then in Addis, now in Darfur. We were having fun in nice hotels in Kenya and Ethiopia, and dodgy guesthouses in Sudan, drinking and playing. But when she started making noises about next steps, that set off alarm bells in my head, dragging me back to the realization that I had a life outside of this little war zone bubble. Soon I would have to go back to that life and the reckoning.

I obviously wasn't rational. Nonetheless, I was functioning at a pretty high level: writing intricate scenarios for a modern-ish fighting force operating in the midst of a complex emergency; continuing to collect information about the status of the rebel forces' disposition and actions, the Government of Sudan's response to the insurgency, and writing reports for the embassy about what I'd learned; at the same time I was carrying on this illicit affair.

But in my head, I was convinced that my life was fucked up, and that all I was doing was hurting other people. I had failed to stop the fighting in Darfur just as I had failed to do so in Kosovo and in Zaire. My writing sucked. My mom had just died. My marriage was a failure. I was a failure. Everything I touched brought pain to others. I wasn't getting better. I was getting worse. The dark stuff in my head triumphed over the rational, work-a-day reality.

I decided to kill myself. I think I did so quite rationally. I thought about it through the morning, scripting the steps and timing, mentally locating the tools I would need and sorting out their acquisition, thinking about the aftermath—both immediate and longer term. By lunchtime I had a plan. By mid-afternoon I had acquired all the tools. Late that afternoon I began work.

I grabbed a couple of beers out of the icebox, wrapped them in a shirt, and put them on the seat of the Toyota. Earlier in the afternoon, I had gone over to the U.S. team house and borrowed a pistol from the Special Forces team sergeant. He loaned it to me, no questions asked, because we had worked together for six months or so previously, and he had no reason to suspect that I was anything other than a competent, professional career officer.

I drove out of town to the west, somewhat dramatically I realized, into the setting sun toward the reservoir. I pulled off the main road to the north side, toward some small villages—just clusters of huts really—and stopped the truck on a low rise just high enough to see the sun falling toward the desert. I opened one of the beers. I started crying but I don't really know why. I was filled with a sense of failure and frustration, a sense of conclusion. Nothing I touched succeeded. Nothing I did was good. I had been through five wars in ten years and done nothing to stop the killing in Rwanda, Kosovo, Afghanistan, Iraq, or Darfur. It felt as if I had reached a logical place in my life to end it.

I opened the second beer, and picked the pistol up off the seat. It felt good in my hand. I felt surprisingly deft with it. I pointed it out the windshield with the magazine resting on the steering wheel and curled my finger around the trigger. I imagined pulling the trigger and the immediate pull the weapon would make as the round fired. There wasn't anything to shoot at out there, so I would have just blown out the windshield. But even if there was something to shoot at, I was holding the pistol in my right hand—I'm left-handed—I probably couldn't have hit it.

I put the pistol back on the seat. I remember a momentary flash of clarity. Who else could I hurt if I did this? My wife, certainly. Anyone else? My sister, maybe. I thought that what I was getting ready to do would leave a hole in some lives. I even thought about someone having to clean up the truck afterwards. Maybe I would do it outside and leave less of a mess.

But the clarity passed and I was overwhelmed with a sense of futility and sadness. I had failed to stop the wars; so many people were dead because of my failures. Images were rushing at me: the forty-five dead from Racak, the raped nun from Bunia, the man with the red-rimmed eyes and his mutilated family near Senik.

I picked up the pistol and charged it—loading a bullet into the firing chamber. My hands were shaking. I put the beer down and took the pistol off *safe*. I was sobbing and talking to myself, to the spheres, to no one. The pistol was ready. I shifted it to my left hand. I looked at it in my hand, lying partly on my lap pointed down a bit. I took a deep breath to calm myself. I was ready.

Then the phone rang.

It scared the hell out of me and I jumped, startled. I almost pulled the trigger. Which would have been highly ironic, to shoot myself in the foot while preparing to shoot myself in the head. I looked at the phone lying on the seat of the pickup and saw that it was my wife, Maureen, calling from Washington, DC. Was this serendipity, karma, luck, or just uncanny timing?

With my thumb, I put the pistol back on *safe* and laid it on the seat. While I talked to Maureen for a few minutes, I stared out through the windshield and watched the sun setting over the rocky brown desert of Darfur. The ringing phone had broken the spell. After the crying and shaking, the moralizing and justifying, the calming of hands and nerves, the intense focus on the immediate act of charging the weapon, and then taking off the safety and preparing to put the barrel in my mouth, the ringing phone pulled me back from the brink. After the phone rang, I could no longer pull the trigger.

I drove back into town. I stopped to return the pistol to the American sergeant who had lent it to me. I went back to the UN guesthouse. That night I read some of the remaining Salinger stories, among them the one titled, "For Esme, With Love and Squalor." There is a point in the story when the protagonist has tea in Devon with a precocious, teenaged girl—the Esme of the title. As she is leaving the teashop, she says, "I hope you return from the war with all your faculties intact." A few hundred words later, in the immediate postwar, readers realize that Sergeant X's faculties are most assuredly not intact. It is pretty clear that somewhere along the way my faculties had become somewhat less intact as well. The Salinger story appeared in *The New Yorker* on April 8, 1950. When I read through it today, I see in it so much of what PTSD does to people: the tics, the anxiety, inability to focus, a quickness to anger, etc.

Salinger, famously reclusive, had gone ashore in the D-Day invasion, and had fought through the Battle of the Bulge and the Heurtgen Forest campaigns with the 4th Infantry Division. Nothing I had done in my wars can approach that type of combat. Which of course makes me feel incompetent and weak. Nothing in my writing will likely ever approach what Salinger had achieved, either.

Over the next week or so, we completed our tasks with the African Union mission. I gave somewhat vague assurances to my UN girlfriend that we would indeed see each other again. I flew out through Addis Ababa and Frankfurt to DC.

At Frankfurt, going through the security checks to board the U.S-bound flight, I pulled my laptop out of my bag and the new *hijab* tumbled out with it. I thought about the intent of the *hijab*—as protection—and I guessed it had done its job. I had survived another trip into a war zone, one where I came perilously close to dying. J.D. Salinger had somehow protected me. If I had been reading Hemingway or Vonnegut, I wonder, would Robert Jordan or Billy Pilgrim have been as effective as Uncle Wiggily?

When I got home I admitted the affair to Maureen. It wasn't the first, so it was kind of a last straw for us. We began sorting through our things and dividing up our life together. I started looking for another assignment and found one at the embassy in Khartoum. I was going back to Darfur.

On September 28, 2005, twenty years to the day after we were married, Maureen and I signed the separation agreement. I flew out to Khartoum that night.

All Things Being Equal...

Late in the evening of the spring equinox, I was sitting in a small room with a rough table, a plastic chair, and a cot with a sagging, smelly mattress on the compound of a medical NGO in a town in eastern Chad. I was going over my notes from interviews earlier in the day, when John Denver came through the door. Ok, so it was not really John, who, having been dead, lo those many years, might have difficulty ambling into my room, but rather it was John Denver's voice that came wafting into the room and began wrestling with the *poomp poomp poomp* of the music playing in the guards' shack on the other side of the whitewashed wall from my bed.

I looked out the screen door to see how it was exactly that John Denver had come to Guereda, Chad singing "Leaving on a Jet Plane," one of the few songs of his that I can still tolerate. I saw the Italian midwife sitting outside under the *boukarou* with her laptop. She had unplugged her earphones to share the music with the Azerbaijani surgeon. Both women smiled and looked a little dreamy as John sang "*...so kiss me and smile for me, tell me that you'll wait for me, hold me like you'll never let me go.*"

Far out.

All things being equal on the equinox, I would probably have chosen something African, or some modern jazz over some smarmy

John Denver tune, but the song the guards were listening to was so distorted, I couldn't tell what language it was in. So, go get 'em, John.

I was in Chad because Khartoum had declined to issue me a visa to enter Darfur. Lots of Darfurian rebels hung out in eastern Chad, and there had been a number of cross-border attacks by Sudanese Janjaweit into Chad, so that's where I went.

I specifically went to Guereda to report on rising ethnic tensions between the Tama and Zaghawa tribes. I had finished my work, but was staying for an extra day because of the visit of the President of Chad, S.E. Idriss Deby Itno. In the midst of the ethnic violence Deby came to try to calm tensions between the tribes. Deby is a Zaghawa. Guereda is the seat of Dar Tama, the land of the Tama people. As a part of the campaign to quell the violence, Deby made changes to the civil administration, changing out the Minister of Defense, the Governor and the Prefect of Guereda, in all three cases replacing an ethnic Zaghawa or Gorane with an ethnic Tama. The new Minister of Defense was a Tama, Mahamat Nour, who, less than twelve months before, had led an unsuccessful armed coup d'état against Deby.

Apparently, all was forgiven.

Or maybe not, forgiveness is complex there.

That morning, just after sunrise, the Sultan's drummers began practicing on his compound—it's hard to call it a palace—next door to the medical compound where I was staying. They did that most of the morning, took a break at noon, then began again after the 2:30 prayers and continued through the afternoon and late into the evening. They were still at it, more or less, when the *poomp poomp poomp* was playing, and John Denver floated in. Their singer, who was not exactly John Denver, ran through his repertoire of epic song-poems, both of them, for about four hours, his voice blaring through the bullhorn attached to the minaret of the Mosque on the Sultan's compound. Sadly, I did not speak whatever language he was singing in, so I missed a lot, but if I were guessing I would have said he was singing the epic story of the Tama people. Or maybe he was simply singing the tried and true theme of all songwriters: I am loving you and you are loving me; we are loving each other and I can't live without you.

Again, all things being equal, I might have chosen John Denver over the unintelligible *poomp, poomp, poomp*, but there was a certain charm to the epic song poems that won me over, particularly given that the next song the Italian midwife played was "Sunshine on My Shoulders." Regardless, I had no choice in the matter, all of these musical selections were provided for me simultaneously.

Son Excellence, Monsieur Le President was coming because the fighting between the Tama and the Zaghawa had slipped into something entirely different. In my notes back at the office I had called it, *"something sinister, something that looks a lot like ethnic cleansing."*

This is how it started. Young, armed Tama men were stopping people in the street in Guereda and asking them their identity, their ethnicity. Those who were not Tama were beaten and warned to get out of town, out of Dar Tama. Sometimes the victims were afraid to stay in Guereda to even get treatment at one of the two NGO-run hospitals there, so they traveled forty kilometers away to a hospital in Dar Zaghawa. Some died on the way. The week before, armed Tama men had gone into the refugee camp in Kounoungo and beaten Zaghawa and Gorane women, to the delighted applause of the Tama women watching.

This is how it spread. Zaghawa extremists stopped a commercial transporter on the road from Guereda to Am Zoer, separated the passengers by ethnicity, and then executed the Tama. We counted seventy Tama men murdered in small villages in three months. Many showed signs of torture or mutilation.

All things being equal, I figured things were getting worse.

The root causes of the conflict are multiple and complex, but there was a common theme: both tribes sought revenge. The Tama sought revenge for generations of abuse at the hands of the Zaghawa and Gorane. The young Tama felt that Nour's appointment as Minister of Defense had immunized them against prosecution for attacks on Zaghawa and Gorane. The Zaghawa, whose Dar spread well across into Darfur, and among whom perhaps seventy-five thousand or perhaps one hundred thousand had died in that war, felt they were victims of a genocide and knew that the Tama took part in some of those attacks while acting as mercenaries, as Janjaweit, for the Government of Sudan in exchange for arms and training for their failed coup d'etat. The Zaghawa militias, in an inspired and ironic bit of literalism, referred to themselves as Zaghawa Janjaweit.

Often, in this part of the world, when there is a killing, the victim's family is awarded a payment—blood money—called *diyah*. Once the family accepts the *diyah*, the case is settled and there can be no reprisals. But sometimes the relationship between the tribes is such that the *diyah* is not allowed. In some cases, members of one tribe consider themselves superior to another. The Arabs there and in Darfur feel that they have a master-slave relationship with the non-Arabs. Generally, one cannot accept *diyah* from a slave. In these cases there is only the *ridah*—*ridah* means calming. The *ridah* calms the immediate situation but doesn't end the dispute. The victims' families reserve the right to seek further compensation, further restitution, revenge. Maybe they seek it; maybe they don't. Forgiveness is complex.

There's another little piece of irony to all this: Arabs in Darfur and Eastern Chad call the Zaghawa and other non-Arab tribes *zurg*, meaning black and *abid*, meaning slave. And, although generally one cannot accept *diyah* from a slave, Arabs in Darfur will accept *diyah* from Zaghawa. Zaghawa in Chad consider themselves superior to the Tama and refuse to accept *diyah* from them, only *ridah*. This is how killings become blood feuds that last for generations.

All things being equal, it seemed nothing was equal.

And I kind of got it, I mean I understood what was going on, but I nonetheless had grown up in a world where tribe and clan and vengeance were just words and not ways of life, so there really was no way I would ever completely get it. And so, of course, the killing and dying went on, and it spiraled into something like ethnic cleansing and then John Denver wafted into my room singing "Leaving On a Jet Plane," and the guards outside were listening *poomp poomp poomp* to some song that may or may not have been in French, and the Homer of Guereda was singing *The Iliad* and *The Odyssey* of the Tama people only there was no Wine Dark Sea in that one, just, I presumed, lots of killing and dying.

Into this entered the president. He arrived, and made some speeches and appointed new authorities to assuage one side, then worked to find some way to assuage the other side. And maybe it would work like a *diyah* or maybe it would only calm things, like a *ridah*.

And, oh by the way, eastern Chad was a sideshow compared to the real killing, the hundreds of thousands of dead in Darfur. But you have to give these things time.

The French Lieutenant's iPod

THE FRENCH LIEUTENANT AND I were riding beside one another in a rattletrap, thirty-year old, Soviet-made cargo helicopter. We were returning to Abeche in eastern Chad from a refugee camp called Kounoungo about 120 kilometers away. Kounoungo is close to the Darfur border and is home to refugees who were driven from their homes by the war. Given all that, it wasn't an especially giddy flight.

We were quiet, partly due to the fact that we were dealing with a very depressing problem. The war had been going on for four years, and those people were no closer to going home than they had been two years before when I first came to Darfur. But we were also quiet because we'd just more or less witnessed two senseless killings and then walked away, because we were worried that something worse might happen. Something worse than two men killing each other, that is.

The war in Darfur and Chad was part of an on-again-off-again war the leaders of Chad, Sudan and Libya had been fighting since 1971. More often than not, the political leaders had been able to pit one tribe against another, exploiting ethnic tensions by manipulating access to scarce resources. But when this didn't work they would have a go at each other with their nations' standing armies. The fighting I was trying to stop was just another round in the long war. Those men were only the latest to die.

In 2003, at about the same time the Darfur crisis moved from rebellion to war and genocide, a young Chadian military officer had left the ranks to form a rebel band just across the border in Darfur. The man, Mahamat Nour, was a Tama tribal leader. As he left Chad for Sudan, he took hundreds of young Tama men with him. The Sudanese government, keen to see a change in the government of Chad because that regime supported the Darfurian rebels who were fighting the Sudanese, gave Nour weapons, support and sanctuary for his nascent rebellion.

In return, Nour and his fighters did the Government of Sudan's bidding, fighting as part of the Janjaweit militias, and killing, burning and raping among the Zaghawa, Fur and Massaliet villages in West Darfur. Civilians in the path of these atrocities fled across the border into Chad. The United Nations established relief camps in eastern Chad for refugees. Once the camp at Konoungo was established, 18,000 refugees from the war moved in.

Konoungo itself is a fine place for camels. The land is hard and rocky, desiccated. A family can scratch out a meager garden of sorghum and beans, but nothing will flourish if the rains don't come. The rains hadn't come for five years. The refugees received shelter, food and water from the UN, but the local townspeople received little or nothing. The refugees are ethnic Zaghawa; the townspeople are ethnic Tama.

And into this we landed, the French lieutenant and I, sent here by our governments to report on what was happening back to our respective capitals. We often traveled together when the African Union's peacekeepers had space on their aircraft for us, and on that day we were standing in the market area of the camp interviewing refugees about the ethnic tension, when we heard an exchange of gunfire a couple of hundred meters away. There had been bandits in the area and the local gendarmes were eager to capture them.

Given the proximity and intensity of the gunfire, we figured something might soon be happening over at the medical clinic, so we walked across the field in that direction, trailed by the dozen or so refugee kids who were our unofficial escorts in the camp. They didn't have much to do, school only runs for part of the day. So when a couple of *khawajah*—white people—arrived, it must have felt like they'd just gotten one hundred channels of cable TV and a jumbotron.

The clinic wasn't much to look at really. It was just a couple of white tents erected by a western medical NGO. There was always a line of patients outside. Maybe even more that day since it was one of the days the NGO doctor visited. The doctor was Azerbaijani and had come on a year-long contract to work for a not-quite-western salary because it was better than anything she could get in the former Soviet republics. She was a surgeon who spent much of her time delivering babies and taking bullets out of young men. She was small and pretty with a thatch of dark curly hair she kept mostly tied back, and she looked as out of place there as I did.

Some of the people waiting in line to see her watched us walk up and made a space for us in the shade provided in the lee of the tent. I smiled and said *shoukhran*—thank you—and touched my right hand to my heart.

We waited outside the clinic for a few minutes until, predictably, a small truck arrived bearing the bodies of the men killed in the firing we heard. What happened is seemingly relatively simple: two men shot each other in the wadi—the dry creekbed—just outside the refugee camp. One man was a bandit, robbing refugees and local townspeople as they walked through the wadi to market. The other was a gendarme trying to arrest the bandit. But this wasn't just a cops and robbers story, and these weren't just two dead men. No, that would be too simple.

One man was a Zaghawa and the other a Tama. In the fragile, precarious existence between refugees and locals, ethnicity was an accelerant: it increased the volatility of the spark. Those killings might have been the spark that would ignite a prairie fire of ethnic violence across Dar Tama.

The doctor came out of the clinic into the gravel parking area where we were standing to pronounce the two men dead, for surely they were dead and this was just a formality. The dead men were laid out in the back of the pickup, their legs and arms akimbo and entwined as they would never have been in life, but uncaring in death, I supposed. It was hot, and already flies were buzzing around them, attracted to the blood on their shirts and the moisture around their eyes and mouths.

I exchanged glances with the doctor. We'd been in a catch-as-catch-can relationship for a few weeks, and I had sought comfort in her arms after investigating some truly grisly stuff. Just the previous week, several Zaghawa men had been pulled off a bus by a group of armed Tama men. Their bound and mutilated bodies were found a couple of days later along the edge of the road. A lone survivor was made to witness the tortures and murders. He was badly beaten, then released and told to warn others what would happen to any Zaghawa who stayed in Dar Tama. There had been other things, too. Not long before that... well, never mind. Suffice to say, it was a cruel, nasty war even as these things go, and each of these events served to magnify the unease most everyone felt, and ratchet up the tension a little bit more.

The doctor put her hand on my shoulder, and pulled herself up into the bed of the pickup. She left her hand on my shoulder perhaps a second longer than was necessary. I supposed I was the only one who noticed, but I did notice, and I knew she was thinking about me, worrying probably. She knew I had been falling apart for a couple of years.

She squatted down and put her fingers along the dead gendarme's carotid artery for a few seconds, checking one side then the other. She shook her head slightly. He was dead. She moved on to the dead bandit and repeated the fingers to the throat thing. He was dead, too. She stood and moved back to the edge of the tailgate. The French lieutenant reached up to help her down. She took his hand, then stepped down off the back of the truck.

One of the peacekeepers stepped up into the bed of the pickup, pulled the dead bandit's corpse up into a sitting position and braced it against his knee, then beckoned for me to take a photograph. I remember thinking, please don't open his shirt, just as he began to pull at the buttons of the man's bloody yellow shirt to open it and expose the wounds in his chest. The dead bandit's head lolled about, and one of the other officers reached over the edge of the truck's bed to hold it up so his face would show in the photo. I looked at his chest and it was covered in blood. I could see the bullet hole and without really thinking I was pointing my little camera at it, and I was pressing the button and checking the shot, and then nodding to the officer, who dropped the dead bandit's corpse back onto the bed of the truck and moved to pick up the dead gendarme's corpse. And we went through the same series of tasks with him opening the gendarme's bloody camouflage tunic and me pointing the camera at the man's bloody chest except that by then I was shaking on the inside and trying not to. Then I had the shot, and I put my little camera away.

I'd seen lots of this stuff. But I wasn't inured to it. Others seemed somehow unmoved, but I simply could not steel myself against a visceral reaction to the dead, the mutilated, the humiliated, no matter how many times they confronted me.

These men were just the latest in the line of dead in the wars I've reported. And while they all looked different, they bled the same. These bled just like all the others: just like the Kosovars, just like the Serbs, just like the Hutus and just like the Tutsis, just like the Afghans, just like the Iraqis, just like the Darfuris. They all looked different, but they all bled the same, and they all died the same. The only other constant seemed to be me wandering around pointing my camera at corpses and taking notes in my little spiral notebook.

I turned on my heel back towards the hospital tent's door, and saw the doctor standing there in the shade. She had surgery to conduct inside but was waiting there just long enough for me to see her. She smiled a little, and gave me a look that I think meant she wanted me to know she cared and was concerned about me. I nodded, and looked down at the ground because I was embarrassed. And then she was gone.

I caught myself looking down at the ground and shaking my head almost imperceptibly, so I straightened up and pushed my sunglasses back up a little. I paused and took stock of what I knew. I'd seen enough to write my report.

The peacekeeper stepped off the back of the truck, and as he did, the dead gendarme's head plopped over, and I saw that his eyes were still open. They stared blindly, open, flat and dull, into the sun while I stared mutely at him. And as I looked at him, I thought of the line in *The Odyssey* where Agamemnon's ghost recounts his murder at the hands of his wife Clytemnestra:

"As I lay dying, the woman with the dog's eyes would not close my eyes even as I descended into Hades."

I paused for a second and wondered what this guy had seen as he lay dying. I wondered if he was watching us as he descended into… where, hell? I worried that if his eyes were open he wouldn't have his *obolus*, the pennies on his eyes to pay his toll, and I wondered if Charon would ferry him across the Acheron without payment. The guy was just a cop trying to do his job, trying to arrest some kid who was robbing refugees. I mean really, robbing refugees, how low is that?

The bandit kid was probably with Nour, burning villages and raping as part of the Janjaweit. He might have taken part in the attacks that displaced some of the people in this camp. He had probably been fighting and killing since he was twelve or thirteen. Now, dead, he looked about sixteen lying in the bed of the truck. He'd survived the war only to get killed right near his hometown while robbing refugees. And he took the cop out with him. I couldn't bring myself to reach out and close the gendarme's eyes, but when nobody was looking, I reached into my pocket and slipped a Chadian coin under his collar, for Charon, just in case.

Someone in the group suggested we get back to the helicopter. The peacekeepers were concerned about more gunplay or an uprising from within the camp. I couldn't tell if it was my feeding off their nervousness or what, but there was definitely a weird vibe. So, we made our way back to the field next to the market where the aircraft sat. The pilots must have sensed something, too, because they had already done their pre-flight checks. We trundled aboard the aircraft and sat side-by-side on the bench seats along the fuselage. As the crew chief was closing the door, the engines whined, and the big five-bladed rotor started to turn overhead. I looked out through the portside windows and saw the crowd of people standing around the aircraft in a loose circle watching us. The show was departing, I thought. But that wasn't it. They were watching us leave, wondering why the hell we had come in the first place.

Before the shooting had started, some of the tribal leaders had been complaining that western diplomats came out to the camp every couple of weeks, they all made promises to improve things and to end the genocide that drove the refugees here in the first place, but nothing ever happened. The leaders told us they had a hard time rustling up a crowd to meet with visiting dignitaries because people were tired of telling the same stories over and over for nothing.

Then we were lifting off. And just as the downdraft from the rotor was roiling the dirt and rocks into a whirlwind among the crowd, a squadron of seven or eight gun trucks arrived, bad-assing their way in from the northeast, each truck laden with eight or nine troops and a heavy machine gun or recoilless rifle.

As we passed over the formation, the refugees' attention shifted away from our helicopter. It was clear that we could no longer do anything for them or to them. Some turned their attention to the Chadian troops who had just arrived to give chase to the other bandits and to avenge the death of their comrade, while others settled back to the issue at hand, the sale of a few peanuts or a couple of AA batteries on a razor-thin profit margin.

And just then there was something about the way the light hit the glass or the smell of the dust in the air or the shudder of the helicopter as it turned, something, and I knew that it was my last field mission. I was done. I'd seen enough.

So the French lieutenant and I sat side by side in the aircraft flying back to Abeche, both settling into the recesses of our iPods. I chose The Stones' "Gimme Shelter"; he chose "Civil War" by Guns 'N Roses.

The War at Home

2006-2010

All romantics meet the same fate someday:
Cynical and drunk and boring someone in
some dark café.

JONI MITCHELL
The Last Time I Saw Richard

Who Will Apologize?

A T MY REQUEST, in May 2006, the State Department's Regional Medical Officer for psychiatry sent me home from Darfur. In official Department parlance, I was being medically evacuated, medevac'd. In the patois of the Foreign Service it was a "psych-evac," or maybe a "psycho-vac." I had come perilously close to being dead by my own hand. Closer to being dead, I guess, than at any other time in my career in any of those other wars. It's not that I was bulletproof; it's just that I wasn't doing the kind of work that normally gets people killed. I wasn't a special operator or an infantryman. Nope. More or less what I did was I talked to people and wrote down what they said. I was pretty good at that part. I also tried to stop them from killing each other, but I failed more often than not at that.

How many are dead because I had failed to take action? I suppose it does no good to ask, because it's impossible to determine. Maybe the number is too high to be believed. But maybe it's zero. Maybe, as Jack Zetkulic told me that day in Kosovo, there was nothing else I could have done. I don't think that's true, but even if it were, I don't think anyone could ever convince me of it. The truth lies somewhere in between. Regardless, in the spring of 2006, I had reached a breaking point.

The Department posts doctors, nurse practitioners, and other medical staff at embassies around the world—the bigger the embassy, generally, the more medical staff there is. Sudan had a nurse practitioner for the daily medical care of the staff. There were doctors in Nairobi, and they made a circuit visiting embassies in the region. One of those doctors was a psychiatrist, and it was to him I turned when I knew I had had enough. He curtailed my assignment to Khartoum; I received orders to return to Washington.

This meant that my psychological health problems were now a matter of record. I had crossed a line from quietly talking with doctors to admitting to the Department's administrators, personnel officers, and security agents that I was broken. There would be consequences, of course, but at the time I didn't really care. I just needed help.

It took a week or so to get the orders written, find a new assignment in Washington, and pack up my stuff. I hung around the embassy's political and defense attaché offices where I had served. I turned over my phone and email lists to the officers who would pick up my portfolio. But I spent most of my time writing a long cable back to Washington detailing why I was convinced that the Department's policy direction in Darfur was doomed.

By regulation, Foreign Service officers can write cables to the secretary dissenting U.S. policy. The mechanism for sending these cables is referred to as the Dissent Channel. It is a special handling procedure for messages that allows FSOs to say their piece about a policy without forcing them to resign in protest. It is very rarely used.

After nearly two years in Darfur, I believed I knew what was necessary to stop the violence. I was considered one of the U.S. government's experts on the war. My cables back to Washington were widely read and circulated among the policy and intelligence communities. The deputy secretary of state had mentioned my work in congressional testimony and public speeches.

So, in my last week at the embassy, while I was packing out, I wrote a cable titled, "Darfur: Who Will Apologize?" The title played off President Clinton's half-apology to the people of Rwanda for failing to intervene in the 1994 genocide there. In the cable, I explained why I thought the policy then in place for Darfur was doomed, and offered suggestions on what was needed to fix the policy—what it would take to stop the killing.

While officially it's not necessary to show these cables to the ambassador or the chief of mission, I did so. I sent a more or less final version to our chief of mission, Ambassador Cameron Hume, who was at the peace talks in Abuja, Nigeria. Cameron told me in an email that he fully supported the use of the Dissent Channel, but that the results were often considerably less dramatic than the drafting officer imagined. He continued, explaining that the cables were sent directly to the secretary's policy planning staff, a group of fewer than a dozen officers and political appointees, and circulated among the most senior officials in the department. One of the officers on the staff, the officer responsible for that particular region or issue, would then draft a cable in response to the Dissent Channel cable and send it to the drafting officer. Very few people would actually see either cable.

Cameron made me a counter offer. He said we could work on a cable together, one that probably neither one of us would like, or I could send my original cable through open channels—meaning many, many more people would see it—but he would put a paragraph atop the cable with his comments. I took that option and a day or two later, the cable went out.

The cable is classified as confidential, so I cannot reproduce it here—I can't even see the cable because I no longer have a security clearance. But it was leaked—I do not know by whom—to Smith College English literature professor Eric Reeves, whose main work seemed to be publicizing war crimes committed by the Sudanese government and its proxies, and criticizing the U.S. government's policies. Reeves apparently passed the cable to Nicholas Kristoff at *The New York Times*, who reported on it. The cable was also one of the 250,000 cables released to Wikileaks by Army private Bradley Manning, so it's out there.

No senior official of the Department ever responded. And most assuredly, the policies didn't change. That's not surprising on either count. Since we did send it outside of the Dissent Channel, no one was mandated to respond; and I don't think anyone who sends a cable like that expects to change policy. It's mostly an exercise in futility, but one that is occasionally necessary just to get different ideas on the table or something that needs to be said to get it off one's chest.

A year later, in June 2007, the American Foreign Service Association presented me its William R. Rivkin award for "intellectual courage and the creative use of dissent," based on the cable— Ambassador Cameron Hume had nominated me for the award. The ceremony was held on the 8th floor of the Department, in the diplomatic reception rooms. Hundreds of people were present; former Secretary of State Lawrence Eagleburger spoke. I was terrified. I forgot my notes and had to speak off the cuff. Reporters interviewed me and the stories ran in newspapers around the country and on NPR.

I flew out of Khartoum and into Washington a few days after the cable went out. First thing, I needed a place to live. I wanted to be in the heart of the city, so I found an apartment on Capitol Hill. My dog Jack and I moved into a one-bedroom English basement apartment a block away from the Eastern Market and two blocks from a Metro stop.

I suppose only the medical officers knew at the time that I had been psych-evac'd. And I found it odd that there was no medical follow-up—no mandatory psychological testing or any evaluation at all upon my return.

So I rode my bike back and forth to work each day. I took Jack to the dog park a few blocks away and let him romp with the other dogs—the crowd that frequented the park with their dogs was about as much community as I thought I could manage. I knew all the dogs' names but not the names of their owners. In the evenings, Jack and I would hang around together. I would sit outside in my canvas yard chair, reading or listening to music and tossing the tennis ball for him a few yards to the cast iron fence that surrounded my little yard.

I could smell meat grilling on barbecues up and down the block. Neighbors would walk by, and sometimes we would exchange a glance and a nod, but more often than not the fence served its purpose of protecting me. That fence was only about two and one half feet high, but it felt like a combat perimeter around my position. Everything inside was safe; everything outside was dangerous. I stayed inside the wire, watchful. I was back in the United States, but I wasn't home.

Newly divorced, I was alone in the city. But I wasn't ready to go out. I wasn't ready to have a social life. Where would I go? I didn't know anyone. I wasn't about to go to nightclubs with the young, cool crowd. Hell, I was in bed before things really got going at those places. I didn't really want to go to the bars over on Pennsylvania Avenue, either. Nice hangouts, all. But I just wasn't ready for a scene.

Late at night I would hear people on their way home from the nearby bars. Women walking down the sidewalks, their high heels sounding like horses' hooves on cobblestones in slow motion. Groups of young men slapping their sneakers down on the pavement and jerking one another's chain over some unmanly act committed earlier.

One evening I went down to RFK Stadium to watch the Nationals play. It was a beautiful summer night, kids were playing in yards and on the sidewalk, people were sitting out on their porches and stoops along East Capitol Street beyond Lincoln Park. I bought a ticket for a seat at field level out on the third base line. I got a beer and a hot dog, and began to make my way to my seat.

About half way down the aisle I realized that it was a mistake. There were just too many people, too much noise, too much everything. I started to panic. I spun around and, feeling like a fish swimming upstream, got back up the aisle as quickly as I could before I went into full panic mode. I could feel my breath shortening and my heart rate quickening.

Back on the concourse, I thought maybe I could work my way through the panic attack—I wanted to try at any rate. I decided to look for empty space rather than just leave. Up was the answer. In those days, the Nationals were probably drawing 10,000 fans per game. Up a little from the bad-old-days of the Expos in Montréal, but still one of the lowest draws in the majors. I figured there would be lots of space upstairs, so I found the ramp and headed up.

RFK stadium was one of those 1970s' all-purpose venues. It hosted football, baseball and soccer, concerts, and big rallies. So there was plenty of room at the top. I climbed until I was high up on the first base side. There were still people around, misanthropes like me, I assumed. How many of those people were as screwed up as I was? There were tons of seats closer to the field, and the ushers were pretty easy about people moving down into most sections. But even way up near the overhang, from where you could barely tell which side was which on the field, there were still a few of us hanging around, lots of seats between us, alone together. The beer guy even came by, but only once in a while. I got my breathing and heart rate under control, and after a while, I stopped shaking. It was a start.

Plan B

A<small>T WORK</small> I <small>LANDED</small> in an office full of introverts, so I felt right at home. There's a joke at the State Department that you can always tell who the extroverts are when you meet them because they'll stare at *your* shoes while they talk to you. I was happy to be in an office full of people who wanted to sit quietly in their offices and be an expert on some aspect of African politics and economics. My principal job was to follow the war in Darfur and Chad, and prepare in-depth analyses for the Secretary and other senior leaders.

I settled in to the job a little, but had made plans for a vacation trip to New Zealand; so in September I headed west. Just before I shut down my phone ahead of take-off from Dulles Airport, I got a text from my boss telling me that I had been selected for promotion in the Foreign Service.

I'm sure my promotion packet looked different than anyone else's in the stack. It would have been filled with letters explaining what I was doing while I was away from the Foreign Service in Afghanistan and Darfur, my two Bronze Star Medal certificates from Afghanistan, and copies of Army Officer Efficiency Reports with big blocks of text blacked out because they were classified. I was number 53 of 53 officers selected that year, but in is in. I asked the flight attendant for a glass of champagne once we reached altitude.

Once I was back from vacation, one of my jobs was to support the President's Special Envoy to Sudan, Andrew Natsios. He worked directly for the President, but sat in an office at the Department.

Natsios's job was to design, coordinate, and implement U.S. policy towards Sudan. It can only be described as a shitty job. The U.S. government's foreign policy apparatus has four big horses: the Departments of State and Defense; the intelligence community, led by the Central Intelligence Agency; and the U.S. Agency for International Development (USAID). In theory, policy is coordinated by the White House—foreign policy in particular through the office of the National Security Advisor. But in fact, U.S. policy on Darfur at that time was a train wreck. Each of the foreign policy agencies had its own agenda and none of the leaders were willing to compromise very much or able to force another to do so.

The State Department was re-building its operational capacity in Sudan. In the years immediately prior to this, State had not staffed the embassy in Khartoum with American officials. The local staff worked in the building, the Americans—including the chief of mission—operated either from Nairobi or Cairo. Once they came back it took a while to get the operation up and running, to build relationships, and get back to normal. Although Secretary of State Powell stepped up and properly denounced what the Sudanese were doing in Darfur as genocide, that still didn't force the hand of the White House or of the other agencies.

Across the river, Secretary Rumsfeld and his staff at the Pentagon were none too keen to get involved in a third ground war in a Muslim nation, especially one in Africa. I was told that the Chairman of the Joints Chiefs had set a strict limit on the number of military officers in Sudan—at five—and was briefed weekly on the situation there. Regardless of what State wanted, Rumsfeld and his team were determined to limit the requirements levied on the Department of Defense. At a public forum held at the U.S. Holocaust Memorial and Museum in August 2013, Michael Gerson, one of President George W. Bush's senior advisors and speechwriters, called the Defense Department's inaction on Darfur "near insubordination."

Job One at the CIA was to capture and kill terrorists. The leadership at Langley took this seriously, of course, and since Osama Bin Laden had lived in Sudan for years, it made sense to talk to the Sudanese. But, this was where things got complicated. The Agency's primary interest in Sudan lay in counter-terrorism operations—it's important to note here that I knew nothing about that side of the mission because I wasn't involved in them, and they were completely stove-piped. To those of us outside that lane, it felt like anything that wasn't directly involved in forwarding the counter-terrorism mission wasn't really important; therefore, Darfur wasn't really important. Cooperation between the U.S. intelligence community and the Sudanese must have been pretty good because *The New York Times* reported that the CIA had flown Salah Gosh, the chief of Sudanese intel, back to the U.S. not long after Colin Powell had stated that the government of Sudan was committing genocide in Darfur. So much for continuity of policy across agencies.

The folks in the U.S. government who had the best relationships with the Sudanese in general were the development and relief experts at USAID. Their individual and organizational experience was based primarily on years of working Operation Lifeline Sudan, a relief operation run out of Uganda that supported the people of South Sudan during the generation-long, brutal and deadly civil war with the north. The good relations USAID officials had with the Sudanese were strictly with the southerners, though. As a matter of fact, once the embassy had been established in Khartoum the chief of mission wanted to consolidate all the staff in that city. But a few USAID officers refused to move from Nairobi. They claimed they wouldn't move to Sudan unless they could live in Juba, the capital of the south.

The White House was supposed to be coordinating all of this, but never seemed able to do so. So Natsios—and his successor, Ambassador Richard Williamson— had to navigate this bureaucratic nightmare. I was their intelligence briefer and liaison to the intelligence community.

Part of Natsios's strategy was to convince the Sudanese that he actually had a plan that could allow them to move forward with the already-agreed Comprehensive Peace Agreement between Khartoum and Juba, continue cooperating with the CIA on counter-terrorism, and yet would force them to stop killing their own citizens in Darfur. He called this "Plan B." In a press briefing in November of 2006, Natsios laid out some deadlines for Sudan to meet, the goal being to allow a larger and more capable peacekeeping force into Darfur. He said that if the Sudanese didn't comply, the U.S. would resort to Plan B. But he didn't explain what Plan B was.

In fact, I was part of Plan B. Andrew asked DoD to send a few U.S. military officers to the Darfur border in Chad. The Defense Intelligence Agency complied, mobilized me for a few months, and sent me and four other officers to Chad. We were to look around, make assessments of the infrastructure—airfields, military bases, road networks, availability of fuel and water, etc.—with an eye to potentially launching a peacekeeping operation, a no-fly zone, or maybe even some sort of combat operation across the border into Darfur. So five U.S. colonels, all Africa specialists, traipsed around eastern Chad for a couple of weeks. One by one, the other colonels all left. I stayed for four months. This was when I was traveling around with the French lieutenant, and John Denver dropped in.

Chad was one of, if not the most, difficult operating environments I'd ever experienced. This was partly because, for most of my time there, I was operating singleton: out by myself, garnering what support I could from the UN or NGO aid workers, or the Chadian Army.

I had a Toyota pick-up truck provided for me by the embassy's defense attaché, and I was using my personal laptop, because the ones from the embassy were all inoperative. I had a mobile and a satellite phone, and a diplomatic passport. It was great in some ways: I could go wherever I needed to whenever I could get there. But it was also pretty depressing being out there alone. I made some friends, including the NGO doctor I started dating. I traveled around the east following up on leads, meeting with Darfurian rebels who came across the border, tracking down reports of fighting along the border, incursions by Sudanese Janjaweit, skirmishes between Chadian Army and rebels, and ethnic violence. I wrote notes on my laptop and sent them to the defense attaché in Ndjamena via my personal Yahoo! account on a UN satellite email system that I waited in line with aid workers to use. This part of the work was a security officer's nightmare. But we got the job done. Eventually, DIA sent me a modified commercial satellite uplink system so I was at least able to stay off the UN's satellite system.

The work and the place were both fascinating. Chad has never really known a peaceful transition of power from one government to another. There is always some conflict brewing across the border in Darfur or the Central African Republic, and everyone in power seems to be related to everyone else in power. To top it off, now there is oil money.

I did about four months there reporting on the war, learning what I could about the Janjaweit, and keeping an eye on the Darfurian rebels who sought to consolidate their forces in and around the refugee camps. I was perhaps the most effective I had ever been at reporting. But in the end, that mission would bring about the end of my career.

Walking the Halls

IN THE SPRING OF 2007 I came back to DC and returned to my office full of introverts. Because I had been promoted, I was made a division chief, overseeing the work of analysts covering East and Central Africa and serving as a deputy to the office director.

Natsios left, Williamson came in. I stayed with some friends I had known since Kosovo and spent time looking at condos downtown.

Before I headed out to Chad, I had dropped off Jack with my friend Mikey and his kids in Florida. Mike and I had known each other for over twenty years since we had served as lieutenants together in the 11th Armored Cavalry Regiment on the inter-German border. He had a 5,000 square foot house, a boat, and a couple of young daughters; so I thought he was a good choice to ask to take Jack while I was in Chad. He agreed, and I dropped Jack off with him just before I flew out.

When I got back I learned that his daughters were so attached to Jack—go figure—that taking him back would have been cruel and unusual. Jack was probably happier in that big house with lots of people than he would have been with me anyway. I bought a two-bedroom condo a twenty-five minute walk from the office and settled in.

I felt like I was ready to start dating. I went out with an Army intelligence officer who was writing a long graduate program paper about Darfur—we met because she wanted to interview me as part of her research. She was cute, blonde, and fourteen years younger than me. It was nice but not right.

I tried Internet dating on Match.com. It's funny how people with similar profiles know each other. Within two weeks, I went on meet-up dates with four women who were friends or who had worked together in politics. Weird. Most of those dates didn't work out, but one was really good. Carole was a Harvard grad who had been in and out of politics and government for twenty years. She was out of government at the time, trying to re-construct an acting career she had dropped to join the Clinton campaign in 1992. It was good. We kept going out.

I was settling down a little, but I wasn't really home. Through all of this I was still struggling. I was on meds and seeing a psychiatrist once in a while. I had episodes where the fear or the sadness was simply overwhelming. Unlike in Afghanistan, when the images of the dead were clear, when I knew what was just over the horizon—at least for a while until the Prozac had kicked in—there was never anything identifiable, just some arbitrary, tortuous fear or sadness pummeling

That fear, as strong as it was, was no more rational than the moments on the train where, every morning, sitting with my bag on my lap, I had shaken uncontrollably, in terror for my life, afraid of some unknown something, some invisible, ethereal vapor—an attack no one else seemed to realize was imminent.

Sometimes just saying the words would be enough: Senik, Racak, Kisangani, Bunia, Muhajeriyah, or Guereda. Sometimes it would be something else, a smell or a sound that would bring it on. Being in a crowd was bad. Even on my meds, sometimes it still came. I could feel it begin right in the center of my chest. It started with a hollow feeling. I could feel my chest tightening and my breath shortening. It would spread out along my arms and up the front of my body. Most times I would try to stop it. I would control my breathing and I'd think through why it might be coming—cognitive therapy. I would flex and stretch to fight the adrenaline. I walked around and looked at other things.

But sometimes I would let it come on, allowing it, no, urging it to come and wash over me, tossing me about, shaking me loose from the moorings of my normal life, the life the Chirpy Bastards could see. I wanted it. I wanted it to take me somewhere. I wanted it to show me what I was afraid of. I would go with it willingly. It had been with me so long that I didn't really fear the sensation. I trusted it. It had been part of me so long it had changed my chemistry like my drug of choice. It was mine. It was me.

So when I would let it just come, it would grow and spread and take over my body as it got stronger. And my hands would shake and I'd lose the sensation of touch and feeling in my fingers. My gut would wrench, and I would cross my arms across my chest and rock back and forth. Then, when I couldn't sit any longer, I would roll into a ball and rock, and feel it laughing at me. Laughing because it—the crazy—knew it was stronger than I would ever be. Laughing because I always thought I could take it but it always won. It always took me further than I wanted to go, but never far enough to show me what was really out there.

Once in a while it would show me some pictures on the big screen. Of course, it always waited until it was fully in control, until it had me shaking and barely breathing and rolled up in a ball, to start the show. And they would always be the same pictures, so I knew what to expect, and that made it worse. The bodies in the well, the butchered family, Senik, the bodies in Podujevo, the Serb with the gun to my head—all the Oscar-winning performances.

But some things were easy. I could get my work done. I knew the players and organizations operating in Darfur and Chad as well as anyone in the U.S. government. Analysts and organizations from across the community invited me to brief them on the war. I was in and out of CIA, DIA, NGA, and NSA regularly. Tactical and biographic analysts envied the data bases I had built while I had been operating in the area. I shared them widely, moving them off the laptop I had used in Darfur and Chad—my personal MacBook—to the classified systems the intelligence community shared.

This was a mistake. There are rules I should have followed

and didn't.

Back in the U.S., and particularly inside the Building as it's called in the State Department, there are rules. Having operated so far and so long outside the low hum of bureaucracy, I had discounted how important some rules were taken to be. I'd transferred unclassified data from one computer network to another, this one a classified network in a quick and efficient, but un-approved method. Maybe I did it more than once. I don't know. It was a simple electronic transaction like sending an email with an attachment. I used a thumb drive given to me in Chad by someone in the defense attaché's office; when I was done with it I gave the thumb drive to some officers at DIA.

One of my regular tasks was to brief senior officials on the war in Darfur. I met the man who had been nominated to become the next U.S. Ambassador to Chad, and spent time talking to him as he prepared for his confirmation hearings. Before he left for post, he selected me to be deputy chief of mission (DCM), his number two at the embassy in N'Djamena.

This changed everything for Carole and me. If we were serious, she would have to go with me—which meant we'd have to be married. If she were going with me, she'd need language training—which meant we'd have to be married. So we decided to take the leap after only having known each other for about nine months. We went to California to spend Passover with her family. After the Seder, we drove up the coast to Big Sur and got married on a deck overlooking the Pacific Ocean. We were deliriously, giddily happy.

Back in DC, she enrolled in French language training. I went to a mandatory training course for DCMs. I was surrounded by senior officers going out to Japan, Poland, Saudi Arabia, and other big, important countries. I was probably the most junior officer in the course.

One afternoon in the middle of class, the course director handed me an envelope. Inside was a note that instructed me to be at an office in the Building the next day at 9:00 a.m. to be interviewed by Diplomatic Security agents.

I went to the interview. I had broken rules regarding the protection of classified information when I transferred the data on the thumbdrive to the network. They asked some questions and I answered them; I thought we were done. In the previous twenty-four-plus years of my service I had never had so much as a security infraction, much less a violation. This sort of thing usually resulted in a minor admonishment or a formal note marking the infraction.

But, two weeks later the phone rang on my desk. The woman on the other end told me my security clearance had been suspended, and that I was to turn in my diplomatic passport and State Department access badge. I could no longer access computers or any classified information.

This is an administrative death sentence to an intelligence officer or a senior foreign affairs officer. I did as I was told, and returned my passport and access badge to the security agents that afternoon. I stopped in at a bar on the walk to the Metro and had a beer. I wondered what I was going to do.

My boss told me to try to stay current on the goings-on in Darfur, but not to bother coming into the office. I couldn't work, no one could share classified information with me, and I would have needed an escort to even walk around in the office. I did some research and learned that these types of cases could take six to seven years to resolve—some took even longer—and for that period the officer was usually stuck in a make-work job with no chance of promotion, no opportunity to do substantive work, not really working at all. In the patois of the Department, this is called "walking the halls."

So I sat at home. With nothing else to occupy my mind, I became paranoid. I spent every day listening for the turn of wheels in the drive, for the knock on the door and the flash of the badge when the security agents came to arrest me.

I was terrified that I would relapse under the stress. My lawyer advised me not to reveal my mental health problems and the consequent memory issues, to the security agents. I couldn't imagine they didn't already know, but in all the interviews, it never came up. It was in my records, so surely, I assumed, they had access to it.

In interview after interview, I couldn't answer their questions. I just didn't remember what they wanted to know, and I didn't have the thumb drive. They brought in a supervisor. I still couldn't resolve their questions.

When, late in the year, a colleague was arrested and admitted to spying for the Cubans, I began to understand their tenacity. They thought they had in me another major case, another big spy. In fact, they had a middle-aged guy with PTSD who couldn't remember a simple electronic transaction: the transfer of a couple of documents from one computer system to another with a thumb drive.

I talked to the lawyers and learned that I could just walk away, and all the pain would end. I discussed it with Carole, and we decided I would retire. I notified the Department and my lawyers that December 31st would be my last day in government service.

But making this decision didn't lower the stress level much. After the initial giddiness had worn off, I was still at home every day with nothing to occupy my mind. The stress of the investigation sent me reeling. I wasn't sleeping enough. I was drinking too much. I started to have the images in my head again.

Carole and I had only been married a few months, and suddenly I was under investigation and at risk of losing my job or maybe going to jail. I know she was worried about me. I didn't go to work, I couldn't. I sat at home every day reading articles on the internet and watching the window for agents coming to arrest me, listening to every car that passed on the street, and fearing it would be the one.

The agents never came, the cars never stopped. But every day I sat, paralyzed by fear, waiting for the knock on the door, imagining the arrest and seizure of assets, visualizing my life crumbling around me.

I wasn't sleeping well, so in the middle of the night I would go upstairs and sit in the dark. Carole would come upstairs in the mornings to find me sitting alone, shaking and crying, terrified of that unknown something out just beyond the perimeter.

Obviously, she knew my history. She worried. "Promise me you won't kill yourself," she said. "Promise me you'll ask for help, that you'll come to me before things get that bad."

"Again," I whispered.

"What?" She asked.

"Before things get that bad, again," I said.

Once I had decided to retire, she took a job on Capitol Hill as communications director for the congressional committee in charge of the Obama inaugural ceremonies.

As the clock ticked down to the inaugural, she couldn't miss work to care for me. So, I got a dog. One of Carole's friends runs a rescue group that drives a van every weekend down to South Carolina to pull dogs out of kill-shelters before they are put to the needle. We picked a dog called Cotton out of the line-up one weekend and brought him home. He was skinny and petrified, but I thought there was something behind the eyes that looked promising. We renamed him Harry.

He had some dings in the flap of his ear—he was said to be half Labrador and half coonhound, so he had some ears—and a couple of scars on his muzzle that the vet said would probably never go away. The woman at the rescue shelter said he had been used as a bait-dog in a dog-fighting ring. I had to do some research to figure out what that meant.

"They use very sweet-natured dogs to train other dogs to fight, because those dogs will not fight back—they're called bait dogs," said Dr. Patricia Latas of the Humane Society in an interview that I had heard on the radio. The humans who run dog-fighting rings tie the good-natured, sweet dogs to poles so they can't escape the attacks of the fighters. Apparently, few bait dogs survive the process. When we heard this, instead of thinking that we had a challenge on our hands, we were immediately suspicious of the gut-grab sell, such as when a humanitarian aid NGO shows a starving kid with big eyes on its ads to get you to donate.

Harry had spent ten months in a shelter before we got him. He needed contact with humans and was deathly afraid of a cage. Hounds are master escape artists. He broke out of every crate we put him in, and twice broke out of our house and through a hole in the fence. After a neighbor brought him home once, we spent a couple thousand dollars replacing the fence—money we were planning to spend on a trip to Paris. The second time he scaled the six-foot fence and went on the lam for five days. On day two, we later figured out, he was hit by a car. The vets who treated him afterwards assured us he was looking for us, not running from us. But it was a traumatic time for him and us. He had $7,000 worth of surgery, repairing all four paws and re-building his shattered ulna.

It wasn't until Harry had been shaved for surgery that we knew the bait-dog stories were true. The puncture and rip scars all over his neck, shoulders, and legs said what he couldn't.

For the next few months, Harry and I sat at home: me waiting for the security agents to come with a warrant for my arrest, and Harry healing and gaining weight. I still wasn't sleeping well, so in the middle of the night if I got up to go upstairs to my office Harry would be right behind me. He would curl up on the floor directly behind my chair, so if I moved he'd know it. During the day he would position himself between me (wherever I was) and the door, doing his best to be my protector and staying in sight of me to help calm him down. It got to the point where Carole started calling him Velcro.

Weeks went by after we got him back, but I couldn't leave him at home. He was still too freaked out to be alone, so he came along with me in the car wherever I went. He owned the back seat of my car. The vet behaviorist said we would probably never be able to leave him alone or let him off leash. But we began to try.

It took four months to get him to the point where I could leave him for an hour. Then, once, I was late, and he panicked. We had to start over: one minute, two minutes, five minutes. We put him on Prozac. Every morning I'd roll a couple of the pills in a ball of cream cheese and give it to him. I'd take my meds right alongside him. Together, slowly, we began to heal.

Carole and I went to a show at The Kennedy Center on New Year's Eve. It ended just before midnight, and we headed home to have a dessert and some champagne. At midnight my retirement from government service became effective. For the first time in twenty-five years, I was unemployed.

The Whole Megillah

HE OLD GUY IN FRONT OF ME was using one of those canes with
four rubber tips at the base as he crept towards the hospital door.
It was the last week of July in Washington DC. The temperature was
at least ninety degrees with intolerably cruel humidity, and he was
wearing a tan golf jacket that, as I passed him, I saw was zipped up
to the neck. It made me feel even hotter just to look at it. At least he
had on a ball cap—one with "World War II Veteran" stitched on the
front—to keep the sun off his head.

Like me, he was carrying a large brown folder. Mine held my
medical records, some service documentation like orders and award
certificates, and notes from my combat deployments. It was my first
visit to the VA hospital.

The Washington VA medical center is as charmless a building
as one could imagine: a big white box in the center of half a dozen
parking lots that are constantly in overflow. In short, it looks like most
big hospitals in any major city. And in many ways, I suppose, it is
like any other hospital: filled with the sick and infirm, health care
and administrative staff scurrying about, bad coffee. But in one very
important way it is entirely different. It is the place where combat
veterans enter the system for treatment of wounds, both physical and
psychological.

Walking in from the parking lot, I started to feel all the familiar sensations: the stress rising in my gut, vision focus narrowed, breathing short and irregular, the memories of five wars and images of the dead hovering just offstage.

Inside the door, there was an information desk with a guy in a wheelchair behind it wearing a DAV piss-cutter cap. He looked me up and down, no doubt making some sort of judgment about me. I couldn't imagine what it might have been. I stammered a bit, explaining that I'd come for my first appointment. My hands were shaking, so I held them down below the edge of the counter. He quietly told me where the registration office was, and pointed the way. Walking through the lobby, I imagined everyone was looking at me, thinking, "Look at the psycho boy, home from the war and broken— what a pussy." I felt like it was my first day in high school, and I was dressed in a bright pink tutu. I took a number and waited.

The waiting room was actually a part of the main lobby, so it was noisy and there were lots of people walking past. I kept my head down until my number was called. Inside the office a woman looked over my paper work—I had brought some of my DD214s, the document that details a veteran's military service showing training, awards and decorations, combat time served, etc.—then she started entering my data into the system. She was perfectly pleasant and did a good job of ignoring my symptoms, until she asked if I wanted to go to the emergency room instead of the green clinic. Maybe I should have.

At my psychological screening, upstairs in the mental health wing, away from the general medical patients, I was interviewed by someone new to the system, maybe a recent Ph.D. graduate, with a more qualified, I assumed, supervisor attending. I had to detail all my problems in full. I started at the beginning in Rwanda, then to Kosovo, then Afghanistan and my treatment there for PTSD, then Iraq, then Darfur and my failed suicide attempt, on and on through the drive to the hospital that morning. Staring at the floor, wringing my hands, I quietly described my memory loss, my unbridled fear and anxiety, my inability to control images of the dead appearing in my head at all hours of the day and night, my weird hyper-vigilance issues. I even included the wholly irrational things like getting lost in my own neighborhood, going to the grocery at midnight because no one else would be there, my anxiety while driving because I couldn't control what that lunatic in the Lexus—what is it with Lexus drivers anyway?—was going to do, and why the hell didn't anyone use turn signals anymore or return their shopping carts to the front of the store instead of leaving them in the middle of the god-damned parking lot. At that point, the supervisor sniggered.

There was an ugly silence in the small room for a few seconds with the only sounds being the air conditioning blowing through the grate in the wall and someone's heels clicking down the hallway outside the closed door. I looked up. The interviewer looked stricken, and her supervisor quickly looked down at her notes.

Shame welled in my throat and my eyes. My humiliation was absolute; even the doctors were laughing at me. Welcome to the VA, psycho boy.

Psychiatric care isn't a one-time shot. You don't just show up, and say, "Hey, doc, I'm a freaking nut-job, can you fix me?" Then get a dose of Prozac and be cured. Frankly, I don't think I'll ever be cured. I don't think I'll ever be fully home. It's a process, everyone says. So, despite my humiliation, I kept going to the VA for treatment. At each visit, and I suppose there were five or six to the main hospital, I was seen by a different doctor or psychologist. I would answer the same questions about my service and the effect it had on me. At every session I had to go into detail about what had happened to me. All the while, I wondered if the doctors couldn't have simply pulled up from their online records the long document I had written when I filed my claim.

I felt like they were trying to get me to recant, or to catch me in a lie. Each time I felt like I was being pushed back a little in my recovery process. The providers always asked questions about whether I had felt my life was in danger, whether or not I had seen dead bodies, or if I had seen friends wounded or killed. The military doctors always used the phrase, "Do you think you are a threat to yourself or others?"

But the VA docs came right out and asked, "Do you have thoughts of suicide?"

In time, I found a therapist I could work with at one of the Vet Centers nearby, and stayed away from the big hospital. There, I was seen quickly, and the social worker was competent—himself a Vietnam combat veteran.

But still, every time I approached the clinic, I could feel the anxiety coming on. My gut wrenched and my breathing sped up. I had panic attacks in the lobby, and was barely able to walk to the elevators. After a while, the panic would start days before the visit. I was going to the clinic for treatment, and for two or three days before the visit, the stress would build. No sleep, fear, wrenched guts. But I kept going.

I also filed a claim with the VA for service-related disability. Like so many other veterans in the system, the adjudication of my claim for benefits was slow in coming. One year to the day after I filed the claim, the Veterans Benefits Agency notified me I could come to a hearing to help determine the validity of my claim. I called as soon as I got the letter and made an appointment.

The day of the hearing I also had a medical treatment appointment at the Vet Center. Even after a year of driving to the clinic for my appointments once every two weeks, I panicked on the way there and got lost. Hours later, at the appointment, I was still a mess. It's called a Compensation and Pension or C&P hearing, but it's held in a consultation room in the hospital and involves a one-on-one conversation with a health provider. As always, I had to explain my entire case to the psychologist. He sat at his desk with a file about four inches thick in front of him. I was in a low chair at desk-side with a lamp shining in my eyes. I had brought notes. I went through them almost line by line, detailing my symptoms—lost sleep, hyper-arousal, quickness to anger, fear, sadness, sense of isolation—the whole megillah. It took about twenty minutes.

As I walked out, I was trembling and felt nauseous. I got to my car and just sat for a few minutes. I couldn't get control of my body or my mind. I was alone in the middle of the parking lot, crying, and staring at my hands shaking in my lap. I looked out the windshield;

the image of the Darfuri boy walking in front of my truck that day five years before flashed in my mind. I could see his stained *thawb*, his dusty brown sandals, his unkempt hair as he tugged on the rope to pull his camel along. I looked onto the seat beside me, fully expecting to see the pistol. A sound came out of my mouth like I had just let slip a lifeline that would pull me out of quicksand, and my gut wrenched.

Three months later, I received a letter from the VA. "Dear Mr. Capps, We've made a decision on your claim for benefits..." I was officially a combat disabled veteran.

Writing My Way Home

THE STREETS WEREN'T VERY CROWDED. It was late fall, getting on to winter in DC. I was on my way home from a graduate writing workshop. Things had gone well in the class. The week before, I had circulated among my classmates and the instructor a snippet of what would become this book, and that night I had received mostly positive feedback with a few really insightful comments on how to improve the piece.

I was nearly finished with a dual concentration degree program—studying fiction and non-fiction writing. I had reached that point in any program where you can begin to see the end and wonder what comes next.

As I was navigating through Northwest DC, dodging taxis, pedestrians, and ninety-pound, Pilates-sculpted housewives from Potomac driving 4,000-pound SUVs, I wondered what I would do with my new education. I was using VA benefits—for the record, that part of my experience with the VA was pretty painless—and I have to admit I felt a little guilty about getting to go to school mostly for free on the taxpayers' dime. I felt like I needed to be able to demonstrate the value of the investment the taxpayers had made in me.

At about the same time, a story came out in *The Baltimore Sun* that went viral among the veterans' community. A young Iraq infantry veteran had been tossed out of a local community college because of an essay in which he wrote that war, particularly killing in a war, was a drug and that he was addicted to it. Charles Whittington had been encouraged to write about his experience by his English composition instructor. He turned in his essay, received an A, and it eventually wound up in the campus newspaper.

What Whittington wrote, especially in a post-Virginia Tech (and pre-Newtown) massacre world, scared the hell out of people. Students, faculty, administrators and staff apparently worried that there was some psycho vet addicted to killing running loose on campus. The administration demanded that Whittington undergo a psychological screening and barred him from campus until the results were in.

In my view, the college administration had failed the young veteran. But I also thought that the community of veterans and, more broadly, the community he lived in had failed him as well. I had just a few weeks earlier been given a copy of Jonathan Shay's *Achilles in Vietnam*. Shay is a psychiatrist, now retired from the VA hospital in Boston where he treated patients, many of whom were Vietnam veterans, for over thirty years. In his book, Shay compares the actions of Achilles and others in Homer's *Iliad* to the situation of many of the veterans he has treated. He also writes about how the Greeks revered their returning warriors, in contrast to how America treated (and treats) its returning veterans.

I guess I had just read the part about how Greek warriors were required to speak in public in order to communalize their combat experience among the citizens who had sent them to war. Shay wrote:

Any blow in life will have longer-lasting and more serious consequences if there is no opportunity to communalize it. This means some form of social ceremony and informal telling of the story with feeling to socially-connected others who do not let the survivor go through it alone.

By the time I got home from class, I had the germ of an idea. I would try to give other veterans the skills and confidence they needed to tell their own stories as a way of communalizing their experience among the 99% of Americans who had sat out the wars in Afghanistan and Iraq. In the process, I would pay back the taxpayers by giving away (thus communalizing) what I had learned in school on their dime. I spent some time over the holidays thinking about it, talked to a bunch of people, and in early 2011, I created the Veterans Writing Project.

I knew after reading about Charles Whittington's experience in college that I wanted to work with student veterans returning from the wars. So I wrote a letter to each of the five big universities in Washington, DC—Georgetown, George Washington, American, Catholic, and Howard— in which I told them that they had a problem that they were likely unprepared to deal with, and how I could be of help to them. In retrospect, this was both foolish and a bit audacious. No one likes to be told they are doing their job poorly, especially by someone who has pretty much zero experience in the field. Not surprisingly, none of the universities bothered responding.

But a couple of months after I had written the letters, I received an email from the Veterans' Services Office at George Washington University inviting me to a meeting. I met with the university's veterans' service staff, and bluffed my way into their agreeing to sponsor the VWP for one set of seminars on campus that summer. We called them the "Open Seminars" as they were open to any veteran, any service member, or any military or veteran's family member.

Classes were to begin in four weeks. I had bupkis: no curriculum, no syllabus, no students. I decided the most important step at that point was to develop some sort of a curriculum; the rest would logically follow, I presumed. I convinced the director of my graduate program to give me a semester's credit through an individual study program to create a curriculum for the seminars. I asked several of my instructors to help, and one was actually assigned to oversee the project.

I had a rough outline completed by the time the first seminar rolled around. The university and I jointly had corralled eight participants. For the next thirteen weeks I furiously wrote chapters in the curriculum: sending them by email up to my advisor, then presenting each chapter, as it was completed, to the participants— whose numbers waxed and waned throughout the summer—then editing and excising as sections succeeded or failed. By the end of the semester, I had a tested curriculum. I called it *Writing War: A Guide to Telling Your Own Story*.

I began recruiting others to help me. I made a specific decision that all of our instructors would meet three strict criteria: working writer, graduate of an MA or MFA program, combat veteran. I quickly found two other veterans who met these requirements: an Air National Guard Chief Master Sergeant, and a former Marine corporal. I recruited a Board of Directors that included a Vietnam veteran with thirty years of Washington DC political journalism and a couple of books behind him; a former president of the Society of American Military Psychiatrists, who was a veteran with seven or eight published books as well; an accountant who was also a Vietnam vet; a couple of political communications professionals who were military family members; and a Naval Academy graduate who had served under Admiral Zumwalt in Vietnam, and had helped raise the funds for the Navy Memorial in Washington.

In September, I entered the thesis phase of grad school. I turned in 150 pages of writing, about half of which were comprised of non-fiction essays that have since become chapters in this book; the other half was fiction, the opening of a novel that takes place in 1916 in The Sudan. I also had meetings with administrators from George Washington University. The university was making a significant investment in student veterans and was interested in continuing our relationship, even assigning sponsorship of the seminars to the director of the University Writing Program instead of the Veterans Services Office. The writing program director agreed to sponsor a set of seminars each semester and to work towards the creation of a permanent home for the VWP as part of a Center for Writing and the Military at GWU.

Our model evolved a bit. I wrote the curriculum so that it could be taught over a fourteen-week college semester and allow the participants to workshop their writing among their classmates—like many other writing programs. But it would also be possible to teach the seminars over a weekend, albeit without the workshopping. That's the model we began to use at GWU and it became our standard. In time, we were running seminars outside the DC area in North Carolina, New York, Pennsylvania, Iowa, and Kentucky.

Just about the time that the first semester test program was finishing up, I received an email from a senior official at the National Endowment for the Arts, who wrote that he had heard about the program I had developed at GWU and was interested to know if I would help them develop a program for working with wounded service members at Walter Reed National Military Medical Center.

I went to the NEA and discussed the project with some of their leaders. I agreed to help create a curriculum for the program called Operation Homecoming, which would take place in a newly created facility on the campus of Walter Reed called the National Intrepid Center of Excellence (NICoE). It is DoD's premier research and treatment facility for PTSD and Traumatic Brain Injury. The instructors for Operation Homecoming would all come from the VWP.

In developing the NEA curriculum I did some in-depth research on therapeutic writing. The guru of this work is Dr. James Pennebaker, a researcher from the University of Texas. Pennebaker met with us as I was developing the curriculum and clarified for us some of his research. He also gave us some course corrections. I spoke with Dr. Jonathan Shay (*Achilles in Vietnam* and *Odysseus in America*), a MacArthur grant recipient, to help choose scenes from *The Iliad* to use as prompts in the class. I also spoke to Dr. Robert Spolsky from Stanford, another MacArthur grant recipient, to hone the language we used in our script.

Since none of our instructors was a clinician, we worked alongside therapists who were in place to take over if any of the service members needed an intervention. At first it was a challenge working with others dealing with PTSD. So many of the (almost entirely) men who came through the program were survivors of much worse than anything I had ever gone through. But I could see that many of them had the same symptoms that I was (and still am) trying to control. For me, that one afternoon a week teaching at NICoE became the best day of the week.

Most teachers I know will tell you that they learn from their students as much as the students learn from them. If there was one thing I learned in the NICoE classes it was that the idea of a moral injury is real. Brett Litz, a psychologist working at the VA hospital in Boston, defines a moral injury as one that stems from "perpetrating, failing to prevent, bearing witness to, or learning about acts that transgress deeply held moral beliefs and expectations."

Much of Shay's work circles back to this idea as well, that things happen in war that are so antithetical to our core beliefs that survivors cannot reconcile actions seen, committed, or left undone with the person they had been and the beliefs they had held before the war.

I wrote about moral injury for *TIME* Magazine in September, 2011:

> ...*it might help to think of morality in wartime as operating within both the laws of war and the rules of honor, integrity, and morality that are ingrained in each of us as a member of society and within our specific culture. If a soldier were to commit an atrocity, that would break both the legal and the moral or spiritual rules. International tribunals and courts-martial help to sort out the former, but what about the latter? And what about actions that don't rise to the level of atrocities? Actions an individual soldier commits, or in some cases actions a soldier might not take, seem to be at the core of this phenomenon. Some of us have been taught that killing is never acceptable. Much of this type of thought springs from a theological fount, and many have sought status as a conscientious objector to avoid direct combat roles during wartime. But others, including those who might not share a strict interpretation of the sixth commandment, might feel an extreme sense of guilt at having killed in wartime. This is where we start to get into the realm of moral injury.*

I've felt for years that my PTSD is as much, if not more, based on things left undone—lives I feel I might have saved—as anything I had seen or done. Because of my work at Walter Reed working with and speaking to so many other veterans suffering from PTSD, I'm convinced of the existence of moral injuries and our need for a better understanding and treatment of them. Our work in the VWP focuses on two outcomes. The first is to give veterans (and, of course, their family members) the tools to make sense of what has happened to them. Consider this quote from WWI British nurse and poet Vera Brittain in her book *Testament of Youth:*

> *Only, I felt, by some such attempt to write history in terms of personal life could I rescue something that might be of value, some element of truth and hope and usefulness, from the smashing up of my own youth by the war.*

Writing helps us make sense of what has happened to us. It gives us the skill to shape our stories. But what do we do with them then?

Our second goal is to help our participants bear witness. Consider this: from a Memorial Day speech given by Oliver Wendell Holmes:

> *The generation that carried on the war has been set apart by its experience. In our youth our hearts were touched with fire. It was given to us to learn that life is a profound and passionate thing. While we are permitted to scorn nothing but indifference, we have seen with our own eyes, and it is for us to bear the report to those who come after us.*

We stress to our participants that, by selecting writing as a medium, they have chosen to write their story, or at least a story. And by doing so, they are bearing witness. Even if the only objective is to put the story away in a closet for the grandkids to read at some later date, it is bearing witness. Putting the story out into the public eye through publication is a way of further bearing witness, and this act alone adds the author to a long line of writers who have written about personal and societal trauma in war.

Bearing witness is an important way by which veterans can not only remain connected to service and other veterans, but can also continue to reach an audience and possibly develop new circles of friends. Isolation, whether physical or emotional, is a significant issue for returning veterans. Imagine serving in combat with a small group of men and women, and then watching that group dissolve on return to the U.S. The absence of proximity to comrades, the lack of a sense of mission, and the diminished level of adrenaline-producing activity can all be partially addressed by bearing witness.

Encouraging veterans to bear witness by publicly telling their stories gives them a mission. It can reinforce the idea that they remain a part of the war. It might give them a voice in exposing the shortcomings or folly of a certain policy. Or, in a post-war environment, it may offer them a chance to memorialize the effort, to provide clarity and understanding. Warriors are patriots. Leaving service, whether by choice or because of wounds or injuries, is traumatic in itself. Staying engaged or re-engaging can help to assuage feelings of guilt or abandonment.

This is difficult work. It challenges the participant to confront painful and disturbing memories. It is sometimes traumatic in itself to open these memories up and re-live them. But it is important to do so. Consider these few lines from Siegfried Sassoon's poem "Remorse":

> *Remembering how he saw those Germans run,*
> *Screaming for mercy among the stumps of trees:*
> *Green-faced, they dodged and darted: there was one*
> *Livid with terror, clutching at his knees...*
> *Our chaps were sticking 'em like pigs... "Oh hell!"*
> *He thought—"there's things in war one dare not tell*
> *Poor father sitting safe at home, who reads*
> *Of dying heroes and their deathless deeds."*

Sassoon is clearly addressing the divide between the soldier in the field and those sitting safely at home. But he is also getting at something more, the idea of moral injury. The things that poor father sitting safe at home most needs to know are the things that keep the warrior up at night in remorse and guilt, fear and unforgetting. These are the things that non-combatants most need to understand through our bearing witness, and that warriors need to forgive themselves for by understanding them. These actions and the horrific memories, remorse and anxiety that follow, are part of the human cost of war.

Epilogue

Ever tried. Ever failed. No matter. Try again.
Fail again. Fail better.

SAMUEL BECKET
"Westward Ho"

Forgive and Forget

As Kurt Vonnegut wrote in *Slaughterhouse-Five*, "And so it goes." The ritual is the same every morning: head downstairs, push the button on the coffee maker, let the dogs out, turn on the radio to get the news, head back to the kitchen for my meds. I keep the bottles lined up on top of the microwave. Off come the tops, one by one, and out come the pills: the oblong white one; the white ovoid; the yellow and white capsule; the round white disk; the little pink one—a sip of water, and down the hatch.

This new cocktail of drugs seems to be working better than the last. My psychiatrist is even making noises about reducing some of the dosages. I've been on some of these for seven years now, so it's about time. All the ones I've tried that failed are arranged on my desk upstairs. You can tell which insurance plan I was on by the pharmacy labels. The cheapies from the VA stand out as well: brown bottle, yellow top = VA. They didn't seem to help much, so the bottles are still pretty full.

I'm getting better, but I'm not safe at home yet. The monsters are still out there. I've shaken, and cried, and embarrassed my wife and myself because I've been simply terrified of some unknown something coming over the hill. I've been too scared to go out to a movie. I had to leave Dodger Stadium on a beautiful afternoon because I couldn't control the shaking and fear that enveloped me like a parachute collapsing on a jumper.

The crying and fear and shaking are still here. They are closer to the skin than blood to a razor. I've stopped counting how many times I've poured too much alcohol into myself and forgotten to take my prescribed medication—the stuff that says on the label, "Do Not Drink Alcohol While Taking This Medication."

It's a process, everyone says. I haven't felt the urge to pick up that pistol and drive alone out into the desert again. But I suppose I'll always worry about something coming out of the shadows and pulling me back there.

I started writing what would become this book while I was still in Kosovo. I remember sitting down with my laptop at a little table in my room in Pristina after the bombing campaign and typing the words, *Yellow. Their skin was yellow. They had dirt under their fingernails and their feet were dirty.* I remember that night specifically. It was the first time I let my guard down about how messed up I was, because of what I had been a part of, and had witnessed first-hand.

One of my colleagues, our team's financial management officer, came by my room to ask me something, and sat down to have a drink. He had joined the team after the bombing campaign, and somehow we got onto what things had been like on the team in the early days of the war. I told him about that day in Senik. He left embarrassed half an hour later because I was crying and unable to get control of myself. It was the last time I let myself go like that publicly, because I knew that if I did, word would get out that I was broken, and I would be sent home.

That was in 1999, and I was already screwed up then. When I gave this manuscript to my publisher in the fall of 2013, I was still trying to get better. In the interim I wrote nearly every day: sometimes a crisp, dry piece for work; sometimes a messy, stream-of-consciousness freakout; sometimes a revision.

In Afghanistan, in 2002, and despite how messed up I was, I started working on the chapter about Podujevo. What I wrote then as a post-script to that story is as much a meditation on memory as a snapshot of that place and time. It fits better here than at the end of that chapter:

I didn't solve the mysteries. Maybe someone has in the years since. The war crimes tribunal continues to indict both Serbs and Albanians for war crimes and crimes against humanity. As I write this, it is over four years later. I have moved from Kosovo to Rwanda, to Washington, and now to Afghanistan. I started writing this piece in Afghanistan after I awoke in the middle of the night with an image of the body in the second house in my head. I don't often dream of Kosovo, so I took the dream as a sign that it was time to start writing again.

I finished the first draft a few days later on the same day I received an email from one of my colleagues, a young Kosovar who had been my translator for months during the war, who was enrolled in college in the U.S.

"Our friend Fatmir was indicted by the tribunal," he wrote. Fatmir had nothing to do with the killing of those people in Podujevo, but it makes me feel that perhaps some of the crimes of Kosovo will be solved.

I can easily recall much of what happened while I was in Kosovo. My memory is also well supported by my notes and by emails I had written home. Most of what happened on that wet morning is clear, and I assume it will remain a part of me forever. But I have a very unfocused memory of the bedroom where the last body lay (and even later, at home, I found that some of my notes from that room are useless scribbles). I can summon a memory of the floor being wet and littered with broken red tiles. I remember the figure 4 formed by the victim's legs. When I try, I can bring up flashbulb images of the walls and of a large bed, beside which lay the body. But I am, in fact, not confident of those memories. The first house and the outbuilding: yes, those memories are clear and I am certain of them. I remember the last house. I remember walking to it. But I wonder if I am imagining more.

I didn't cry during my first year in Kosovo. I often think about the not crying and wonder if I should have—or more properly, if I needed to. I have cried since. I don't know if I cry for the dead or just because I didn't then. In Kosovo, I mostly just looked and listened. I took notes and walked away. That day, Mimi and I and our guide got into our truck and drove back to Podujevo and had coffee. Our guide talked about the politics of the city and I took notes so I could write a second report about that when we returned to our office that evening.

I remember putting my arm lightly around Mimi's shoulders as we left the compound and asking her if she was all right. She confidently said she was. I guessed that if she was all right, then I was supposed to be all right, too. So I was; I was all right. I said I was all right, and I was all right, for a short while at least.

Mimi was eighteen at the time. She was fearless. I tried to be, but I wasn't. I remember her because I want to. I want to remember her courage and her loyalty. She had been with me in Senik, too. I want to remember her being all right.

But as much as I want to remember Mimi, I want to forget some things we did and saw together—some of the awful memories. I know it is important that society have and keep a memory of these things. It's important to remember who was killed. Not just that some people died, but who was killed and when and how and why they were killed—especially if we never learn by whom. We have a collective memory of the horrors of wars. We all recognize words like Srebrenica and Auschwitz as code words for horror. But they are code for collective memories of collective horrors. We don't necessarily remember the specific individual horrors of war even though we remember the Hiroshimas. We must have a memory of the smells and the sight of the bodies and the look on that girl's face as she fought her anguish. Someone has to remember these things. It's important that we, our society, have these personal memories. But sometimes I wish they weren't mine.

But they are mine, and they stay with me, and they keep coming back. Not every day, but often enough that I want them to stop. Most times when they come, I can clench my teeth and turn the music in my headphones up loud and make myself think of something else. I can usually walk away from them as easily as I do from a project on my laptop. But sometimes I cannot walk far enough to get these filthy pictures out of my head. When I can't, my hands shake. I lay my head in them and rub my eyes and run my hands across the top of my thinning hair. I shudder in a warm room. My stomach twists and knots in a visceral reaction.

I write in hope that by writing down these memories I can give them away like a penitent in a confessional. Maybe if I can confess my memories to someone I can be absolved of them. Maybe if I can give the memories away or at least share them, they won't be so awful. Maybe they'll only be bad. Bad would be ok. Bad would be all right. But I haven't yet been able to give them away. They stay with me in a cruel validation of the aphorism that no good deed goes unpunished. So if I'm stuck with them, I guess the best I can hope for is that they only come back when I want them to—only when I need them. I will need them someday. I'll need them when someone says these things don't or didn't happen. I'll know they did and they do. So, for now, when the pictures come back to me uninvited, I take a deep breath and I try to be *All Right*.

Each week, in the graduate writing program at Johns Hopkins, I would bring some short piece of writing about my experience in Kosovo or Darfur to class and my fellow students would critique it in workshop. I know several of them found the writing disturbing: all stream of consciousness, profanity-laced, filled with violent images and descriptions of my collapse. But one classmate suggested I craft an essay about one aspect of my story for a magazine she edited. It would run in July, a traditional time for non-military themed magazines to place patriotic or other military themed articles. We had about nine months and used all of it.

Over a few weeks, I pulled together about a thousand words

detailing my collapse and the bureaucratic framework surrounding it. For the first time, I admitted openly my flirtation with suicide. I even joked about it a little. I wrote about the contradictions inherent in the military medical system: that doctors have divided loyalties, owing privilege to patient conversations, but at the same time owing equal responsibility to the service to protect interests and security and operational effectiveness. I wrote about service members' anxiety over asking for help because they fear ridicule, loss of position and potential for promotion, or being charged with cowardice—and yes, that has actually happened. But, mostly I wrote about my own collapse.

Putting the words onto the page was hard enough, but sending those words out for publication was terrifying. It meant publicly admitting what I had tried to hide for so many years: that my mind was broken. To hell with it, I thought. I've lost my career, my twenty-year marriage fell apart, I've moved on to a new life. Let's air the laundry of the old and start anew; maybe I can help someone else in doing so.

So I did. I laid it out in the same language I had used in all those reports: crisp, dry accounts of the moral failures of an individual, but also of the government. Then I waited. With every piece of professional writing there is editing and some back and forth with the editor. This is especially true for a peer-reviewed health policy journal. I was fascinated by the idea that these editors were trying to find peers to review my essay. How many others were there with a story like mine? Few, I supposed. But in time and after several rounds of editing, the journal hit the stands. I was out.

The Washington Post and NPR had first dibs on interviews and a review of the essay itself. *The Post* was kind, complimentary even. Reading an excerpt from the essay into a microphone at the NPR studios was a struggle. Keeping the emotion out of my voice—not breaking down into tears—took a few takes. Afterwards, I rode the train home, shaking and struggling not to collapse into a ball of goo on the floor.

The reaction of my friends and colleagues was most surprising, particularly that of the colleagues from Darfur where I had nearly taken my life. "I never knew," was the phrase I heard most often. 'How could you not have?' was what ran through my mind in response. Surprisingly, none of my friends or colleagues from Afghanistan ever commented on the piece. Maybe it's because they aren't NPR listeners or don't read health policy journals and just don't know. Maybe it's because they're embarrassed that one of their own had broken so easily.

Once that story was out, I kept writing. I published mostly policy commentary for *TIME, Foreign Policy,* and *The American Interest.* But I was also writing this book. I published essays that became the chapters "Yellow" and "The French Lieutenant's iPod" in literary reviews.

I wrote what I remembered. I wrote because it helped me control the memories. I wrote because it helped me understand.

This book is what I remember. It is what I found in those metaphorical boxes I had stuffed under the bed—the things that came out once those boxes were rattled in Afghanistan.

It's what I found in my notebooks from Kosovo, from Central Africa, from Afghanistan, Iraq, and Darfur that I had stuffed in a plastic bin in the back of a closet. I wrote mostly from memory, picking out moments from each major deployment that stuck with me or haunted my dreams. But I used notebooks from my deployments to confirm details. Scribbled inside are the names and places and times and dates and numbers I needed to remember for my reporting from the field.

I read the notebooks as if I were a researcher filling gaps in an oral history. I wrote what I remembered, and then pored over the journals to confirm or refute what I remembered and had written in the first draft. Sometimes I had remembered that an event took place in one village, when in fact it had occurred some place else. I had forgotten the names of some villages, of some people. I used the notebooks to correct those gaps. I also emailed friends and colleagues with specific questions. Most were helpful, while some ignored the questions.

Digging through the notebooks and asking colleagues what they remembered was part of the revision process. Revising an essay or chapter is one thing, but I can't edit what's in my head. There really is nothing like Alexander Pope's line, "the eternal sunshine of the spotless mind." There is no forgetting, no changing the past. Not yet, anyway.

Besides, I don't want to forget. I want to remember, but I want to be in control of the memories, which is something I have been unable to do for years. I'm still living in my own private Idaho in some ways because I don't yet have full control over my mind. I have a sign in my office about either controlling the story or allowing the story to control you that might as easily be applied to one's memory as story. Some days the fight ends in a draw, but I feel as though I'm winning more and more often. Writing is the most effective tool I've found to help get the memories under control.

At times I thought of trashing this project. Putting all the files under the physical bed, or in the real attic, and moving on. I have at times seen this book as my confession of weakness and cowardice. Not the cowardice where one turns and runs in the face of a determined enemy onslaught. That kind is understandable, to me anyway. No, mine is moral cowardice: failing to take action to protect the survivors in Senik; fighting harder to get into Racak; being complacent about injustice and hatred, about humiliation and dishonor, about murder and rape. It has seemed to me at times that it was the mere memory of ten years of failure, of weakness, of all the dead I did not save, that broke my mind. Were I more religious, I would call these sins of ommission rather than sins of commission.

Through it all, the sane part of me wondered why would I want to expose my weakness, my failures. The crazy part urged me on at night, whispering: "Keep writing."

I think a lot about what I did in these wars and what more I might have done. Maybe I did all I could, all that I was capable of doing. Maybe not.

Could I have stopped the killing of over a hundred thousand

Hutus in Zaire in 1996? No.

Could I have convinced the United States government to intervene politically or militarily to do so? No.

In point of fact, I tried and failed. Standing on the roof of an Entebbe airport building, fuming and cursing the general and his bosses all the way up the chain to President Clinton, I should have learned to keep my role and my place in perspective. But I didn't. For whatever reason, that failure seemed very personal to me. I believed I had failed the refugees through my fecklessness, my inability to convince a major general to deploy his troops into a sovereign nation in the grip of a civil war that would become what many now refer to as Africa's World War.

I wanted to be the man. I wanted to be the guy who found a hundred thousand people that the satellites and surveillance aircraft couldn't. Maybe I was. My partner and I put that video in front of the general. But I was greedy. I also wanted my nation to fly to their rescue, to wrap the American eagle's wing around them as protection, to ride to the rescue like the cavalry. They didn't. "It's the UN's problem now," the general said.

Could I have stopped the ethnic cleansing in Kosovo? No.

Could I have prevented the killing of forty-five innocent Kosovars at Racak? Maybe.

There was a myth among my colleagues at the Department of State that I was the first observer into Racak, that I had discovered the bodies. I heard someone repeat this even as recently as June 2009. I usually tried to correct the record, but that time I let it go. I didn't feel up to going into the story. To do so would be to have to explain how I felt about not trying harder to get into the village on the first day. It would have meant admitting that I didn't do everything I could have. It would have meant admitting that I am in some way culpable for those deaths.

It's hard to explain why I feel this way. When I think about Racak, I try to accept that I could not have stopped the killing. I now realize that my boss in Belgrade was right. I know these things intellectually. But it is hard to understand them emotionally. It's hard to understand why these things happen. I know how they happen. I know intellectually how societies are motivated to pit one ethnic group against another. I know how people's minds can be manipulated to dehumanize an entire group of people. I've seen enough of these things that I can explain the steps involved in a coldly rational way. But I can't explain what in human nature allows a group of men to take another group of men away from their families and their warm houses up to a frozen hilltop and shoot them dead.

It's hard to explain evil.

Richard Holbrooke's book on the former Yugoslavia is titled *To Stop a War*. Holbrooke was a larger-than-life figure. He was twice an ambassador—to Germany and at the United Nations—and twice an Assistant Secretary of State —for Asia and Europe. I served as Holbrooke's driver a few times in Kosovo. He was there to stop a war. I was a junior officer on my second assignment in the Foreign Service. I was there to pretty much do what I was told. Is it folly to think I could have done much more than I did? Even looking back I think not. I suppose in the end it's a question of scale.

Could I have stopped the genocide in Darfur? Of course not. But I did help keep one village from being destroyed. I may have saved some lives there, so I guess I got better at this work as I went along. I was certainly less fearful of taking some sort of action in Darfur than I had been in Kosovo or Zaire. If I were to judge myself on the ability to stop a war or an act of genocide, I would fail. But if I were to judge myself on finding a way to keep one village from being destroyed, I might pass, or at least fail better.

In 1998, just before I had deployed to Kosovo, I met a man in Montreal who helped me grasp how important one small action can be. At the time, I was a consul working in the non-immigrant visa section of the American Consulate in Montréal. He appeared at the window applying for a visitor's visa to the U.S.

"What is the purpose of your travel to the United States?" I asked the man, only cursorily looking up to confirm that the face at the window matched the face in the passport picture.

"I have an interview at the United Nations," he said. "A job interview," he quickly added, handing me a letter from the United Nations inviting him to a job interview in two weeks. It looked official.

"Do you have any family here with you in Canada?" I asked.

"Yes, my wife and six children are here," he said.

Well, that's something, I remember thinking.

"Do they like it here?"

"Yes, but they would rather be somewhere warm."

Somewhere like Florida, perhaps, I thought.

"When was the last time you were in the C.A.R.?"

"Oh, it has been five years. I've been here since I began my studies," he said.

I had been there the year before, in 1996, when the army of the Central African Republic had mutinied after too many months of not being paid. The American ambassador had ordered all non-essential Americans out of the country and I had flown in on a Marine aircraft to help run the evacuation. In about ten days the expatriate population of the small country had dropped by ninety percent as the French and American militaries conducted what the military calls an NEO: a Non-Combatant Evacuation Operation.

"I was there in May, last year," I said.

"Oh, that was a very dangerous time," he said. Vincent was his name. "My children were there then."

"So what were your kids doing in Bangui during the mutiny?"

"Oh, well, you see, until then they were living there. It is so much cheaper for them to go to school there. Plus, it is very cold here," he replied.

"Did they have any problems during the fighting?"

"Yes, sadly, our house was looted and they had to be evacuated," he looked a little wistful.

Suddenly, it dawned on me. Those kids I loaded in the aircraft and evacuated to Canada, they were Vincent's kids.

"How many kids do you have," I asked glancing at his application, "and how old are they?"

"Six." He pulled a picture of them out of his wallet showing them all sitting around a Christmas tree.

I told my colleague in the booth I would be back in a second. I slipped out the door and pulled Vincent over to a bench in the waiting room.

"I evacuated your kids out of Bangui."

He was as shocked as I was. He told me how the Canadian ambassador had called him from Yaoundé and let him and their mother speak to all of the kids. They'd arrived in Montreal a couple of weeks later and, aside from the cold, had adjusted well.

Vincent got his visa. He went to New York and got his job as an agricultural economist with the United Nations. A few weeks later, he brought the kids by the consulate. The kids looked great and had no idea who I was, although the older kids remembered an American at the airport. At least they said they did.

I've lost track of Vincent now, but I hope he and his family are all some place safe and warm.

They say time heals all wounds. I know it's even beyond cliché to say that, and I don't really believe it. If it were true, the Hatfields and McCoys wouldn't still be feuding in West Virginia. Or Darfurians would only need the *ridah*, the calming. There would be no *diyah*, no restitution for a crime. One would simply let time wash the memories like a bloody bandage, fading the stains from crimson to pink to white.

For me, time has passed and some memories have faded. Some of the images have changed. I can't remember the grieving father's face from Senik. I can't remember details of the woman who wanted me to evacuate her son. I wonder if, having smothered so much for so long of what I'd felt then—confusion, fear, revulsion, anger—I can no longer remember those faces because I have subconsciously suppressed the images. Or maybe those images, those people, have become spectral, symbols representing events and actions that are, in my mind, larger than life.

If so, then those memories are like actors in a morality play, one seen clearly but remembered only in fits and starts. They inhabit a dusky netherworld of fear and ambiguity. They exist to remind me of my fears and my failures. And they remain the central characters in these acts of war.

But some memories of Senik—the sticky, sweet smell of blood and wounds, and the sounds of the picks and shovels attacking the rocky ground—have become a permanent part of my memory. The image of the women's bodies on the trailer, the yellow pallor of their skin, the crimson of the blood staining the white bandages, the blue of the UN tarp, stubbornly clings to the rim of my memory. The weary disdain so evident on the old man's face and the bright reds and oranges of the scarf covering what remained of that young woman's head, these are mine for life.

I wonder sometimes if those people remember that an American diplomat had abandoned them? I suppose they remember that the Red Cross and the United Nations did not abandon them, and that UN and Red Cross workers came to take them to safety. Maybe the woman who pushed her child at me that day remembers. Maybe the old man, shot or wounded by shrapnel, remembers. If he survived, that is.

I wonder if they can forgive. Is it in them to forgive my ignorance and my cowardice? I wonder if it is in me to forgive myself. I haven't yet.

As pieces of this book have been published, read and reviewed, readers, friends, editors, and commentators have taken note of my use of the word cowardice. "Don't be so hard on yourself," one said. "It's more fearfulness than cowardice," said another.

Lord Moran's classic treatise on the psychological effects of war, *The Anatomy of Courage*, devotes an entire chapter to cowardice. Moran writes that the Army Act's (the early 20th Century British version of the Uniform Code of Military Justice) definition of a coward is "someone who displays an unsoldier-like regard for his personal safety in the presence of the enemy by shamefully abandoning his post or laying down his arms." This seems reasonable to me.

The Uniform Code of Military Justice explains that cowardice is "misbehavior motivated by fear," and further that the offense of cowardice is, "Refusal or abandonment of a performance of duty before or in the presence of the enemy, as a result of fear..." When the Taliban fired rockets at our base in Afghanistan, I didn't fall apart. I got up, grabbed my weapon, and went to where I had been instructed to be. When the thug in Recane held his pistol against my head, I didn't piss my pants. I waited for an opportunity to act, and I did. When the lady tried to hand me her child, I told her I couldn't take it because the rules of our mission wouldn't allow it. I was afraid I would be sent home and our mission might lose its status if I had. I failed to act because of fear—but the only enemies present were my ignorance and anxiety; we weren't at war.

So maybe my actions that day in Senik don't meet the official definition of cowardice; it's not cowardice to work within the rules of my mission. But it's certainly not courageous to hide behind the skirts of diplomatic bureaucracy.

I've thought a lot about those guys with the pistols outside Recane. They were bullies. They wanted to feel big. I suspect they did. They scared a couple of diplomats and a Kosovar woman. And, even though the bombs didn't fall until a few months later, they eventually did. I doubt that village was hit, because most of the bombs actually were aimed at Serbia proper rather than Kosovo. Maybe I should have felt big after the bombing campaign. But I didn't. I felt we had failed in our mission to stop the violence. Realistically, I now know that it wasn't possible. But that has taken me a while to understand.

The wars in Afghanistan and Iraq were so big and my role was so small that it's hard to even consider what more I might have done. I do wonder, though, had I been stronger, smarter, more competent, whether Habibullah and Dilawar might still be alive. I don't know. I failed, the system failed, they died.

By the time I got to Darfur, I was pretty broken. At the end of my two tours there, I knew I was finished. I knew that day in Chad with the French lieutenant that I was done. I knew when that peacekeeper pulled the gendarme's body up onto his knee so I could shoot a picture that, undoubtedly, I'd seen enough, probably too much. I wrote then that I sometimes felt like I was still in all those other places, in all those other wars. Or that maybe all those other places and all those others wars were still in me. I didn't know then; I still don't now.

What I do know is that the killing and dying go on. I probably have written five hundred thousand words about the root causes of the conflicts that I was involved in, citing historic grievances and ethnic rivalries manipulated by despotic leaders through the inequitable distribution of resources, and still they continue—only the venues change.

There will always be wars and there will always be dead guys. But someone else is out there now. Godspeed to them. I've done my share. I'm going home.

Acknowledgments

There are too many people to thank. Here are a few of them: Barbara Capps, Maureen Capps, Carole Florman. Scott Babe, M.D., Gil Becker LCSW, Ron Koshes, M.D., Michael Coffey, Ellen Ficklen, Tim Schaffner, John Wright. Sanija Berisha, Shaun Byrnes, Anne-Sophie Ducreux, Zola Dowell, Mimoza Jupa, Morgan Morris, Jack Zetkulic, Valon Zharra. Jack Bailey, Telesphore Kagaba, Don Koran, Nan Mattingly, Rich Skow. John Longenecker, H.K. Simmons. A.M.F., Tahmina Tagizada, J.J.W., Rich Williamson. Harry S. Moskowitz.

Glossary of Military and Diplomatic Terms Used

—BCP. Bagram Collection Point. A temporary holding facility for captured Al Qaida and Taliban on the U.S. airbase at Bagram, Afghanistan.

—Case Officer. An intelligence officer trained in specialized techniques—tradecraft—to recruit and manage agents and networks of agents operating against a hostile nation or entity. In the U.S. Army they are also known as Area Intelligence Officers.

—CENTCOM. U.S. Central Command. The four-star-level command based in Tampa, FL that oversaw operations in Afghanistan and Iraq.

—CJ2X. Director of Human and Counterintelligence Operations. Derived from the standard numeric breakdown of staff offices where S1 is personnel, S2 is intelligence, S3 is operations, etc. The "C" represents the fact that the position oversees coalition forces, the "J" attests to the joint nature of the position (encompassing more than a single service-Army, Navy, Air Force, Marines), the X represents human intelligence, particularly controlled or clandestine operations.

—DATT: Defense Attaché. A military officer serving on diplomatic duty usually in an embassy representing the Secretary of Defense to the host nation's military and advising the Ambassador on military issues.

—DCM. Deputy Chief of Mission. A senior diplomatic officer in an embassy, second in rank only to the Ambassador.

—DIA. Defense Intelligence Agency.

—DRC: Democratic Republic of the Congo. Formerly Zaire.

—DS. Diplomatic Security. A bureau in the Department of State with responsibility for providing security for embassies and missions overseas, offices in the U.S., and senior officials. See also RSO.

—EOD. Explosive Ordnance Disposal. Bomb disposal and weapons experts.

—FAR. *Forces Armées Rwandaises*. The Rwandan Army before and during the genocide of 1994. Also, the Ex-FAR: former FAR troops in DRC.

—FDLR: *Forces Démocratiques de la Libération du Rwanda*. A Hutu rebel group operating in DRC. Some members are former *Interahamwe*.

—FSO. Foreign Service officer. An American diplomat.

—ICS. Internal Communications System.

—*Interahamwe*. "Those who struggle together," (Kinyarwanda). The executors of the genocide in 1994.

—ICRC. International Committee of the Red Cross.

—KBR. Kellogg Brown and Root. A U.S. contracting firm that provides logistics support to military operations including food service.

—KDOM. Kosovo Diplomatic Observer Mission. A small international mission operating in Kosovo from summer 1998 through winter 1999 with teams from the U.S., Canada, the EU and the Russian Federation.

—KLA. Kosovo Liberation Army. See also UÇK.

—KVM. Kosovo Verification Mission. A mission under the control of the OSCE in Kosovo during late 1998 and early 1999 principally organized to verify the agreement between Milosevic and the Holbrooke made in October 1998 that pushed the VJ out of Kosovo.

—M240. A 7.62mm light machine gun.

—MI. Military Intelligence.

—MP. Military Police

—MUP. *Ministarstvo Unutrašnjih Poslova*. Serbian Ministry of the Interior special police.

—NGA. National Geospatial-Intelligence Agency

.—NSA. National Security Agency.

—NGO. Non-Governmental Organization.

—Operations Center. Within the State Department, the office that maintains communications with overseas embassies and missions, monitors communications and coordinates action. The staff of the Ops Center are known as The Watch.

—OSCE. Organization for Security and Cooperation in Europe.

—RPG. Rocket Propelled Grenade.

—RSO. Regional Security Officer. In an embassy, the staff member tasked with managing the guards and advising the ambassador on security matters.

—RPF. Rwandan Patriotic Front. The rebels who defeated the Interahamwe and ended the genocide in 1994.

—SAPI. Small Arms Protective Insert. A ceramic plate that fits inside updated military body armor; designed to stop small arms fire.

—SF. Special Forces. U.S. Army Green Berets

—Toyota War. The war fought between Chad and Libya in 1987 during which the Chadian troops used Toyota pick-up trucks as their primary means of tactical movement. Chad won, Libya lost.

—UCK. *Ushtria Çlirimtare e Kosovës*

—UÇK. (Pronounced Oo-Cheh-Kah) The Kosovo Liberation Army.

—UPDF. Ugandan Peoples' Defense Force. The Ugandan Army.

—UNHCR. United Nations High Commission for Refugees.

—USG. United States Government.

—VA. Department of Veterans Affairs.

—VJ. *Vojska Jugoslavije*. The Serbian Army under Milosevic.

—Watch, The. The Foreign Service staff who man the State Department's Operations Center.

Permissions and Credits:

Laura Silber and Allan Little: *Yugoslavia: Death of a Nation*. Copyright © 1997, Penguin Books, NY

Siegfried Sassoon: "Remorse," from *Counter Attack and Other Poems*, published 1918. Accessed on Bartleby.com, http://www.bartleby.com/136/34.html

Vera Brittain: From the Foreword to *Testament of Youth*. Copyright 1933, Vera Brittain. Penguin Books, NY, 1994 ed.

Joseph Conrad: *Heart of Darkness*. Copyright 1899, Joseph Conrad. Accessed at Gutenberg.com http://www.gutenberg.org/cache/epub/526/pg526.html

Simone Weil: "The Iliad or the Poem of Force." Essay written in 1939. Accessed here: http://people.virginia.edu/~jdk3t/WeilTheIliad.pdf

Oliver Wendell Holmes: From a speech given on Memorial Day (May 30th) 1884 in Keene N.H. Accessed here: http://people.virginia.edu/~mmd5f/memorial.htm

Joni Mitchell (from jonimitchell.com): "The Last Time I Saw Richard." Copyright © 1971, Joni Mitchell Music.

Warren Zevon: "I'll Sleep When I'm Dead." Copyright © 1975 Warren Zevon and Elektra Records, from the album, "Warren Zevon"

Jonathan Shay: *Achilles in Vietnam*. Copyright © 1995, Simon & Schuster, Inc., NY

John Denver: "Leaving on a Jet Plane." Copyright © 1966 Cherry Lane Music Company. (via Cherry Lane Music company website)

Photo Captions and Credits:

Cover Photo: Eric Kroll and James Reed

Author in Kosovo, October 7, 1998. Kisna Reka, talking with Kosovars displaced by fighting in the area. AP Photo, Santiago Lyon. By permission.

Author in Rwanda, Fall 2000. In the south of the country near Rusumo. Courtesy of Ron Capps. By permission.

Author in Afghanistan, early spring 2003, at a Special Forces camp near the Pakistan border. Courtesy of Ron Capps. By permission.

Author in Darfur, Fall 2005, leaving a meeting with Sudanese Liberation Army commanders. Courtesy of Ron Capps. By permission.

Author in Washington, DC, Fall 2011, teaching a Veterans Writing Project seminar. Courtesy Dept. of Defense from *Soldiers* Magazine: photo by Jacqueline Hames. By permission.

Author in Washington,DC, Spring 2013. With Harry. Courtesy of Dept. of Veterans Affairs: photo by Robert Turtil. By permission.

Author's Notebooks. Courtesy of Ron Capps. By permission.

Maps:

All maps are original and created by Martin Lubikowski.

Courtesy of ML Design. By permission.

Cover and Interior Design: James Kiehle

Library of Congress Cataloging-in-Publication Data

Capps, Ron.

Seriously not all right : five wars in ten years / Ron Capps.

pages cm

Summary: "For more than a decade, Ron Capps, serving as both a senior military intelligence officer and as a Foreign Service officer for the U.S. Department of State, was witness to war crimes, ethnic cleansing, and genocide. From government atrocities in Kosovo, to the brutal cruelties perpetrated in several conflicts in central Africa, the wars in both Aghanistan and Iraq, and culminating in genocide in Darfur, Ron acted as an intelligence collector and reporter but was diplomatically restrained from taking preventative action in these conflicts. The cumulative effect of these experiences, combined with the helplessness of his role as an observer, propelled him into a deep depression and a long bout with PTSD, which nearly caused him to take his own life. Seriously Not All Right is a memoir that provides a unique perspective of a professional military officer and diplomat who suffered (and continues to suffer) from PTSD. His story, and that of his recovery and his newfound role as founder and teacher of the Veterans Writing Project, is an inspiration and a sobering reminder of the cost of all wars, particularly those that appeared in the media and to the general public as merely sidelines in the unfolding drama of world events"-- Provided by publisher.

ISBN 978-1-936182-58-9 (hardback) -- ISBN 978-1-936182-59-6 (pdf) -- ISBN 978-1-936182-60-2 (epub)

1. Capps, Ron. 2. Intelligence officers--United States--Biography. 3. Diplomats--United States--Biography. 4. War correspondents--United States--Biography. 5. World politics--1989- 6. Military history, Modern--20th century. 7. Military history, Modern--21st century. 8. Post-traumatic stress disorder--Patients--United States--Biography. 9. Authors, American--Biography. 10. Veterans Writing Project. I. Title.

CT275.C2795A3 2014

616.85'2120092--dc23

[B]

2013045595